REVELATION: *ALL* OF GOD'S WORD REVEALED

Brian Young

CREATION INSTRUCTION ASSOCIATION

Copyright 2000 by Creation Instruction Publishing

All rights Reserved. No part of this book may be reproduced or transmitted in any form or by any means, electronic or mechanical, including photocopying, recording, or by any information storage and retrieval system without permission in writing from the publisher.

Unless otherwise stated, Scripture is taken from the Holy Bible: NEW INTERNATIONAL VERSION, 1973, 1978, 1984 by the International Bible Society. Used by Permission of Zondervan Bible Publishers.

ISBN #1-928765-03-3

Library of Congress Control Number: 00-133399

Any questions or comments may be directed to:

Brian Young – CIA
Box 304
Plentywood, MT 59254

Other resources available through CIA:

For a free newsletter, From the Beginning, write to the address shown above. Also, CIA has many videos and books available that deal directly with the creation/evolution debate. For a more dynamic approach, contact Brian Young to speak personally at conferences, local churches, or for seminars today.

Printed by Maverick Publications
PO Box 5007 Bend, Oregon 97708

INDEX

IMPORTANT NOTE	4
A MUST READ INTRODUCTION	5
CHAPTER 1	11
SECTION 1 SEVEN CHURCES	11
CHAPTER 2	21
CHAPTER 3	29
CHAPTER 4	37
SECTION 2 SEVEN SEALS	37
CHAPTER 5	45
CHAPTER 6	49
SEVEN SEALS OUTLINE	57
CHAPTER 7	59
CHAPTER 8	69
SECTION 3 SEVEN TRUMPETS	70
CHAPTER 9	75
CHAPTER 10	85
CHAPTER 11	91
CHAPTER 12	109
SECTION 4 OPPOSING KINGDOMS	109
CHAPTER 13	117
CHAPTER 14	129
CHAPTER 15	143
SECTION 5 SEVEN BOWLS	143
CHAPTER 16	147
CHAPTER 17	157
CHAPTER 18	167
CHAPTER 19	175
SECTION 6 BELIEVERS HOPE	175
CHAPTER 20 INTRODUCTION	186
CHAPTER 20	189
SAINT OR SINNER?	197
1000 YEARS ARE OVER	210
CHAPTER 21	219
CHAPTER 22	229
REVELATION OUTLINE	239
INDEX	241
ABOUT THE AUTHOR	246

Important Note:

The book of Revelation has often been viewed as a book that cannot be understood and, therefore, is often skipped over when reading the Scriptures. The fact is, Revelation is very plain and very little of it is new information because many of the Old Testament books are simply elaborated on in the New Testament. There are many labels describing peoples' interpretations of Revelation, (millennial, premillennial, postmillennial, historic premillennial, amillennial) but we are not going to take any of these approaches as we often get preconceived ideas from these labels and the text does not always warrant these beliefs in their entirety. We will therefore simply call ourselves Christians and let God's Word speak for itself.

A deep trap I believe Satan uses against us while studying this book is to depart from what God says and start putting in our own opinions and words. There are many different views and interpretations of Revelation, but we are going to take a strict Biblical interpretation and try to leave out any presuppositions. Too often people try to impose their views upon the text instead of letting their doctrines flow out the Scriptures. I believe you will find much more than you ever imagined in reading through this book with the Holy Spirit as your guide.

Another aspect I believe is important to realize is that we, in the United States, are really the only country that has time to worry about prophecy. Many Christians in most other countries are already experiencing great persecution because of their faith. Revelation is not intended mainly to predict our future and waste our time trying to figure out what lies ahead in this lifetime. Its intent is to point us to Christ and to what He has prepared for us in heaven. We should not get caught up in trying to predict which country does what and who the Antichrist may or may not be, rather, knowing God's Word in Revelation will prepare our hearts and give us understanding when the time comes. This book should give you a spiritual, heavenly focus, not a selfish, earthly one. It should give us a sense of urgency that causes us to look at our future with spiritual eyeglasses rather than always being near sighted and concerned about what car, boat or other toys we may have in the next five years. It is to help us prepare our hearts and set our minds on things above; that we may not be distracted by earthly possessions and cares below.

You will find a general outline in the back of the book. Let us begin!

Introduction

The last book of the New Testament was written by John near the end of the first century while he was exiled to the island of Patmos (1:9). It is the only book with a specific promise of a blessing for its readers (although Scripture as a whole offers the same promise).

Revelation is a very orderly and symbolic but yet, literal book. The number seven dominates the text and is found 54 times. A few examples follow:

1. seven churches (1:4,11,20)
2. spirits (1:4; 3:1; 4:5; 5:6)
3. candlesticks (1:12,13,20; 2:1)
4. lamps (4:5)
5. stars (1:16)
6. seals (5:1;5:5)
7. horns (5:6)
8. eyes (5:6)
9. angels (8:2,6)
10. trumpets (8:2,6)
11. 1,000's (11:13)
12. heads (12:3; 13:1; 17:3;7,9)
13. thunders (10:3,4)
14. crowns (12:3)
15. plagues (15:1,6,8; 21:9)
16. mountains (17:9)
17. divisions of letters (Ch. 2)
18. kings (17:10,11)
19. beatitudes (1:3; 14:13; 16:15; 19:9; 20:6; 22:7; 22:14)
20. judgments (11:3; 12:6; 14; 13:5)
21. I am's (1:8,11,17,18; 21:6; 22:13,16 -- John's gospel also has seven "I am's."
22. songs, and benedictions (4:9-11; 5:8-13; 7:9-12; 11:16-18; 14:2,3; 15:2-4; 19:1-6).

There are also many connections between Revelation and Genesis. Perhaps that is why Scripture seems to make reference to a future restoration of Edenic principles: "The LORD will surely comfort Zion and will look with compassion on all her ruins; He will make her deserts like Eden, her wastelands like the garden of the LORD. Joy and gladness will be found in her, thanksgiving and the sound of singing" (Isa 51:3). A *small* sample of such connections follows:

1. There is gold in the new city (Rev 21:21) and the Garden of Eden (Gen 2:12).
2. A river flows from the throne (Rev 2:10) and from the garden (Gen 2:10). The Tree of Life resides in both Eden and in the city (Gen 2:9; Rev 22:2).
3. Both the garden and the city have been specially prepared for man (Gen 2:8,9; Rev 21:2).
4. The garden was a type of paradise with no sin and the city is a paradise with no sin.
5. God walked with man in the garden as He will in the new city (Gen 3:8; Rev 21:3).

Further we see that in Genesis the terms Eden and the Garden of Eden are often used interchangeably. However, in Genesis 2:8 we see that the Garden was planted on the east side of the land of Eden, hence the Garden OF Eden. Once the fall came, Adam and Eve were driven out of the Garden and must have gone through an eastern gate, because after they left, God put a cherubim there to keep everyone out. The cherubim were only placed on the east suggesting that this was the only place the Garden was accessible. In fact, the ancient word "paradise" even means "an enclosed garden." Taking this a step further. When Cain was driven away he went further east (Gen 4:16) and, therefore, further away from God and His paradise. This is also why the Tabernacle always had its entrance from the east side. The only way to enter our paradise (heaven) is from the east. In Ezekiel 47:1-2 we see the River of Life flowing from the throne, and it appropriately flows east. The Wisemen who came to see the baby Jesus came from the east (Matt 2). Likewise, the Jews have the Eastern Gate cemented shut in Jerusalem because only the Messiah is able to go through that gate. It is believed that when Christ returns He will go through the Eastern Gate or sometimes called the Golden Gate.

We see further evidence that the Garden of Eden foreshadows our heavenly home when we look at the River of Life that flowed DOWN from the center of Eden and separated into four other rivers. This means the Garden was a mountain. As a matter of fact, even Ezekiel calls Eden a mountain when talking of Satan: "You were in Eden, the garden of God; every precious stone adorned you: ruby, topaz and emerald, chrysolite, onyx and jasper, sapphire, turquoise and beryl. Your settings and mountings were made of gold; on the day you were created they were prepared. You were anointed as a guardian cherub, for so I ordained you. You were on **the holy mount** of God; you walked among the fiery stones" (Ezek 28:13-14). This is why God makes so much of mountains in Scripture. For example, Isaac was nearly sacrificed on Mount Moriah where the temple was later built. The Commandments were given on Mount Sinai. Jesus was Transfigured on a mountain, tempted on a mountain, ascended from a mountain, and gave His Sermon on the Mount from a mountain. Elijah called down fire while on Mount Carmel. When sin came into the world, Adam and Eve were restricted from the Mountain of God. Likewise, later only Moses, the priests and the 70 elders were allowed to meet God on Mount Sinai, and even then only after making atonement through a sacrifice (Exo 24). Any one else who touched the mountain would die. Clearly mountains represent not only the Garden of Eden, but heaven, the very thing Eden symbolized. We read in Revelation: "And he carried me away in the Spirit to a **mountain great and high**, and showed me the Holy City, Jerusalem, coming down out of heaven from God" (Rev 21:10). That is also why we read in Hebrews: "But you have come to **Mount** Zion, to the heavenly Jerusalem, the city of the living God. You have come to thousands upon thousands of angels in joyful assembly" (Heb 12:22).

We also read of the rivers and the surrounding area of the Garden: "The name of the first [river] is the Pishon; it winds through the entire land of Havilah, where there is gold. (The gold of that land is good; aromatic resin and onyx are also there) (Gen 2:11-12). Note that there are three articles found here:

gold, resin and onyx. First let us address the onyx. In Exodus 25:7 and 28:9-12 we see that the High Priest was to wear two onyx stones with the names of the 12 tribes of Israel on them. The purpose of these stones was explained, "Fasten them on the shoulder pieces of the ephod **as memorial stones** for the sons of Israel. Aaron is to bear the names on his shoulders as a memorial before the LORD" (Exo 28:12). A memorial of what? The only time we see this stone prior to this is in the Genesis account of Eden. When the people looked at the priest they were to see a Holy Man like Adam in heaven. We will examine the priest in a moment, but for now realize that God wanted the people to see that He was going to restore them to the Edenic paradise once again.

Second, we deal with the resin or bdellium. Later on we see that the Israelites received manna from heaven while in their desert wandering. We read, "The manna was like coriander seed and looked like resin" (Num 11:7) The word for resin is the same Hebrew word (*bedolach*) used in Genesis for resin and is nowhere else used in Scripture. In Exodus we are told the color of the manna eaten by the Israelites: "The people of Israel called the bread manna. It was white like coriander seed [same Hebrew word for resin] and tasted like wafers made with honey" (Exo 16:31). Therefore, if the manna was white and it looked like resin, the resin in Genesis must also be white. That makes clear the reference in Revelation: "He who has an ear, let him hear what the Spirit says to the churches. To him who overcomes, I will give some of the hidden **manna**. I will also give him a **white** stone with a new name written on it, known only to him who receives it" (Rev 2:17). This resin in the Edenic paradise foreshadowed the white stone to come, where we will receive a new name which only comes by being made new in the spirit. It is also worth noting that the references to resin and onyx were made to the Israelites while they passed through the area believed to be Havilah, the general location of the Garden of Eden.

Thirdly, the gold was significant. We know that the Temple foreshadowed heaven: "They serve at a sanctuary that is a copy and shadow of what is in heaven" (Heb 8:5). That is why the Temple was covered in gold (Ex 25, 1Kings 6). The clothing of the High Priest was also layered with gold (Ex 28). It should be no surprise then, that so many Old Testament passages use the imagery of precious stones to foreshadow salvation. A few examples follow:

- "Herds of camels will cover your land, young camels of Midian and Ephah. And all from Sheba will come, bearing gold and incense and proclaiming the praise of the LORD" (Isa 60:6).
- "Surely the islands look to me; in the lead are the ships of Tarshish, bringing your sons from afar, with their silver and gold, to the honor of the LORD your God, the Holy One of Israel, for He has endowed you with splendor" (Isa 60:9).
- "O afflicted city, lashed by storms and not comforted, I will build you with stones of turquoise, your foundations with sapphires. I will make your battlements of rubies, your gates of sparkling jewels, and all your walls of precious stones" (Isa 54:11-12).

It should be no surprise then that Revelation describes our paradise in such a way: "The wall was made of jasper, and the city of pure gold, as pure as glass. The foundations of the city walls were decorated with every kind of precious stone. The first foundation was jasper, the second sapphire, the third chalcedony, the fourth emerald, the fifth sardonyx, the sixth carnelian, the seventh chrysolite, the eighth beryl, the ninth topaz, the tenth chrysoprase, the eleventh jacinth, and the twelfth amethyst. The twelve gates were twelve pearls, each gate made of a single pearl. The great street of the city was of pure gold, like transparent glass" (Rev 21:18-21). Gold was significant not only in the beginning, but also is in the end.

I said I would discuss the Holy Priest who foreshadowed the redeemed man. The priest was to wear white linen (Exo 28) just as in heaven we too receive white linen to wear: "Fine linen, bright and clean, was given her to wear. (Fine linen stands for the righteous acts of the saints)" (Rev 19:8). Further we see that part of the curse was sweat, "By the sweat of your brow you will eat your food until you return to the ground, since from it you were taken; for dust you are and to dust you will return" (Gen 3:19). That may be why no clothing was to be worn that made the Holy man sweat, "They are to wear linen turbans on their heads and linen undergarments around their waists. They must not wear anything that makes them perspire" (Ezek 44:18). In heaven, the curse is wiped away, and as a model of the redeemed man, no curse should be found. Also on the priest's chest was a gold plate engraved with the words, "Holy to the Lord" (Ex 28:36) showing the symbolic removal of the curse upon the priest. We already discussed how his breastplate was covered with gold and precious stones.

The garden was also abundant in vegetation, another symbol of prosperity. In more places than we have room to mention, trees are used in reference to Godly men (Gen 18:4-8; 30:37; Jud 3:13; 4:5; 1 Kings 19:5; John 1:48 etc.). We see that every blessed man is seen as having his own vine or tree for protection and comfort. We read of these blessings, "During Solomon's lifetime Judah and Israel, from Dan to Beersheba, lived in safety, each man under his **own vine** and fig tree" (1 Ki 4:25). Likewise our heavenly home is described with such blessing: "In the last days the mountain of the Lord's temple will be established as chief among the mountains; it will be raised above the hills, and peoples will stream to it. Many nations will come and say, 'Come, let us go up to the mountain of the LORD, to the house of the God of Jacob. He will teach us His ways, so that we may walk in His paths.' The law will go out from Zion, the Word of the LORD from Jerusalem. He will judge between many peoples and will settle disputes for strong nations far and wide. They will beat their swords into plowshares and their spears into pruning hooks. Nation will not take up sword against nation, nor will they train for war anymore. **Every man will sit under his own vine and under his own fig tree, and no one will make them afraid,** for the LORD Almighty has spoken" (Mic 4:1-4). We also read in Zecheriah, "In that day each of you will invite his neighbor to sit under **his vine and fig tree**, declares the LORD Almighty" (Zec 3:10). It is for the purpose of showing blessings that planting and flourishing is almost always used in reference to God's work throughout Scripture. Psalms states, "He is like a tree planted by streams of water, which yields its fruit in season and whose leaf does not wither. Whatever he does prospers" (Psa 1:3). In Jeremiah we read, "But blessed is the man who trusts in the LORD, whose confidence is in Him. He will be like a tree planted by the water that sends out its roots by the stream. It does not fear when heat comes; its leaves are always green. It has no worries in a year of drought and never fails to bear fruit" (Jer 17:7). Isaiah writes, "In days to come Jacob will take root, Israel will bud and blossom and fill all the world with fruit" (Isa 27:6). Even the lampstand in the Temple was described as a tree with branches and yet pure gold (Exo 37:17). The Cedar walls within the temple [a model of heaven] were carved with flowers, palm trees and vines (1 Kings 6:15-36), all showing God's abundant blessings through Edenic symbolism. In celebrating the Feast of Tabernacles or the Feast of Booths the Israelites were to make booths of foliage and palm branches to symbolize God's protection. During this time they were to leave the security of their homes and walled cities to live out in the open in unprotected booths. God promised that He would protect and watch over them, they didn't need to trust in walls or other means of security: "Three times a year all your men are to appear before the Sovereign LORD, the God of Israel. I will drive out nations before you and enlarge your territory, and no one will covet your land when you go up three times each year to appear before the LORD your God" (Exo 34:23). This feast should have reminded them of the Paradise of Eden and the Paradise to come. During this time they were told to sacrifice 70 bullocks (Num 29:12ff) to symbolize the original 70 nations of the earth in Genesis 10. Therefore, they were celebrating the gathering of the nations into God's eternal Kingdom when atonement would be made for them. Interestingly enough, the Israelites forgot about this feast and did not practice it until their return from Babylon (Neh 8:13-18). It would be through Israel that Christ would come (Rom 9:5) to redeem and restore His people for a paradise much better than that of Eden, this time it would be heaven. As Jesus said, "In My Father's house are many rooms; if it were not so, I would have told you. I am going there to prepare a place for you. And if I go and prepare a place for you, I will come back and take you to be with Me that you also may be where I am" (John 14:2-3).

One could go on and on making comparisons, but these should suffice in showing that Revelation is not a separate book from the rest of Scripture, it is merely the conclusion, the last act, and without it, the story of salvation is incomplete.

Why is it written in symbolic form? Most commentators will agree that symbolism is not weakened by time and, therefore, it was applicable during Jesus's day as well as our own. The same imagery used in Daniel and Ezekiel will be seen in Revelation. In Revelation 22:10 God tells John NOT to seal up the words of this book, but in Daniel 12:4 God told Daniel to seal up the words until the end. Therefore, we are glimpsing at what Daniel saw, but was unable to tell us.

Regarding its basic layout, we begin with seven churches, seven seals, seven trumpets, and then seven bowls.

CHAPTER 1

Section 1 (Revelation 1:1-3:22)
Seven Churches

Rev 1:1-3 The revelation of Jesus Christ, which God gave Him to show His servants what must soon take place. He made it known by sending His angel to His servant John, who testifies to everything he saw--that is, the word of God and the testimony of Jesus Christ. Blessed is the one who reads the words of this prophecy, and blessed are those who hear it and take to heart what is written in it, because the time is near.

In these verses we have a preface showing not only the importance of this book, but also how it came down to us. First of all, it is the revelation of JESUS CHRIST. Many think this book is the revelation of doom and gloom, but it begins by stating the complete opposite. Revelation is *apokalupsis* in the Greek and it means "unveiling" or "revealing." So, here we see that Jesus Christ is going to be unveiled in a way not yet seen.

This revelation was given to show what must **soon** take place. The Greek word *tachos* means shortly, hastily or speedily, implying one of two things (or both):

1) That the events you will read will begin very shortly in history.
2) The time frame for these events will cover a short period.

I am inclined to believe "soon" means both occurring soon and taking place rapidly as the rest of the text will explain later.

We see a type of hierarchical descent in these verses; e.g. God gave this revelation to Jesus, who then gave it to the angel, who gave it to John, who is now giving it to us.

It is rather ironic that this book is the only one in all of Scripture that gives a specific blessing to its readers, especially when this particular book is the most misunderstood and unread out of the 66. (Promises of blessings also occur in 22:7; 14:13; 16:15; 19:9; 20:6; 22:14). We have an encouragement to read, hear and meditate upon the words within because the time is near. For centuries people have been saying the time is now, and for centuries people have been wrong. So what does "near" mean? We will examine this further as we go, but for now suffice it to say that the signs the Lord is revealing today seem to suggest that the time is, indeed, at hand for our generation. As Paul wrote, "And do this, understanding the present time. The hour has come for you to wake up from your slumber" (Rom 13:11).

Rev 1:4-5a John, to the seven churches in the province of Asia: Grace and peace to you from Him who is, and who was, and who is to come, and from the seven spirits before His throne, and from Jesus Christ, who is the faithful witness, the firstborn from the dead, and the ruler of the kings of the earth.

Here we have the greeting as commonly seen in other epistles with the author listed first, followed by the address to the audience; in this case, the seven churches in Asia. Note the difference; however, that Paul wrote seven different letters to seven different churches while here John writes one letter to seven different churches. Why seven? Seven represents the number of completeness and, in a sense, this is written to all churches. The fact that seven is symbolic does not mean that perhaps only six churches received the letter. No, literally seven churches received the letter because it symbolized completeness. This may be likened to a wedding ring symbolizing unity while it remains a literal ring. Keep this idea of symbolism in mind as we continue in Revelation.

It is interesting that Revelation begins with words of grace (v. 4) and ends with grace (22:21). Here, grace and peace comes from the Trinity:

1) *God Himself*, Who is, Who was and, Who is to come. This not only shows God's eternal character being unconstrained by time as we know it, but also perhaps to God's characteristics during the church ages. The law Giver of the Old Testament, the God Incarnate of the New Testament, and the Judge of the time to come. We will see the same title in Revelation 1:8, 4:8; 11:17; and 16:5.
2) *From the seven Spirits*- or the Holy Spirit. Most think this alludes to the seven-fold Spirit in Isaiah 11:1-2 which says, "A shoot will come up from the stump of Jesse; from his roots a Branch will bear fruit. The Spirit of the LORD will rest on Him-- the Spirit of wisdom and of understanding, the Spirit of counsel and of power, the Spirit of knowledge and of the fear of the LORD--. We will see these seven Spirits again in 3:1; 4:5; and 5:6. In Revelation 5:6 we see that these seven Spirits are represented by seven eyes. This is significant as we see God tell us about these seven eyes (Spirits) in Zecheriah: "I see a solid gold lampstand with a bowl at the top and *seven lights on it*, with seven channels to the lights. . . .(These seven are the eyes of the LORD, which range throughout the earth)" (Zech 4:2,10).
3) From *Jesus Christ* (v. 5). Christ is the **Faithful Witness**. The word for witness in the Greek is *martus*, which is where we get the English word for "martyr." We read in Isaiah, "See, I have made him a *witness* to the peoples, a leader and commander of the peoples" (Isa 55:4). Even Jesus Himself had earlier said, "for this reason I was born, and for this I came into the world, *to testify* to the truth. Everyone on the side of truth listens to Me" (John 18:37). Christ indeed was martyred for our sins, but more than that, was raised from the dead and is thus the **firstborn from the dead** (see Romans 6:9; 8:34). In Colossians we read, "And He is the head of the body, the church; He is the beginning and the *firstborn from among the dead*, so that in everything He might have the supremacy" (Col 1:18; see also Ps 89:27). Therefore, Christ

is **Ruler of the kings of the earth**. The Greek word for "ruler" given here is *archon* and means "first" or "chief" of all. Jesus is King of kings and this will be written on His thigh in Revelation 19:16. Timothy testifies that Christ is "God, the Blessed and only Ruler, the King of kings and Lord of lords" (I Tim 6:15).

Revelation 1:5b-8 To Him who loves us and has freed us from our sins by His blood, and has made us to be a kingdom and priests to serve His God and Father--to Him be glory and power for ever and ever! Amen. Look, He is coming with the clouds, and every eye will see Him, even those who pierced Him; and all the peoples of the earth will mourn because of Him. So shall it be! Amen. "I am the Alpha and the Omega," says the Lord God, "who is, and who was, and who is to come, the Almighty."

John continues to give praise to Him who freed us from the bondage of sin so that we have become slaves to God (Rom 6:22) and a kingdom of priests (I Peter 2:5; Exodus 19:6). As priests we will serve God, (Rev. 22:3) yet, at the same time, we will reign with Him (Rev 20:6; 5:10; II Tim 2:12).

Take note of the two-fold doxology "to Him be *glory* and *power.*" This will later become three-fold (4:11), then four-fold (5:13), ending in a seven-fold doxology (7:12).

The picture of Christ in the clouds is significant because clouds are often used with God's presence. For example, at Mt. Sinai the law was given (Ex 19:9), at the transfiguration the clouds enveloped them all (Mat 17), the temple was filled with a cloud (Ex 40:35), a cloud led the Israelites in the wilderness (Ex 13:21). The Old Testament often uses the word, Spirit and Cloud synonymously: "The Lord will wash away the filth of the women of Zion; He will cleanse the bloodstains from Jerusalem by a spirit of judgment and a spirit of fire. Then the LORD will create over all of Mount Zion and over those who assemble there a cloud of smoke by day and a glow of flaming fire by night; over all the glory will be a canopy" (Isa 4:4); and "Because of Your great compassion You did not abandon them in the desert. By day the pillar of cloud did not cease to guide them on their path, nor the pillar of fire by night to shine on the way they were to take. You gave Your good Spirit to instruct them. You did not withhold Your manna from their mouths, and You gave them water for their thirst" (Neh 9:19-20). This as well illustrates a type of Edenic paradise to come. At creation, we begin by seeing the "Spirit of God hovering over the waters" (Gen 1:2). In so doing, light was brought out of darkness. Likewise, the Cloud in the wilderness separated light from darkness: "Coming between the armies of Egypt and Israel. Throughout the night the cloud brought darkness to the one side and light to the other side" (Exo 14:20). This light then led the way to the Sabbath rest during Creation, but it also led to the Israelites Sabbath rest of the promised land. Hebrews clearly tells us that the Promised land was a Sabbath rest (Heb 4). If you have not read Hebrews chapter four go and do so because it gives tremendous insight into the importance of the Sabbath rest. There we see that heaven also is called our Sabbath rest: "There remains, then, a Sabbath-rest for the people of God" (Heb 4:9). The Cloud lead to the Sabbath rest of creation, to the Sabbath rest of the Promised Land, and now to the Sabbath rest for all of God's people.

Christ coming on the clouds has already been predicted in the New Testament where it reads, "At that time the sign of the Son of Man will appear in the sky, and all the nations of the earth will mourn. They will see the Son of Man coming on the clouds of the sky, with power and great glory" (Mat. 24:30; see also Mat 16:27; 26:64). This may have come from passages like those in Zecheriah: "they will look on Me, the One they have pierced, and they will mourn for Him as one mourns for an only child (Zech 12:10; see John 19:34). Also, "After that, we who are still alive and are left will be caught up together with them in the clouds to meet the Lord in the air. And so we will be with the Lord forever" (1 Th 4:17). In the Old Testament Daniel writes, "In my vision at night I looked, and there before me was One like a son of man, coming with the clouds of heaven" (Dan 7:13). Ezekiel says, "for the day is near, the day of the LORD is near-- a day of clouds, a time of doom for the nations" (Ezek 30:3). Clearly these verses are not unique to Revelation.

This section closes with God proclaiming to be the Alpha and the Omega, the First and the Last. We will see this description again in verse 17; 21:6; and 22:13. And added to our earlier description in verse four, is God as the Almighty. Out of the twelve times God is called by this name in the New Testament, nine of them are here in Revelation (4:8; 11:17; 15:3; 16:7,14; 19:6; 21:22). See Romans 9:29; 2 Corinthians 6:18; and James 5:4 for other examples.

Rev 1:9-11 "I, John, your brother and companion in the suffering and kingdom and patient endurance that are ours in Jesus, was on the island of Patmos because of the word of God and the testimony of Jesus. On the Lord's Day I was in the Spirit, and I heard behind me a loud voice like a trumpet, which said: "Write on a scroll what you see and send it to the seven churches: to Ephesus, Smyrna, Pergamum, Thyatira, Sardis, Philadelphia and Laodicea.

John has been exiled because of his faith to Patmos, a small island (4 X 8 miles) in the Aegean Sea, during one of the most cruel time periods of history; the reign of Domitian. Domitian was a Roman emperor who intensely persecuted Christians. Eusebius, an early historian, records that John was released by the emperor Nerva (96-98 AD).

Much debate has been done as to whether the "Lord's Day" refers to Sunday, or in a stricter sense, "the day of the Lord" which refers to the end times. Some argue that it cannot refer to the end times because the second chapter is talking about the present churches, while others say it can't be the Sabbath because nowhere else in Scripture is it called the "Lord's Day." Regardless, it was a special day.

The command to write what was seen to the churches shows it to be for generations to come and, therefore, is also applicable for us today. The churches are listed in a geographical circle about 50 miles apart from each other, starting with Ephesus and moving clockwise around to Laodicea. The fact that these churches are listed in some order gives further testimony to the orderliness of God and the book of Revelation as a whole.

Rev 1:12-16 I turned around to see the voice that was speaking to me. And when I turned I saw seven golden lampstands, and among the lampstands was someone "like a son of man," dressed in a robe reaching down to His feet and with a golden sash around His chest. His head and hair were white like wool, as white as snow, and His eyes were like blazing fire. His feet were like bronze glowing in a furnace, and His voice was like the sound of rushing waters. In His right hand He held seven stars, and out of His mouth came a sharp double-edged sword. His face was like the sun shining in all its brilliance.

This scene is important as it gives the setting for the judgment seat. John turns to see who is speaking and sees seven golden lampstands. This may have been a rather familiar sight since the temple had lampstands similar to the Menorah today (Exodus 25:31; Zech 4:2; Rev 2:1). What are these lampstands? They are literal lampstands among the throne, but they also represent the seven churches as plainly stated in verse 20.

Among these lampstands (churches) is none other than Christ Himself. Understanding that these seven churches represent all churches throughout history, He is then among His churches today as well. Christ is said to be "like a son of man." This term is used for Jesus more than 80 times in the Gospels alone. We will see it again when Christ begins to reap the harvest: "I looked, and there before me was a white cloud, and seated on the cloud was one *"like a son of man"* with a crown of gold on His head and a sharp sickle in His hand" (Rev 14:14).

The court is being prepared for the final judgment upon all sinners. We see a wise and powerful judge described with white hair, blazing eyes, and bronze feet. Daniel gives similar insight to this event: "As I looked, *thrones* were set in place, and the *Ancient of Days* took His seat. His *clothing was as white* as snow; the *hair of His head was white like wool*. His throne was flaming with fire, and its wheels were all ablaze. A river of fire was flowing, coming out from before Him. Thousands upon thousands attended Him; ten thousand times ten thousand stood before Him. The *court* was seated, and the books were opened" (Daniel 7:9-10; see also Ezek 1:26). White hair not only speaks of His everlasting nature (Is 9:6), but also of wisdom: "The glory of young men is their strength, gray hair the *splendor* of the old" (Prov 20:29), and "Gray hair is a crown of splendor; it is attained by a righteous life" (Prov 16:31; see also Lev 19:32). Further reference to the flaming eyes and bronze feet can be found also in Daniel which reads, "His body was like chrysolite, *His face like lightning, His eyes like flaming torches,* His arms and *legs like the gleam of burnished bronze,* and His *voice like the sound of a multitude*" (Dan 10:6). Regarding the voice, we read, "I saw the glory of the God of Israel coming from the east. His voice was like the *roar of rushing waters*" (Ezek 43:2); "The voice of the LORD is *powerful*; the voice of the LORD is *majestic*. The voice of the LORD *breaks the cedars* (Psa 29:4-5). See also Ps 93:4.

This "One like the Son of Man" is also wearing a robe with a golden sash just as seen in Daniel 10:5. This shows Him to represent a high priest because in Old Testament times the high priest wore a long robe similar to this (Ex 28:4; 29:5). Also, we read in Isaiah, "Righteousness will be His belt and faithfulness the sash around His waist" (Isa 11:5).

In His hand He holds seven stars which are the angels of the churches as explained in verse 20.

Out of His mouth comes a double edged sword which is the Word of God (Heb 4:12, Eph 6:17), sharp enough to divide even the soul and spirit. It is with this Word that God will judge the heart: "Repent therefore! Otherwise, I will soon come to you and will fight against them with the sword of My mouth" (Rev 2:16); and "Out of His mouth comes a sharp sword with which to strike down the nations" (Rev 19:15). Isaiah wrote of Christ: "He made my mouth like a sharpened sword" (Isa 49:2). See also Isa 1:20.

Christ is coming in all His glory as His face *shines in all its brilliance*, just as it did at the Transfiguration (Mat 17). After all, Jesus is the Morning Star (Rev 22:16, 2 Peter 1:19) and in His full glory He will judge the Antichrist: "And then the lawless one will be revealed, whom the Lord Jesus will overthrow with the breath of His mouth and destroy by the *splendor* of His coming" (2 Th 2:8).

Rev 1:17-18 When I saw Him, I fell at His feet as though dead. Then He placed His right hand on me and said: "Do not be afraid. I am the First and the Last. I am the Living One; I was dead, and behold I am alive for ever and ever! And I hold the keys of death and Hades."

Although John walked with Jesus he never saw Him in all His glory -- until now. Upon seeing this John fell to the ground just as Daniel did (Daniel 10:7-10; 8:17), as well as Ezekiel (Ezek 1:28). However, at the touch of His hand strength is given (Dan 8:18). It is interesting to see the "I am" come after "Do not be afraid," because the first "fear not" in the Bible comes right before the first "I am" way back in Genesis 15:1. God is the First and the Last, the eternal God; a concept we cannot even begin to understand. "Christ Jesus died, but more than that, was raised to life, and sits at the right hand of God" (Rom 8:34). "Seeing what was ahead, he spoke of the resurrection of the Christ, that He was not abandoned to the grave, nor did His body see decay. God has raised this Jesus to life, and we are all witnesses of the fact" (Acts 2:31-32). Indeed Jesus is the Living One who will judge and cast His opponents into Hades (Rev 9:1 20:13).

Rev 1:19-20 Write, therefore, what you have seen, what is now and what will take place later. The mystery of the seven stars that you saw in My right hand and of the seven golden lampstands is this: The seven stars are the angels of the seven churches, and the seven lampstands are the seven churches.

Verse 19 gives us a basic outline to the entire book of Revelation. John is commanded to write what he has seen (Ch. 1- what we just covered), what is now (Ch.2-4), and what will take place later (Ch. 4 on).

The seven stars and seven lampstands seen in verses 12-16 are here explained. The stars, or angels, have also been interpreted as pastors, but the text doesn't warrant this interpretation. The word "elder" (synonymous with "pastor" in the New Testament) is used 12 other times in Revelation and could have been used here, but was not. The same word used here occurs 67 times throughout Revelation, always referring to angels.

This begins the first of a series of seven churches. The question arises: Are these churches representative of only seven single churches? No. As mentioned earlier, seven is a number of completeness. Each church represents not only a living, functioning church in John's day, but it also represents an attitude that is predominate among churches in a given time period. Almost every church today can find some characteristic in all seven of these churches just as we can find murder in all parts of the country. However, in general, Washington D.C. is known for its violence, San Francisco is known for homosexuality, etc. Likewise, each church (and time period) is known for a dominating trait.

There are those who reject this interpretation, usually based upon fear of being labeled as having a particular belief as mentioned in the introduction. However, when taken into context with the rest of the churches and Revelation as a whole, it is evident that these churches have a dual meaning. This will become clearer as we go. For now a quick explanation of the outline in the back of this book may be of help.

Each of the seven churches cover a time period in which a predominate attitude exists, right up to the last church (Laodicea), which represents roughly from 1900 to the present. Each church is given seven characteristics or points:

1. A general introduction such as "to the angel of the church at Ephesus write . . . ."
2. A characteristic of Christ which is repeated from the first chapter. It usually begins as, "These are the words of Him who. . .." This attribute fills a void or need for this particular church characteristic. For example, in the last church representing the present time, God as Creator is the attribute. This is certainly relevant for our day. The rest of these attributes will be discussed as we go.
3. A statement of knowledge such as, "I know your deeds, your hard work . . .." What is stated is a church characteristic which represents the general attitude of society during a given time period.
4. An admonition or warning such as, "Yet I hold this against you. . .." This, again, is an attitude prevalent in society during a certain range of time in history.
5. Christ's second coming predicted: "If you do not repent, I will come. . .."

6. An urge to hear what the Spirit says to the churches: "He who has an ear let him hear . . . ."
7. A blessing is given: "To him who overcomes, I will give..."

Immediately after the time period of the churches, seven seals are opened. When the seventh seal is opened, seven trumpets sound. When the seventh trumpet sounds, seven vials of judgment are poured out. One can see that these events are progressively faster and faster. Taking this all in context, if the seven vials take place during the seventh trumpet, and the seven trumpets take place in the seventh seal, would not the seven seals begin taking place during the time period of the seventh church?

We read in Romans that the whole creation has been groaning as in the pains of child birth. Labor pains get quicker and quicker all the time, just as the events here in Revelation do. To explain, let us assume that each seal covers roughly the same amount of time. . .say seventy seconds each (490 seconds total). If all seven trumpets take place in the seventy seconds of the last seal, then each seal is roughly only 10 seconds long (10 X 7 = 70 seconds for *all* seven). If the seven vials all take place in the 10 seconds of the single seventh trumpet, each vial would be just over one second each, etc. (1.42 sec/vial X 7 vials = about 10 seconds). Again, I am not proposing these as literal times, but simply as an illustration of the layout of Revelation. With the churches, seals, trumpets, and vials, that pretty much covers Revelation. We will continue to follow this line of thinking and things will become more clear as we go.

One more pattern is seen in each of the series of sevens. It appears that each section (churches, seals, trumpets and vials) can be separated with the first four following a certain theme, the next three following another. Further, the last set of three (fifth, sixth, seventh) can be divided with a period of silence or some type of interlude between the second and third (sixth and seventh). In short, they are split 1,2,3,4**5,6 break 7. It is interesting to note that Christ was born four thousand years after creation (according to Biblical genealogies) and now we are about two thousand years after His resurrection. According to this pattern, that leaves only one millennium. With the coming of Jesus we switched themes from the Old Covenant to the New Covenant (Romans 7:6). Also, in the creation week we see the first four days having the theme of material creations while the last two are dealing with living creatures. The sixth and seventh day are separated as on the seventh day, God rested. Again we see a four, two, one split. The following is an example showing how the seven seals follow this pattern:

1. *White Horse*   (first four follow one theme & often successive).
2. *Red Horse*
3. *Black Horse*
4. *Pale Horse*
    5. <u>**Scene in Heaven**</u>   (next two follow another theme).
    6. <u>**Sun, Moon, Stars changed.**</u>
        7. **Trumpets sound to prepare for war**.
          (Last one separated by an interlude).

When all of this matches throughout the entire book of Revelation, and perhaps creation, does it not seem fitting for the seven churches to also represent seven church ages? Keep in mind the many connections between the paradise of Eden and the eternal paradise of the New Jerusalem (Rev 21). Just as many of the traditions and procedures in the Old Testament foreshadowed Christ, so also the garden foreshadowed the New Jerusalem. (For example: The Old Testament Passover lamb's blood was put on the doorframe to deliver people from death, and Christ's blood, our Passover Lamb, delivered us from death). Let us examine what Scripture says in the following chapters!

CHAPTER 2

Rev 2:1-7 To the angel of the church in Ephesus write: These are the words of him who holds the seven stars in his right hand and walks among the seven golden lampstands: I know your deeds, your hard work and your perseverance. I know that you cannot tolerate wicked men, that you have tested those who claim to be apostles but are not, and have found them false. You have persevered and have endured hardships for my name, and have not grown weary. Yet I hold this against you: You have forsaken your first love. Remember the height from which you have fallen! Repent and do the things you did at first. If you do not repent, I will come to you and remove your lampstand from its place. But you have this in your favor: You hate the practices of the Nicolaitans, which I also hate. He who has an ear, let him hear what the Spirit says to the churches. To him who overcomes, I will give the right to eat from the tree of life, which is in the paradise of God.

Ephesus, as a capital, was one of the largest cities of Asia and this perhaps contributed to its immorality and idolatry. The fertility goddess, Artemis (Diana) was believed to have fallen from the sky and come to rest in Ephesus. Diana brought in a tremendous amount of wealth, as many trinkets of her were sold here. In Acts 19:25-41 the men who made a living on selling these idols tried to put an end to Paul's preaching. Priscilla is left here in Acts 18 and Timothy was also left as pastor here.

The attribute of Christ is "Him who holds the seven stars in His right hand." This comes directly from Rev 1:16. The stars represent the angels of the churches and the lampstands represent the churches themselves. The reminder of Christ's presence is to encourage them to return to the zeal they had at the beginning of their conversion.

This church was known for its hard work, perseverance and intolerance and is, overall, a great church even now, 40 years after it was started by Paul. They practiced church discipline as they tested false apostles and did not tolerate them (1 John 4:1). For the name of Christ they endured persecution and hardship with joy (Romans 5:3).

However, warning went out to remember their first love and the height from which they had fallen. When Paul writes his letter to the Ephesians he states, "Grace to all who love our Lord Jesus Christ *with an undying love* (Ephesians 6:24). Often times new converts to the faith display a wonderful zeal and love for the Lord, but as time goes on the fire turns into mere glowing embers, which get dimmer and dimmer with time. Here we see a call for the church to return to this zealous service and praise for our Lord Jesus Christ.

If they do not return to the attitude they had at first, they run the risk of having their lampstand (church) taken from it's place. One more word of encouragement is given as they have been opposing the practices of the Nicolaitans. Who these Nicolaitans are we cannot be sure. The word comes from the Greek, "*Nicao*" meaning to conquer, and "*laos*" meaning laity. So perhaps they were those who opposed the church laity. Certainly they were among those false apostles mentioned in verse two. There was a Gnostic group bearing this name a good time after John's letter, in fact they opposed John's writings. Perhaps they simply took the name from the Nicolaitans spoke of in this passage.

As in all the churches, the admonition to hear this warning is given along with the promise that those who overcome will eat from the tree of life. This will be fulfilled as we see the Tree of Life in the new heaven, the paradise of God (Rev 22:2). The Garden of Eden in Genesis paints a beautiful shadow of what is to come.

The church here not only represents the actual church of Ephesus, but the attitude of society during the time of history from about AD 33 to AD 100. Obviously these are not exact dates, but simply a rough guide. During this apostolic age many early churches had been "falling from their first love" as it was no longer new and exciting. Sometimes, we still fall prey to this today.

Rev 2:8-11 To the angel of the church in Smyrna write: These are the words of him who is the First and the Last, who died and came to life again. I know your afflictions and your poverty--yet you are rich! I know the slander of those who say they are Jews and are not, but are a synagogue of Satan. Do not be afraid of what you are about to suffer. I tell you, the devil will put some of you in prison to test you, and you will suffer persecution for ten days. Be faithful, even to the point of death, and I will give you the crown of life. He who has an ear, let him hear what the Spirit says to the churches. He who overcomes will not be hurt at all by the second death.

The second church of Smyrna was a port city about 35 miles north of Ephesus and was built around 1000 BC. It is noted here for its persecution. It remains today as Ismir, in Turkey, but in times past, displayed an amphitheater which seated about 20,000 people and was one of the finest cities in Asia. Smyrna was not only the birth place of Homer, but was also home to Polycarp, a pastor here until his martyrdom in AD 155.

The word Smyrna is a type of embalming spice called myrrh. As a baby, Jesus was brought gold, incense and myrrh (Mat 2:11). However, in Isaiah 60:6 which predicts the bringing of these gifts, myrrh is left out to show that He would not need this burial spice as He would rise from the dead. If you recall, when Mary went to anoint the body with spices she found the tomb empty (Mark 16:1).

The attribute given here fits the trials the church at Smyrna is facing: persecution. The letter comes from "Him who is the First and the Last, who died and came to life again" (Rev 1:17-18). I believe Polycarp may well have had this in mind while he was martyred on a burning stake. The reminder of life after death should have been a great encouragement to all who were being persecuted here.

The people are described as being financially poor but spiritually rich (Compare this to those in Laodicea (3:17) who are financially rich but spiritually poor). They knew what true riches were (Luke 16:11). This is the only church that is not admonished for doing any bad thing. I believe this is because of its great persecution as "we also rejoice in our sufferings, because we know that suffering produces perseverance; perseverance, character; and character, hope. And hope does not disappoint us, because God has poured out His love into our hearts by the Holy Spirit, whom He has given us" (Romans 5:3-5). What blessings come from our sufferings: "Therefore, since Christ suffered in His body, arm yourselves also with the same attitude, because he who has suffered in his body is done with sin" (1 Pet 4:1). See also 1 Thess 1:6; 1 Peter 2:19; 4:12-13; 1:7.

Just as Ephesus had false apostles, Smyrna had false Jews; people who claimed to be true people of God but actually opposed Him by rejecting Christ and relying on their traditions and laws. These people are called, "a synagogue of Satan." There were indeed a large number of physical Jews living in Smyrna who opposed the church and, in fact, they played a large part in Polycarp's execution.

The church is told to not fear as the "crown of life" awaits and the persecution will be but a short time of ten days. Why the amount of "ten days" is unclear. It may mean simply what it says, ten, 24 hour days. The number ten has been used in other parts of Scripture as a period of testing, but they have been literal days. For example, Daniel and his friends underwent ten days of trial eating only grains (so as not to defile themselves with meat) while captives in Babylon (Dan 1:12-15). After the ten days were over, they were found to be healthy and remained for seventy years in Babylon. With Daniel and Revelation being so closely related, the ten days of testing early on in the book may have some significance. The seventy years of captivity may also have something to do with the many sevens found in Revelation. Either way, the ten days is obviously meant to represent a short period of time and a small price for the eternal crown of life. (A promise that can be trusted from Him who died but came to life again (attribute in verse 8).

As mentioned, there is nothing bad going on at this church so no admonition is given. However the promise of deliverance from the second death is stated. This deliverance takes place in Rev 20:6 which reads, "Blessed and holy are those who have part in the first resurrection. The second death has no power over them, but they will be priests of God and of Christ and will reign with Him for a thousand years." What is this second death? "Then death and Hades were thrown into the lake of fire. The lake of fire is the second death (Rev 20:14).

The time frame for Smyrna's characteristics in society is from about AD 100 to AD 300. Historically, this was a period of grave persecutions. From Nero to Diocletian many say there were ten waves of persecution with the worst part being the last ten years under Diocletian. Polycarp himself was martyred under the reign of Diocletian. As Polycarp was about to be burned at the stake he was asked to renounce Christ, but only replied, "eighty and six years have I served the Lord and you want me to recant now, light the flames!" This attitude of perseverance under ruthless persecution is certainly portrayed here in John's letter.

Rev 2:12-17 To the angel of the church in Pergamum write: These are the words of him who has the sharp, double-edged sword. I know where you live--where Satan has his throne. Yet you remain true to my name. You did not renounce your faith in me, even in the days of Antipas, my faithful witness, who was put to death in your city--where Satan lives. Nevertheless, I have a few things against you: You have people there who hold to the teaching of Balaam, who taught Balak to entice the Israelites to sin by eating food sacrificed to idols and by committing sexual immorality. Likewise you also have those who hold to the teaching of the Nicolaitans. Repent therefore! Otherwise, I will soon come to you and will fight against them with the sword of my mouth. He who has an ear, let him hear what the Spirit says to the churches. To him who overcomes, I will give some of the hidden manna. I will also give him a white stone with a new name written on it, known only to him who receives it.

Pergamum was the farthest north of the seven churches. On a clear day the Mediterranean sea could be seen from here. One of its most notable traits was its huge library, which held around 200,000 volumes of books. Egypt refused to sell them papyrus for paper so they resorted to making their own parchments out of sheep skin, and thus the name "Pergamum." Wherever there is great worldly wisdom, folly seems to increase. This appears to be the case here as it was the worst of the seven cities with the largest altar to Zeus in the world. In addition to this, people came from all over the world to see the healing god, Esclepis. Esclepis was a snake wrapped around a pole. This symbol was put on their coins and is one we still see today in the medical fields. This church will be noted for beginning to tolerate and compromise the faith. They also have those among them that are sheep in wolves clothing (Mat 7:15).

The attribute is from, "Him who has the sharp, double edged sword" and comes from Revelation 1:16. The sword is the Word of God, "for the Word of God is living and active. Sharper than any double-edged sword, it penetrates even to dividing soul and spirit, joints and marrow; it judges the thoughts and attitudes of the heart" (Heb 4:12). This attribute is an important reminder for those who have Christ on their lips, but not in their hearts, because God can see the heart whereas we cannot.

God acknowledges Pergamum as the place that Satan has his throne. Perhaps this was in reference to the altar of Zeus or simply to the many pagan religions of which Pergamum was the center. In fact, Alexander Hislop describes in his book, *Two Babylons,* how the pagan priests of Babylon moved to Pergamum after their fall during the reign of Belshazzar. Despite this, however, the people in the church have remained faithful to the true God, regardless of past persecution in the days of Antipas. We do not know who this Antipas was but he was indeed martyred in Pergamum.

Unlike Ephesus and Smyrna, Pergamum was not able to keep false prophets and teachers out of the church. This seems to be a typical cycle in churches throughout history. They start out strong, but as time goes on, compromising attitudes begin to arise (Just as Harvard and Yale began as Christian colleges and are now completely secular). Pergamum had among them those who held to the practices of Balaam. Balaam's name means "not of the people" which is very similar to the Nicolaitans (conquer laity) in verse 15. Balaam was the prophet that served with his lips but not with his heart. Balaak wanted to pay Balaam to curse Israel but Balaam could only spew out blessings upon them from his lips. Motivated by sinful greed, Balaam realized that he could not physically curse Israel so he taught Balaak how to destroy them in other ways. Balaam encouraged Balaak to send his most beautiful women to the Israelites and intermarry (a sin as described in Deut 7:3) among them and lead them astray. The attitude of some in this church may be summed up by Peter when he writes, "They have left the straight way and wandered off to follow the way of Balaam son of Beor, who loved the wages of wickedness. But he was rebuked for his wrongdoing by a donkey--a beast without speech--who spoke with a man's voice and restrained the prophet's" (2 Peter 2:15-16). For more on Balaam see Num 22-29; 31:15-16; Joshua 24:9-10; Duet 23:4-5.

Others followed the teaching of the Nicolaitans who probably opposed what the pastors and laity were doing regarding church discipline and saying that the spirit of compromise was okay, especially with other gods such as Zeus or Esclepis.

He who hears and overcomes will receive the hidden manna and a white stone with a new name on it. The hidden manna is Christ Himself and we celebrate this in Holy communion today. John writes, "I tell you the truth, he who believes has everlasting life. I am the Bread of life. Your forefathers ate the manna in the desert, yet they died. But here is the bread that comes down from heaven, which a man may eat and not die. I am the living Bread that came down from heaven. If anyone eats of this bread, he will live forever. This Bread is My flesh, which I will give for the life of the world. Then the Jews began to argue sharply among themselves, 'How can this man give us His flesh to eat?' Jesus said to them, 'I tell you the truth, unless you eat the flesh of the Son of Man and drink His blood, you have no life in you. Whoever eats My flesh and drinks My blood has eternal life, and I will raise him up at the last day. For My flesh is real food and My blood is real drink'" (John 6:47-55).

The meaning of the white stone was discussed in the introduction where we saw that this is the fulfillment of the Edenic blessing. He who hears will overcome and be brought into the freedom of Christ in Paradise. Also, a white stone was sometimes given to those who were declared innocent. In the Old Testament, the breastplate of the high priest had twelve stones with the name of the twelve tribes, but none of them were white (Ex 28:15-21). Regarding the new name, Isaiah wrote, "The nations will see your righteousness, and all kings your glory; you will be called by a *new name* that the mouth of the LORD will bestow (Isa 62:2), and "to His servants He will give another name" (Isa 65:15). It is interesting that God gives new names with His covenant. When Abram received the promise he became Abraham and this set God as his "Definer."

When we are baptized we are baptized into the Name of the Trinity: "Therefore go and make disciples of all nations, baptizing them in the Name of the Father and of the Son and of the Holy Spirit" (Mat 28:19). We receive a new name at baptism. Circumcision was the Old Testament sign of the covenant as Baptism is the New Testament sign of the covenant. Colossians states, "In Him you were also circumcised, in the putting off of the sinful nature, not with a circumcision done by the hands of men but with the circumcision done by Christ, having been buried with Him in baptism and raised with Him through your faith in the power of God, who raised Him from the dead" (Col 2:11-12). That is why the Jewish people have always officially given their children names at their circumcision. Even Jesus received His name upon being circumcised: "On the eighth day, when it was time to circumcise Him, He was named Jesus, the name the angel had given Him before He had been conceived" (Luke 2:21). Therefore, when we enter our eternal rest, the covenant will be complete and we will receive a new name signifying our new nature being freed from our sinful flesh.

Historically, we are looking at this church representing a time period around AD 300-AD 500. It was then, that the church and world began to mix on a political rather than a spiritual level. As a result, toleration of false teachings and idols became more prevalent. It was during this time as well that Constantine became a nominal Christian. He baptized his entire army, idols became saints and heathen priests became church priests, but not out of devotion to our Lord. The government and church were united into a political arena of Balaam's doctrine of compromise and show.

To review we have seen Ephesus who did not tolerate anything but was loosing it's zeal. Smyrna was also intolerant but was being persecuted and now Pergamum is beginning to tolerate and compromise, losing the true meaning of Christianity. Let this be a warning for us in our attitude of worship and spirituality. Do we compromise God's Word for the sake of personal comfort or finances?

Rev 2:18-29 To the angel of the church in Thyatira write: These are the words of the Son of God, whose eyes are like blazing fire and whose feet are like burnished bronze. I know your deeds, your love and faith, your service and perseverance, and that you are now doing more than you did at first. Nevertheless, I have this against you: You tolerate that woman Jezebel, who calls herself a prophetess. By her teaching she misleads my servants into sexual immorality and the eating of food sacrificed to idols. I have given her time to repent of her immorality, but she is unwilling. So I will cast her on a bed of suffering, and I will make those who commit adultery with her suffer intensely, unless they repent of her ways. I will strike her children dead. Then all the churches will know that I am he who searches hearts and minds, and I will repay each of you according to your deeds. Now I say to the rest of you in Thyatira, to you who do not hold to her teaching and have not learned Satan's so-called deep secrets (I will not impose any other burden on you): Only hold on to what you have until I come. To him who overcomes and does my will to the end, I will give authority over the nations-- 'He will rule them with an iron scepter; he will

dash them to pieces like pottery' -- just as I have received authority from my Father. I will also give him the morning star. He who has an ear, let him hear what the Spirit says to the churches.

Thyatira was a simple trade city located about 40 miles east of Pergamum. It received the longest of the seven letters. Lydia (Acts 16:14) was from Thyatira where she sold a purple dye.

The letter is from "the Son of God, whose eyes are like blazing fire and whose feet are like burnished bronze." This comes from 1:14-15 and is an appropriate judgment figure for such an adulterous church. His eyes search the heart and His feet crush His enemies (verse 27). It seems that Pergamum's virus of compromise had infected Thyatira and infested the greater population.

Verse 19 shows that the church had a few who were growing in faith and were working at improving themselves. However, they were still tolerating that woman Jezebel who claimed to be a prophetess. Paul specifically warns against women speaking in the church, "women should remain silent in the churches. They are not allowed to speak, but must be in submission, as the law says. If they want to inquire about something, they should ask their own husbands at home; for it is disgraceful for a woman to speak in the church. Did the word of God originate with you? Or are you the only people it has reached? If *anybody thinks he is a prophet or spiritually gifted*, let him acknowledge that what I am writing to you is the Lord's command. If he ignores this, he himself will be ignored" (1 Cor 14:34-38). We do not know who this woman was but her name fits her actions. In the Old Testament Jezebel was an evil, immoral, Baal worshiper (1 Kings 16:30-33; 2 Kings 9:22). Here in Thyatira she led people into sexual immorality and eating improper food. She obviously knew she was in the wrong but chose to continue living her life of sin as God gave her an opportunity to repent, (verse 21) but she doesn't. As a result, the Son of God would bring destruction upon her with His feet of bronze. She and her children (verse 23 -followers) would be cast upon a bed of suffering rather than a bed of lust and sinful passion. Each heart would be judged individually by the flaming eyes (verse 18) and each would pay for their own deeds. We read in Romans, "God will give to each person according to what he has done. To those who by persistence in doing good seek glory, honor and immortality, He will give eternal life. But for those who are self-seeking and who reject the truth and follow evil, there will be wrath and anger. There will be trouble and distress for every human being who does evil: first for the Jew, then for the Gentile" (Romans 2:6-9). No one can escape God's judgment!

Verse 24 is stated for the minority, or to "the rest of you" who have not followed the teachings of Jezebel and Satan. Christ asked them to merely hold on to what they had. Don't tolerate anything else, keep the faith and service that you now possess. Those who do so will be given authority over the nations. We will read the fulfillment of this later when John states, "I saw thrones on which were seated *those who had been given authority to judge.* And I saw the souls of those who had been beheaded because of their testimony for Jesus and because of the word of God. They had not worshipped the beast or his image and had not received his mark on their foreheads or their hands. They came to life and reigned with Christ a thousand years" (Rev 20:4).

Verse 27 quotes Psalm 2:9 and describes authority being given not only to the saints, but to Christ as well, "who received authority from His Father." The attribute given in this letter mentions the "Son of God" (verse 18) and is the only time this term for Christ is used in Revelation. However, here we see God is the Father and we will see this again in 3:5 and 3:21. This describes what Daniel wrote when he says, "But the saints of the Most High will receive the kingdom and will possess it forever--yes, for ever and ever" (Dan 7:18) and "Then the sovereignty, power and greatness of the kingdoms under the whole heaven will be handed over to the saints, the people of the Most High" (Daniel 7:27). Paul wrote, "Do you not know that the saints will judge the world?" (1 Cor 6:2). Christ will rule with an iron scepter as Hebrews explains, "But about the Son he says, 'Your throne, O God, will last for ever and ever, and righteousness will be the scepter of Your kingdom'" (Heb 1:8). We indeed have a glorious future in the resurrection of Christ Jesus our Lord, the Morning Star (Rev 22:16).

In Thyatira we see the general attitude of society from around AD 500 to AD 1500, the period we call the Dark Ages. During this time we had impartial burnings at the stake, vast idol and saint worship, the crusades, where murder was done in the name of God, and the growth of the papacy. No wonder Christ is viewed as the Son of God (only true, infallible God to be worshipped rather than saints or popes), whose eyes are like blazing fire (to look into the hearts of the crusaders and church politics), and whose feet are like burnished bronze (to judge the wickedness done in God's name, the claims of infallibility or the need of good works rather than grace alone and Scripture alone).

One can see the logical downward spiral of God's people. Ephesus became bored while Smyrna was persecuted. Pergamum then gave in to allow politics and God's Word to mesh, which automatically led to the full fledged tolerating of Thyatira where political wars were fought using the name of God to justify their sinfulness. Scripture warns us, "You, my brothers, were called to be free. But do not use your freedom to indulge the sinful nature; rather, serve one another in love" (Gal 5:13).

CHAPTER 3

Rev 3:1-6 To the angel of the church in Sardis write: These are the words of him who holds the seven spirits of God and the seven stars. I know your deeds; you have a reputation of being alive, but you are dead. Wake up! Strengthen what remains and is about to die, for I have not found your deeds complete in the sight of my God. Remember, therefore, what you have received and heard; obey it, and repent. But if you do not wake up, I will come like a thief, and you will not know at what time I will come to you. Yet you have a few people in Sardis who have not soiled their clothes. They will walk with me, dressed in white, for they are worthy. He who overcomes will, like them, be dressed in white. I will never blot out his name from the book of life, but will acknowledge his name before my Father and his angels. He who has an ear, let him hear what the Spirit says to the churches.

Sardis was built at a high elevation surrounded by cliffs on three sides. In Old Testament times, the king of Sardis was very wealthy, but overconfident due to its natural defenses. In his cockiness, the king tried to attack Cyrus in Persia but was defeated and retreated back to Sardis. However, Cyrus followed and besieged the city. Meanwhile, Cyrus offered a large reward for any soldier that could find a way to climb the cliff. One soldier found a way and Sardis fell to Cyrus. It was a wicked city and the capital of Lydia (home of Aesop).

This letter is from "the one who holds the seven spirits of God and the seven stars" (from 1:4,16). The seven spirits clearly show God's knowledge of hearts of those in Sardis through the Spirit of understanding, knowledge, wisdom etc. (Is 11:1-2). This church was in desperate need of guidance from the Spirit of God and their spiritual leaders (stars) as this church received no acknowledgment of anything good.

Christ says that Sardis had a *reputation* of being a vibrant and alive church, but in reality they were dead. Apparently they are going through the motions of church life but their lives don't go through the motions of faith. Timothy describes this type as, "having a form of godliness but denying its power. Have nothing to do with them" he warns (2 Tim 3:5). Many churches today have impressive numbers but the spirituality is missing. Any church where the Word of God is not taught as supreme and where the Holy Trinity is not accepted as Three persons in One is no church worth setting foot in, even if the building is beautiful and the pews are full.

Sardis was given the warning to wake up and follow what they knew in their hearts but were not practicing, nor were they repenting of their evil deeds. Their deeds had been found incomplete probably because they went through the motions, but their hearts were not in it, "and everything that does not come from faith is sin" (Rom 14:23). If they do not repent, "**I will come like a thief,**" says Christ "and you will not know at what time I will come to you." Notice the progression through the churches regarding Christ's promised return.

- Ephesus: Repent...do the things you did at first, **If you do not repent, I will come** and remove your lampstand...(2:5)
- Smyrna: Be faithful even to the point of death...(2:10)
- Pergamum: Repent, otherwise, **I will soon come**...(2:16)
- Thyatira: Only hold on to what you have **until I come**... (2:25)
- Sardis: If you do not wake up, **I will come like a thief**...(3:3)
- Philadelphia: **I am coming soon.** Hold on to what you have (3:11)
- Laodicea: **Here I am**, I stand at the **door**... (3:20)
  Chapter 4:1 (End of churches) says, "After this I looked, and there before me was **a door standing open**."

    Here we see Christ predicting His return right up until He says, "Here I am" during the last church of Laodicea when the prediction becomes reality. According to the outline of Revelation, the seals should now be opened and chapter four shows the door open as we view the court room where the judgment will take place and the seals will be opened. Also note that the warning for Sardis is that "**if** you do not wake up, I will come like a thief **and** you will not know at what time I will come to you." Sardis must be alert so that they can see the signs of the end and will be prepared for this day. Many people say we do not know when the end of the world will come. I agree to a point as Matthew 24:36 states, "No one knows about that *day* or *hour*, not even the angels in heaven, nor the Son, but only the Father." Christ says nobody knows the day or hour but what about the year, decade, century etc. Don't take this wrong. I am not saying we should waste our time on trying to pick a year (personally, I don't think we can), but rather be alert for signs of the end because it will *not* surprise us Christians. "Now, brothers, about times and dates we do not need to write to you, for you know very well that the day of the Lord will come like a thief in the night. While people are saying, 'Peace and safety,' **destruction** will come on **them** suddenly, as labor pains on a pregnant woman, and they will not escape. **But you**, brothers, **are not in darkness so that this day should surprise you like a thief.** You are all sons of the light and sons of the day. We do not belong to the night or to the darkness. So then, let us **not be like others, who are asleep, but let us be alert** and self-controlled" (1 Th 5:1-6). Clearly, this day will not come like a thief to those who are in Christ and patiently await His coming.

    Despite the psuedo-christian nature of this church, there are those that have remained faithful. To these people, God has promised them the long awaited, white robe of righteousness that is worn in the eternal paradise (Rev 19:8; 7:14).

    The names of these faithful saints will never be blotted out of the book of life. This shows that ALL people have their names in the book of life and are predestined to heaven, because in order to have your name blotted out, it must be written down already (Eph 1:1-5,11; Rom 8:29-30). However, those who reject the gift of grace through faith in Christ (Rom 5:2) will have their names erased from the book of life. What a joyous sound it will be to our ears when we hear Jesus acknowledge our name before His father and the angels, saying, "Well done thou good and faithful servant" (Mat 25:23). Additional passages about the book of life follow:

- Psa 69:28 "May they be blotted out of the book of life and not be listed with the righteous."
- Phil 4:3 "Yes, and I ask you, loyal yokefellow, help these women who have contended at my side in the cause of the gospel, along with Clement and the rest of my fellow workers, whose names are in the book of life."
- Rev 17:8 "The beast, which you saw, once was, now is not, and will come up out of the Abyss and go to his destruction. The inhabitants of the earth whose names have not been written in the book of life from the creation of the world will be astonished when they see the beast, because he once was, now is not, and yet will come."
- Rev 20:12 "And I saw the dead, great and small, standing before the throne, and books were opened. Another book was opened, which is the book of life. The dead were judged according to what they had done as recorded in the books."
- Rev 20:15 " If anyone's name was not found written in the book of life, he was thrown into the lake of fire."
- Rev 21:27 "Nothing impure will ever enter it, nor will anyone who does what is shameful or deceitful, but only those whose names are written in the Lamb's book of life."
- Dan 12:1 "At that time Michael, the great prince who protects your people, will arise. There will be a time of distress such as has not happened from the beginning of nations until then. But at that time your people--everyone whose name is found written in the book--will be delivered."

The time frame given for the church of Sardis is from 1500 AD to 1700 AD. This period is noted for the reformation of the Catholic church and unmixed condemnation among arising denominations. Even though much good came out of the reformation, it was also marked by a Catholic church filled with deceit and malice. They appeared to be an alive church, yet they were spiritually dead. The reformation was the "wake up" call (verse 2) for the Catholic church. The deeds of a church founded upon good works were found incomplete (verse 2). The desperately needed leadership came through the reformation as Bible reading and believing Christians emerged in full force through the Spirit led efforts of those whose clothes had not been soiled (verse 4).

Rev 3:7-13 To the angel of the church in Philadelphia write: These are the words of him who is holy and true, who holds the key of David. What he opens no one can shut, and what he shuts no one can open. I know your deeds. See, I have placed before you an open door that no one can shut. I know that you have little strength, yet you have kept my word and have not denied my name. I will make those who are of the synagogue of Satan, who claim to be Jews though they are not, but are liars--I will make them come and fall down at your feet and acknowledge that I have loved you. Since you have kept my command to endure patiently, I will also keep

you from the hour of trial that is going to come upon the whole world to test those who live on the earth. I am coming soon. Hold on to what you have, so that no one will take your crown. Him who overcomes I will make a pillar in the temple of my God. Never again will he leave it. I will write on him the name of my God and the name of the city of my God, the new Jerusalem, which is coming down out of heaven from my God; and I will also write on him my new name. He who has an ear, let him hear what the Spirit says to the churches.

Philadelphia was about 28 miles southeast of Sardis and is known for having many earthquakes. It is the sixth of the seven churches and is today called Alasehir. It was founded by King Attalus of Pergamum and named for his brother, thus the name, Philadelphia, meaning "brotherly love."

The letter is written from, "Him who is holy and true, who holds the key of David. What He opens no one can shut, and what He shuts no one can open." This is almost a direct quote from Isaiah 22:22 which were the words promised to Eliakim (servant under Hezekiah). Eliakim's predecessor (Shebna) did evil and, therefore, his position was about to be given to Eliakim who would serve Judah and God faithfully. The Key to the House of David describes the governmental power that rested on his shoulders just as Christ would have the government put on His shoulders: "For to us a child is born, to us a Son is given, and the government will be on His shoulders. And He will be called Wonderful Counselor, Mighty God, Everlasting Father, Prince of Peace. Of the increase of His government and peace there will be no end. He will reign on David's throne and over His kingdom, establishing and upholding it with justice and righteousness from that time on and forever. The zeal of the LORD Almighty will accomplish this" (Is 9:6-7). This description of Christ is similar to the attribute found in Rev 1:18 where the keys being held are of death and Hades. Here, however, they are of David and may allude to opening doors of witness opportunities and evangelism. The qualities describing this church suggest that this city was an evangelistic witness to many even among its surroundings of apostasy.

Verse eight tells about an open door that perhaps was an opportunity to witness. We read, "And pray for us, too, that God may open a door for our message, so that we may proclaim the mystery of Christ, for which I am in chains" (Col 4:3). 1 Corinthians 16:9 also states, "because a great door for effective work has opened to me."

The church has little strength but, "My grace is sufficient for you, for My power is made perfect in weakness" says <u>Christ</u> (2 Cor 12:9). Though they are weak, God will continue to give them strength. We see that not only have they kept God's Word (verse 8), but they must be sharing it as even those who oppose Christ will bow down and acknowledge that God loves them (verse 9; see also Phil 2:9-10). Those belonging to the work righteous synagogue of Satan were seen earlier in Rev 2:9.

Since they have kept God's command to endure patiently, they will be kept *from* the hour of trial coming upon the earth (verse 10). The Greek word for, "from" is *evk* and can mean "out of." Therefore some use this as an argument for the rapture; the belief that Christians will be taken up to heaven and delivered from the tribulation coming up in later chapters. However, these verses do not make this clear and, therefore, can only be hypothetical Scripturally speaking. Another possible hypothesis is that the church of Philadelphia has already died and, therefore, have already been kept out of the tribulation of which we will read about in Chapters 6 and following. Also, in Jesus prayer for the church, we have a remarkable personal note from God. Jesus said, "I have given them Your Word and the world has hated them, for they are not of the world any more than I am of the world. *My prayer is not that You take them out of the world but that You protect them* from the evil one. It is also interesting that in the parable of the harvest the ungodly are judged first, "Let both grow together until the harvest. At that time I will tell the harvesters: **First** collect the weeds and tie them in bundles to be burned; then gather the wheat and bring it into my barn" (Mat 13:30).

"I am coming soon" says Christ who will soon say, "Here I am" to the church of Laodicea (3:20). They are asked to hold on to what they have so they do not lose their crown (4:4).

Those who overcome will be made permanent pillars in the new temple. In the new Jerusalem, the temple is God: "I did not see a temple in the city, because the Lord God Almighty and the Lamb are its temple" (Rev 21:22). We will therefore be a permanent pillar in Christ. We read elsewhere in the New Testament that we are, "members of God's household, built on the foundation of the apostles and prophets, with Christ Jesus Himself as the chief cornerstone. In Him the whole building is joined together and rises to become a holy temple in the Lord. And in Him you too are being built together to become a dwelling in which God lives by His Spirit" (Eph 2:20-22). Peter writes, "You also, like living stones, are being built into a spiritual house to be a holy priesthood, offering spiritual sacrifices acceptable to God through Jesus Christ" (1 Pet 2:5). We, as pillars, will be marked with three things: 1) The name of Christ (Rev 22:4); 2) The name of the new city or new Jerusalem (described in Rev 22); and 3) A new name (2:17).

The time period for Philadelphia is about 1700 AD to 1900 AD. This is a time of great revival and missionary expansion after the reformation. It certainly fits with the characteristics of this church having an open door that no one can shut. These missions have continued even up to the present. This also ties into the four/three split of the sevens discussed earlier. The first four churches are successive but the last three are continuing. For example, the 5th church is marked by the Reformation era, which is still going on today, and the missionary focus of the 6th church continues today as well.

Rev 3:14-22 "To the angel of the church in Laodicea write: These are the words of the Amen, the faithful and true witness, the ruler of God's creation. I know your deeds, that you are neither cold nor hot. I wish you were either one or the other! So, because you are lukewarm--neither hot nor cold--I am about to spit you out of my mouth. You say, 'I am rich; I have acquired wealth and do not need a thing.' But you do not realize that you are wretched, pitiful, poor, blind and naked. I counsel you to buy from

me gold refined in the fire, so you can become rich; and white clothes to wear, so you can cover your shameful nakedness; and salve to put on your eyes, so you can see. Those whom I love I rebuke and discipline. So be earnest, and repent. Here I am! I stand at the door and knock. If anyone hears my voice and opens the door, I will come in and eat with him, and he with me. To him who overcomes, I will give the right to sit with me on my throne, just as I overcame and sat down with my Father on his throne. He who has an ear, let him hear what the Spirit says to the churches."

    Laodicea was an economically rich trade center about 45 miles southeast of Philadelphia. It was one of the most impressive churches on the outside but one of the worst on the inside (spiritually). In fact, in 60 AD they suffered an earthquake and refused disaster relief offered from Rome and rebuilt themselves. They also piped warm water into the city from springs six miles away. Paul mentions this church in Colossians 4:12-16.

    The attribute of Christ assigned to this church is quite appropriate not only for this church but the time period it represents - the churches today. The letter comes from the faithful and true witness, the **ruler of God's creation** (from 1:17-18). Paul also addresses this issue in Colossians describing Christ as, "the image of the invisible God, the firstborn over all creation. For by Him all things were created: things in heaven and on earth, visible and invisible, whether thrones or powers or rulers or authorities; all things were created by Him and for Him. He is before all things, and in Him all things hold together" (Col 1:15-17). Apparently the humanistic philosophies were being accepted at the church of Laodicea, and this is why Paul warns us in Colossians, "See to it that no one takes you captive through hollow and deceptive philosophy, which depends on human tradition and the basic principles of this world rather than on Christ" (Col 2:8). Today, the "human tradition" of evolution has deceived many into following the foolishness of men which leads to destruction. In fact, this is the first time in history that God's own church has ever denied Him as Creator. We, as with this church, need to accept God's Word as true in its entirety and acknowledge Christ as the faithful and TRUE witness. Christ is indeed the Way, the Truth and the Life (John 14:6).

    Christ sees that this church is neither cold, nor hot but wishes they were one or the other. As a result of this compromising and comfortable lifestyle, God will spit them out of His mouth. This church may have had the doctrine of Creation and the Trinity but they would not take a stand for it. How often do we shy away from or ignore important issues simply to remain neutral and keep from hurting feelings or rocking the boat. Too many churches today are more worried about numbers and accommodations than they are about the doctrines and truths in Scripture. As a result of this upbringing, many people today are lukewarm, wanting to ride the fence keeping sight of the worldly things (evolution, music, millions of years) on one side, yet having Christ remain only in their peripheral vision on the other. They think, "as long as I go to church on Sunday I am a Christian." Is this the product of faith? (See James 2:26). This attitude of neutrality is not how Christ would have us be. (2 Cor 3:12; 10:2).

The people in Laodicea believed they were rich and had all they needed (so who needs God?) yet in reality they were poor and miserable lost souls. They were blind to the truths plainly seen in Scripture, and as Romans boldly states, "since what may be known about God is *plain* to them, *because God has made it plain* to them. For since the creation of the world God's invisible qualities--His eternal power and divine nature--have been clearly seen, being understood from what has been made, so that men are without excuse. For although they knew God, they neither glorified Him as God nor gave thanks to Him, but their thinking became futile and their foolish hearts were darkened. Although they claimed to be wise, *they became fools"* (Rom 1:19-22). Compare this to Smyrna in 2:9 where they were financially poor but spiritually rich.

They were counseled to buy gold refined in the fire -- faith rather than material possessions. "These have come so that your **faith--of greater worth than gold**, which perishes even though refined by fire--may be proved genuine and may result in praise, glory and honor when Jesus Christ is revealed" (1 Pet 1:7). Faith is true richness which brings everlasting life and provides white clothes of righteousness (Is 64:6; Rev 6:11; 7:9). As it is now, their eyes were blinded by worldly wealth and philosophies so that they could not see the Truth Himself: "What Israel sought so earnestly it did not obtain, but the elect did. The others were hardened, as it is written: 'God gave them a spirit of stupor, eyes so that they could not see and ears so that they could not hear, to this very day'" (Rom 11:7-8). Faith will provide them with the salve their eyes need, so that as Paul says, "I keep asking that the God of our Lord Jesus Christ, the glorious Father, may give you the Spirit of wisdom and revelation, so that you may know Him better. I pray also that the *eyes of your heart* may be enlightened in order that you may know the hope to which He has called you, the *riches* of His glorious inheritance in the saints" (Eph 1:17-18).

Verse 19 expresses God's love for the church of Laodicea in the fact that He is disciplining them just as we read in Hebrews, "because the Lord disciplines those He loves, and He punishes everyone He accepts as a son" (Heb 12:6).

Verse 20 is especially interesting as it is the close of the promises of Christ's return. Here He says, "Here I am! I stand at the door." The other churches only received warnings like, "I am coming soon," or "I will come like a thief" but now He is here. We read in Matthew, "Now learn this lesson from the fig tree: As soon as its twigs get tender and its leaves come out, you know that summer is near. Even so, when you see all these things, you know that it is near, *right at the door*" (Mat 24:32-33). James 5:9 reads, "Don't grumble against each other, brothers, or you will be judged. The Judge is standing at the door!" Christ is standing at the door (Note in 4:1 that the door is standing open) and knocking. If anyone opens the door, Christ will come in and eat with them at the marriage supper of the Lamb (Rev 19:9). This is the same supper talked about in the parable of the wedding banquet in Matthew 22, of which one should certainly read in connection with this.

To him who overcomes (v. 21) God will give the right to sit with Him on the throne just as Christ does (Heb 12:2; Rom 8:34). This will be fulfilled in

Rev 20:4 as the saints will play a part in judging the world. Paul writes, "Do you not know that the saints will judge the world" (1 Cor 6:2)?

The estimated time frame in history for Laodicea is about 1900 to the present. The reminder of God as Creator is certainly relevant for our society today, as never before has this foundational belief been so controversial. The spirituality of today is diminishing into a "feel good" church atmosphere with little focus on doctrine or inspiration of Scripture. People are compromising with the world in order to have the pleasures of the world, and yet serve the Lord at the same time. These people, as Isaiah writes, "Come near to Me with their mouth and honor Me with their lips, but their hearts are far from Me. Their worship of Me is made up only of rules taught by men" (29:13). In addition, Luke 16:13 states, "No servant can serve two masters. Either he will hate the one and love the other, or he will be devoted to the one and despise the other. You cannot serve both God and money." We are a generation of great financial blessings. Capitalism and materialism run rampant while we attribute it all to "hard work" and "dedication." We are in desperate need of riches that gold cannot purchase - faith that has been refined in fire. The signs are showing that Christ is indeed "at the door" and we will soon see what's behind it as we now embark on chapter four.

CHAPTER 4

Section 2 (Revelation 4:1-8:5)
Seven Seals

Rev 4:1-2 After this I looked, and there before me was a door standing open in heaven. And the voice I had first heard speaking to me like a trumpet said, "Come up here, and I will show you what must take place after this." At once I was in the Spirit, and there before me was a throne in heaven with someone sitting on it.

Chapter four is describing a courtroom scene. This will become more clear as we move on, but for now think of the beginnings of a court case. The courtroom is being filled, the Judge is sitting on His seat, and the jury is being seated as well. Here the courtroom being described is simply the judgment seat in heaven. A judgment is about to be passed sometime during the period of the last church. The exact same vision that is about to be described was seen by Daniel who wrote, "As I looked, thrones were set in place, and the Ancient of Days took His seat. His clothing was as white as snow; the hair of His head was white like wool. His throne was flaming with fire, and its wheels were all ablaze. A river of fire was flowing, coming out from before Him. Thousands upon thousands attended Him; ten thousand times ten thousand stood before Him. **The court was seated,** and the books were opened" (Dan 7:9-10).

As mentioned, we just saw, "Here I am, I stand at the door" (3:20) and now the door is open. The very first words of chapter four are, "After this" implying right after the time of the church of Laodicea in John's vision. We now get to see what is behind that door as we see the Judge and the courtroom being seated in the next two chapters.

The voice which spoke was the same that John heard in 1:10. Therefore, the same view of God in His glory with white hair, blazing eyes and face, a sword coming from His mouth, holding seven stars and standing among the churches (lampstands) was probably seen here. (Look back at 1:10 -1:16 again to see this description). The voice like a trumpet called him "up" to the throne in heaven. Earlier the voice was as rushing waters (1:15). Both describe a powerful and loud voice. Perhaps the trumpet is significant because of 1 Thessalonians 4:16 and 1 Corinthians 15:52 which talk about the trumpet blasts at the end of the world. One must be careful, however, in saying that this voice is the trumpet blowing right now because the seven trumpets do not appear until after the seven seals have been opened in chapter 8. Here God's voice is only LIKE a trumpet.

How John traveled through time and space we do not know as John himself probably did not know. Paul wrote of a similar event when he states, "I know a man in Christ who fourteen years ago was caught up to the third heaven.

Whether it was in the body or out of the body I do not know--God knows. And I know that this man . . . was caught up to paradise. He heard inexpressible things, things that man is not permitted to tell" (2 Cor 12:3-4). (It is interesting to note that it was exactly 14 years earlier that Paul was beaten and left for dead at Lystra as told in Acts 14. Did Paul see the "light at the end of the tunnel," and was he brought back to life? After everyone thought he was dead, he *arose* and went back to town the same day. The following day he walked 30 miles. How could anyone be beaten so severely and do such a thing without Godly intervention?)

The throne John saw is perhaps the judgment seat of which all must stand before. "For we must all appear before the judgment seat of Christ, that each one may receive what is due him for the things done while in the body, whether good or bad" (2 Cor 5:10) and, "For we will all stand before God's judgment seat" (Romans 14:10).

Rev 4:3 And the one who sat there had the appearance of jasper and carnelian. A rainbow, resembling an emerald, encircled the throne.

God, who we just saw sitting on the judgment seat, was now described as having the appearance of jasper and carnelian. These precious stones are valuable as is the message God brings, but that doesn't seem to be the point. It is the brilliance of these stones that is being compared to God's brilliance. We see a very similar picture in Revelation 21:11: "It shone with the glory of God, and its brilliance was like that of a very precious jewel, like a jasper, clear as crystal." It is also interesting to note that the new Jerusalem has a foundation of 12 precious stones, two of which are carnelian and jasper (Rev 21:18-21). Each stone represented a tribe of Israel and it was predicted that these stones would be used (Is 54:11-12), which we will discuss later in chapter 21.

The rainbow is significant in that it not only shows us that God's throne is near, but also in the message it represents. Almost every time God is seen in His glory the rainbow is seen with Him. When Ezekiel saw God this is how he described it, "I saw that from what appeared to be His waist up He looked like glowing metal, as if full of fire, and that from there down He looked like fire; and brilliant light surrounded Him. Like the appearance of *a rainbow in the clouds* on a rainy day, *so was the radiance around Him*. This was the appearance of the likeness of the glory of the LORD" (Ezek 1:27-28). When Christ comes again the rainbow will be with Him: "Then I saw another mighty angel coming down from heaven. He was robed in a cloud, with a rainbow above His head; His face was like the sun, and His legs were like fiery pillars" (Rev 10:1). This coexistence of the rainbow and God is significant because of what the rainbow stands for. The rainbow first appeared after Noah's Flood when God put it in the sky and said, "I have set My rainbow in the clouds, and it will be the *sign of the covenant between Me and the earth*" (Gen 9:13). Though we are often unmindful of the rainbow and its meaning, it never leaves God's presence. His covenant promise is always there with Him shining brightly. When we see God, we also see His promises.

Rev 4:4 Surrounding the throne were twenty-four other thrones, and seated on them were twenty-four elders. They were dressed in white and had crowns of gold on their heads.

Around God's throne were 24 elders on their thrones. In 5:8-10 we see that these elders are saints. People who once lived on this earth, but now are in heaven. Who are these saints? When Peter asked Jesus what reward they would get for following Him, Jesus said, "I tell you the truth, at the renewal of all things, *when the Son of Man sits on His glorious throne*, you who have followed Me will also sit on *twelve thrones*, judging the twelve tribes of Israel" (Mat 19:28). From this passage we can clearly see that the 12 disciples are sitting around God's throne in heaven. But what about the other 12 if there are 24 thrones? We read about following Christ ourselves in Timothy where we see, "Here is a trustworthy saying: If we died with Him, we will also live with Him; if we endure, we will also reign with Him" (2 Tim 2:11-12). Also later in Revelation, "I saw thrones on which were seated those who had been given authority to judge. And I saw the souls of those who had been beheaded because of their testimony for Jesus and because of the Word of God. They had not worshipped the beast or his image and had not received his mark on their foreheads or their hands" (Rev 20:4). Even more straight forward is Paul who wrote, "Do you not know that the saints will judge the world" (1 Cor 6:2)? The other 12 could represent the rest of the saints as 12 does indeed represent completeness, just as three and seven do. See also Luke 19:11-27 and Matthew 25:31-32.

These disciples and saints are dressed in white and have gold crowns on their heads. Both of these are significant in that they show Christ's victorious redemption. The white robes were predicted back in 3:4-5 and is probably the linen clothing explained as the "righteous acts of the saints" in 19:8. The crown on their head is *stephanos* in the Greek and is a type of victors crown, showing them to have been victorious through Christ.

Rev 4:5 From the throne came flashes of lightning, rumblings and peals of thunder. Before the throne, seven lamps were blazing. These are the seven spirits of God. 4:6 Also before the throne there was what looked like a sea of glass, clear as crystal. In the center, around the throne, were four living creatures, and they were covered with eyes, in front and in back.

The throne is the focus point of this chapter because it is here that the Judge resides and announces His sentence upon the earth and those that dwell within. The fact that lightning and thunder came from the throne shows this is indeed a judgment, not a word of peace or comfort. God's thundering voice has often been associated with His deliverance or even the giving of the law at Mount Sinai (Ex 19:16). In Psalms we see, "The LORD thundered from heaven; the voice of the Most High resounded. He shot His arrows and scattered the enemies" (Psa 18:13-14).

The mystery of the seven lamps was explained for us so that there can be no doubt as to their meaning. They are the seven Spirits of God. There is only one Spirit, but it seems perhaps with seven qualities, as described earlier in our discussion on chapter one verse four in connection with Isaiah 11:2.

Other descriptions of God's throne have also described a clear reflecting surface before it. Since the living creatures were also here in verse six, we may have had reference to this "sea of glass" in Ezekiel which states, "Spread out above the heads of the living creatures was what looked like an expanse, sparkling like ice, and awesome" (Ezek 1:22). When Moses went up the mountain and saw God he described it this way: "Under His feet was something like a pavement made of sapphire, clear as the sky itself" (Ex 24:10).

The four living creatures are the cherubim. This explains why the temple in the Old Testament was built the way it was. The temple consisted of an outer court, a Holy Place and a Most Holy Place. The Most Holy Place was where the Ark of the Covenant rested. The Ark of the Covenant represented God's presence and His throne. On top of the Ark of the Covenant were the engraved cherubim. Inside was God's Word in the form of the Ten Commandments. In the Holy Place there were lampstands, a gold table for the bread of the presence, and the altar of incense, all of which are represented in our glimpse of the heavenly throne here. Therefore, one could almost say that the Old Testament temple was more symbolic and the description here in Revelation is more literal, because the Old Testament temple was simply a foreshadowing of the real heavenly throne with real cherubim, not just engravings. That is why the author of Hebrews wrote of Christ "If He were on earth, He would not be a priest, for there are already men who offer the gifts prescribed by the law. They serve at a sanctuary that is a **copy and shadow of what is in heaven**" (Heb 8:4-5).

These cherubim are with God wherever He goes. They are simply the chief angels whom God sits between on His throne as seen from the Psalms: "The LORD reigns, let the nations tremble; He sits enthroned between the cherubim, let the earth shake" (Ps 99:1); "You who sit enthroned between the cherubim, shine forth" (Ps 80:1). See also Is 37:16 and Ezek 9:3; 10:1-3. Even Satan was a cherub, "You were anointed as a guardian cherub, for so I ordained you. You were on the holy mount of God; you walked among the fiery stones. You were blameless in your ways from the day you were created till wickedness was found in you. Through your widespread trade you were filled with violence, and you sinned. So I drove you in disgrace from the mount of God, and I expelled you, O guardian cherub, from among the fiery stones" (Ezek 28:14-16). It was a cherub that guarded the Garden of Eden after the fall into sin as well (Gen 3:24). We will see them many times in Revelation (5:8-9; 6:1; 7:11; 14:3; 15:7; 19:4) and also in other Old Testament references to God's throne. In Ezekiel we see a lengthy but important description of these creatures:

> I looked, and I saw a windstorm coming out of the north--an immense cloud with flashing lightning and surrounded by brilliant light. The center of the fire looked like glowing metal, and in the fire was what looked like **four living creatures**. In appearance their form was that of a man, but each of them had **four faces and four wings**. Their legs were straight; their feet were like those of a calf and gleamed like

burnished bronze. Under their wings on their four sides they had the hands of a man. All four of them had faces and wings, and their wings touched one another. Each one went straight ahead; they did not turn as they moved. Their faces looked like this: Each of the four had the face of a **man**, and on the right side each had the face of a **lion**, and on the left the face of an **ox**; each also had the face of an **eagle**. Such were their faces. Their wings were spread out upward; each had two wings, one touching the wing of another creature on either side, [just as in the Most Holy Place in the temple] and two wings covering its body. Each one went straight ahead. Wherever the spirit would go, they would go, without turning as they went. The appearance of the living creatures was like burning coals of fire or like torches. Fire moved back and forth among the creatures; it was bright, and lightning flashed out of it. The creatures sped back and forth like flashes of lightning. As I looked at the living creatures, I saw a wheel on the ground beside each creature with its four faces. This was the appearance and structure of the wheels: They sparkled like chrysolite, and all four looked alike. Each appeared to be made like a wheel intersecting a wheel. As they moved, they would go in any one of the four directions the creatures faced; the wheels did not turn about as the creatures went. Their rims were high and awesome, and all four rims were **full of eyes** all around. When the living creatures moved, the wheels beside them moved; and when the living creatures rose from the ground, the wheels also rose. Wherever the spirit would go, they would go, and the wheels would rise along with them, because the spirit of the living creatures was in the wheels. When the creatures moved, they also moved; when the creatures stood still, they also stood still; and when the creatures rose from the ground, the wheels rose along with them, because the spirit of the living creatures was in the wheels. Spread out above the heads of the living creatures was what looked like an expanse, sparkling like ice, and awesome. Under the expanse their wings were stretched out one toward the other, and each had two wings covering its body. When the creatures moved, I heard the sound of their wings, like the roar of rushing waters, like the voice of the Almighty, like the tumult of an army. When they stood still, they lowered their wings. Then there came a voice from above the expanse over their heads as they stood with lowered wings. Above the expanse over their heads was what looked like a throne of sapphire, and high above on the throne was a figure like that of a man (Ezek 1:4-26).

After this description it goes on to describe this man in the same way as we saw in Revelation chapter one. As we move into verse seven we will look back upon this description of the cherub.

From these verses we can clearly see that if one cannot understand Revelation, one cannot understand the rest of the Bible either. Revelation has simply restated what has already been said earlier in other Old Testament books.

Thunder, lamps, clothing, sea, and living creatures have all been explained earlier. This is why it is so important to let Scripture interpret Scripture.

Rev 4:7 The first living creature was like a lion, the second was like an ox, the third had a face like a man, the fourth was like a flying eagle. 4:8 Each of the four living creatures had six wings and was covered with eyes all around, even under his wings. Day and night they never stop saying: "Holy, holy, holy is the Lord God Almighty, who was, and is, and is to come."

As in the above Ezekiel passage we see the four living creatures described in the same way. However, where Ezekiel saw four wings, John saw six. This difference may be explained in that there seems to be two types of cherubs. The type with four wings, which serves the same function as those with six, is called a seraphim. "I saw the Lord seated on a throne, high and exalted, and the train of His robe filled the temple. Above Him were seraphs, each with six wings: With two wings they covered their faces, with two they covered their feet, and with two they were flying. And they were calling to one another: '*Holy, holy, holy is the LORD Almighty*; the whole earth is full of His glory.' At the sound of their voices the doorposts and thresholds shook and the temple was filled with smoke" (Isa 6:1-4). It is also important to note that the same message was being sung by both the seraphs and the cherubs.

The fact that God is the One who is, was, and is to come, shows His eternal nature in the past, present, and future. What a glorious day it will be when it will be said, "Holy, holy, holy is the Lord God Almighty, who is and who was." This is exactly what will be said when Christ returns in chapter 11. Once He comes, there is no more need to say "who is to come."

Another important distinction between these angels and the saints is in how they worship God. Here, as it is anytime the angels worship, it is in third person praise. The saints, however, always worship in second person praise using the word "You" to describe God. This difference may be due to the fact that the angels do not understand the Gospel message like we do. After all, Christ did not come to die for the angels, only man. Peter explains, "It was revealed to them that they were not serving themselves but you, when they spoke of the things that have now been told you by those who have preached the gospel to you by the Holy Spirit sent from heaven. *Even angels long to look into these things*" (1 Pet 1:12). Isn't it amazing that we have a gift so special that even angels marvel at it?

Rev 4:9 Whenever the living creatures give glory, honor and thanks to him who sits on the throne and who lives for ever and ever, 4:10 the twenty-four elders fall down before him who sits on the throne, and worship him who lives for ever and ever. They lay their crowns before the throne and say: 4:11 "You are worthy, our Lord and God, to receive glory and honor and power, for you created all things, and by your will they were created and have their being."

As the cherubim worshipped, the 24 elders (saints and apostles) fell prostrate as they worshipped the eternal God. They laid the crowns that were on their heads down in front of the throne. As we mentioned in verse four, these are victors' crowns, and this act of presenting them to God was an acknowledgment of whose victory it really was. Now, in second person praise the elders gave God the glory for His creation and His sustaining power of that creation. This acknowledgment is important because it shows that the world belongs to God. That being the case, He has the right to judge it and that is exactly what He is about to do.

As seen earlier in 1:6 God was praised with a doxology in verse 11. God is such an orderly Creator it is even evident in the praises He receives. In chapter one He was worthy of glory and power; a two-fold doxology. Now honor has been added to that glory and power for a three-fold doxology. In 5:13 praise will be added to the glory, honor and power for a four-fold doxology. It will end in 7:12 with a seven-fold doxology.

CHAPTER 5

Rev 5:1 Then I saw in the right hand of him who sat on the throne a scroll with writing on both sides and sealed with seven seals. 5:2 And I saw a mighty angel proclaiming in a loud voice, "Who is worthy to break the seals and open the scroll?" 5:3 But no one in heaven or on earth or under the earth could open the scroll or even look inside it. 5:4 I wept and wept because no one was found who was worthy to open the scroll or look inside. 5:5 Then one of the elders said to me, "Do not weep! See, the Lion of the tribe of Judah, the Root of David, has triumphed. He is able to open the scroll and its seven seals."

Chapter five continues the courtroom scene started in chapter four. Now, however, Christ is given a scroll that is sealed seven times. The scroll contains words of judgment for the earth and the unbelievers who dwell on it. The best way to view this is as a deed to the earth. Christ is now coming to claim ownership of His creation.

God the Father was still sitting on the throne as seen in chapter four, however, now we see that He is holding a sealed scroll in His right hand. No one on earth or heaven was able to open it except the Lion of the tribe of Judah. We see in Isaiah, "For you this whole vision is nothing but words sealed in a scroll. And if you give the scroll to someone who can read, and say to him, 'Read this, please,' he will answer, 'I can't; it is sealed'" (Isa 29:11). However, because of Christ's ability to open the scroll, "In that day the deaf will hear the words of the scroll, and out of gloom and darkness the eyes of the blind will see" (Isa 29:18). The title, "Lion of the tribe of Judah" was given in Genesis 49:8-10 as a prophecy for Christ. Making this even clearer we see another title; the Root of David. This came from Isaiah 11:1,10, but was also quoted in Romans, showing it to be speaking of Christ. Paul wrote, "And again, Isaiah says, 'The Root of Jesse will spring up, One who will arise to rule over the nations; the Gentiles will hope in Him'" (Rom 15:12).

The scroll being sealed seven times is important for our understanding of the rest of Revelation. As mentioned in the introduction, each set of events (churches, seals, trumpets and vials) climaxes with the seventh one. But the seventh church only brings forth the seals. The seventh seal will only issue in the trumpets.

Each seal that is about to be opened will bring a judgment to the earth. It is interesting that Roman wills were sealed seven times as well, furthering the picture of this scroll as a deed to the earth. When the first seal was broken on a scroll one was able to unroll it a short ways until the next seal appeared. Then the second seal could be broken, and the scroll unrolled further, until the third seal appeared, and so on.

Rev 5:6 Then I saw a Lamb, looking as if it had been slain, standing in the center of the throne, encircled by the four living creatures

and the elders. He had seven horns and seven eyes, which are the seven spirits of God sent out into all the earth. 5:7 He came and took the scroll from the right hand of him who sat on the throne. 5:8 And when he had taken it, the four living creatures and the twenty-four elders fell down before the Lamb. Each one had a harp and they were holding golden bowls full of incense, which are the prayers of the saints. 5:9 And they sang a new song: "You are worthy to take the scroll and to open its seals, because you were slain, and with your blood you purchased men for God from every tribe and language and people and nation. 5:10 You have made them to be a kingdom and priests to serve our God, and they will reign on the earth."

We saw another description of Christ here as the slain Lamb. He was standing in an interesting place; in the center of the throne. God was sitting on the throne and now Christ was in the center of it. It seems that the throne was being occupied by both God and Jesus. This fits into our proper understanding of the Trinity; one God, three persons. In both cases, they were encircled by the four living creatures and the 24 elders (4:4; 5:6). Once again, the 24 elders were bowing down before the throne to worship (4:10; 5:8). Further, to finish out the Trinity, we saw Christ with seven horns and seven eyes. The horns can certainly symbolize power, and the eyes as all seeing and knowing, but sometimes it is too easy to become lost within symbolism. Luke wrote of this horn: "He has raised up a Horn of salvation for us in the house of His servant David" (Luke 1:69, see also Deut 33:17). For now it is best to see them as simply the Spirits of God, clearly described and easily understood. Once more this fits the description seen earlier in chapter one verse four where we saw the seven Spirits of God mentioned. See 1:4 for a commentary on this.

The fact that John saw Christ as both the Lion and the Lamb is important because the Lion is in reference to Him as Judge upon the people of the earth and the earth itself. However, the Lamb shows Him as the Redeemer of those people who follow Him.

When Christ took the scroll in His hand He was worshipped by the elders and the living creatures. One possible explanation comes from what the elders had in their hands. Golden bowls of incense which were the prayers of the saints. If the song they sang is any indication of the prayers offered we see praises were given to God for His righteous deliverance. Also in 6:10 John saw the saints calling out for God to judge the world and avenge their death brought about by these ungodly inhabitants. Hebrews 9:4 shows us a deeper truth with these prayers when it says that the altar of incense [prayers of the saints] was in the Most Holy Place where the Ark of the Covenant was. However, in the Old Testament, the altar of incense was in the Holy Place, not the Most Holy Place. This shows that after Christ the barrier keeping us from Him was broken. This is precisely why the curtain of the temple, separating the Most Holy Place from the Holy Place, was torn in two when Christ died (Mat 27:51). It clearly shows us that Christ is now our mediator to God. We no longer need a priest to offer prayers on our behalf, we do it ourselves. Here the saints themselves offered the prayers to Christ.

The song offered by the elders (saints and disciples) was new, because at this point a new era was beginning. For the first time Christ is going to judge the world because He has gained the right through His death and resurrection. Just as in 4:11 we see the elders were giving their praises in 2nd person, not third person as with the angels. There are many Old Testament references to this new song, many of which come from Psalms: "He put a new song in my mouth, a hymn of praise to our God. Many will see and fear and put their trust in the LORD" (Psa 40:3); "Praise the LORD. Sing to the LORD a new song, His praise in the assembly of the saints" (Psa 149:1); "A psalm. Sing to the LORD a new song, for He has done marvelous things; His right hand and His holy arm have worked salvation for Him" (Psa 98:1). See also Is 42:10 and Rev 14:3-4.

Rev 5:11 Then I looked and heard the voice of many angels, numbering thousands upon thousands, and ten thousand times ten thousand. They encircled the throne and the living creatures and the elders. 5:12 In a loud voice they sang: "Worthy is the Lamb, who was slain, to receive power and wealth and wisdom and strength and honor and glory and praise!"

Now John saw myriads of angels around the throne of God. Daniel likewise was seeing the same judgment day when he wrote, "A river of fire was flowing, coming out from before Him. Thousands upon thousands attended Him; ten thousand times ten thousand stood before Him. The court was seated, and the books were opened" (Dan 7:10). We also see from Jude that many will follow Christ during the judgment, "See, the Lord is coming with thousands upon thousands of His holy ones to judge everyone, and to convict all the ungodly of all the ungodly acts they have done in the ungodly way, and of all the harsh words ungodly sinners have spoken against Him" (Jude 1:14-15, see also Heb 12:22). There can be no question what is about to take place here in Revelation.
Since the angels were giving the praises here, we again see they were worshipping in 3rd person praise just as in 4:8.

Rev 5:13 Then I heard every creature in heaven and on earth and under the earth and on the sea, and all that is in them, singing: "To him who sits on the throne and to the Lamb be praise and honor and glory and power, for ever and ever!" 5:14 The four living creatures said, "Amen," and the elders fell down and worshipped.

These verses mirror the words of the psalmist who wrote, "Praise the LORD from the earth, you great sea creatures and all ocean depths, lightning and hail, snow and clouds, stormy winds that do His bidding, you mountains and all hills, fruit trees and all cedars, wild animals and all cattle, small creatures and flying birds" (Psa 148:7-10). Indeed, all of creation gives God glory. We read in Romans, "The creation waits in eager expectation for the sons of God to be revealed. For the creation was subjected to frustration, not by its own choice, but by the will of the one who subjected it, in hope that the creation itself will be liberated from its bondage to decay and brought into the glorious freedom of the children of God" (Rom 8:19-21). This freedom was now at hand and the living creatures acknowledged and agreed with those praises as they fell down to worship.

The earlier three-fold doxology of glory, honor and power (4:11), now becomes four-fold by adding praise to them. These praises, as discussed above, come from all of God's creation. Another interesting side note involves the four-fold doxology. The next time this doxology is seen it will be in its completion as a seven-fold doxology. In the section on 1:19-20 we discussed the patterns of sevens and how they are split between the first four and the last three. Here again we see a split with the doxologies ending after the fourth one but finishing with the seventh (7:12). This pattern holds true for whatever set of sevens one looks into.

At this point it may be good to do a quick recap of the first five chapters. We will do this periodically to keep the flow of things going smoothly without loosing track of what was previously explained.

1. In chapter one we saw a basic introduction showing us who wrote this, how and from whom John received it, and what he saw while the message was given. We saw a description of a Judge (God) among His churches, holding the angels of those churches in His hands.
2. In chapter two we shifted back to earth to see the churches that God was watching over. They symbolized all the churches throughout time. Each church brought us closer to the present era with their attributes getting worse and worse until finally ending with Laodicea, a lukewarm church who rejected God as Creator.
3. In chapter three we continued through these seven churches.
4. In chapter four we shifted back to heaven and returned to the Judge who was taking His seat on the throne. Around Him were the angels, saints and disciples praising Him.
5. In chapter five we saw Christ with God, having a scroll, or deed to the earth, while the praises continued. He is now ready to open the scroll so that the earth and its inhabitants can be judged. Chapter six will describe each of these seal judgments as the scroll is opened.

CHAPTER 6

Rev 6:1 I watched as the Lamb opened the first of the seven seals. Then I heard one of the four living creatures say in a voice like thunder, "Come!" 6:2 I looked, and there before me was a white horse! Its rider held a bow, and he was given a crown, and he rode out as a conqueror bent on conquest. 6:3 When the Lamb opened the second seal, I heard the second living creature say, "Come!" 6:4 Then another horse came out, a fiery red one. Its rider was given power to take peace from the earth and to make men slay each other. To him was given a large sword.

Way back in Daniel we saw much of the same vision described there as we have seen so far in Revelation up to chapter six, but Daniel did not understand it: "So I asked, 'My lord, what will the outcome of all this be?' He replied, 'Go your way, Daniel, because the words are closed up and sealed until the time of the end'" (Dan 12:8-9). What Daniel did not understand and what was to be sealed up (not written down) is now given to us in Revelation. At the time of the end we will know what is happening if God's Word is used and regarded to. In Matthew we read, "So when you see standing in the holy place 'the abomination that causes desolation,' spoken of through the prophet Daniel-- *let the reader understand--*" (Mat 24:15). Daniel says, "Many will be purified, made spotless and refined, but the wicked will continue to be wicked. None of the wicked will understand, but those who are *wise will understand*" (Dan 12:10). Jeremiah stated twice that, "The anger of the LORD will not turn back until He fully accomplishes the purposes of His heart. In days to come you will understand it clearly" (Jer 23:20, 30:24). Also, Paul wrote, "But you, brothers, are not in darkness so that this day should surprise you like a thief" (1 Th 5:4). It seems that even the trumpets will be heard clearly, "All you people of the world, you who live on the earth, when a banner is raised on the mountains, you will see it, and when a trumpet sounds, you will hear it" (Isa 18:3). It is therefore unnecessary to keep making unclear predictions regarding the fulfillment of these seals since they will be made clear by the Spirit of God when the time is at hand. However, do not let this allow you to slip into complacency regarding the study of God's Word, or perhaps you *will* be surprised. The Spirit, through whom we are given the understanding, works through the Word.

The first of the seven seals was opened by Christ, the Lamb of God. Once open, John saw a white horse being ridden by a man with a crown and bow, going out to conquer. The first question we must ask ourselves is: Who is this man? The second question being: Who, is he conquering? Many say that this is Christ because he was wearing a crown and riding a white horse, which usually would symbolize purity. They add to this the fact that in Revelation 19 we see a white horse with a man wearing a crown going out to conquer the ungodly. He has "King of kings" and "Lord of lords" written on His thigh. In

Revelation 19 there is no question that it is Jesus Christ. Here, however, it is none other than one attempting to be *like* Christ, in other words, the Antichrist. There are a few reasons for us to believe this. First, the crowns of the two riders here and in chapter 19 are different. Here it is the victors crown, *stephanos*, but in Revelation 19 it is *diadema*, from which we get the royal diadem, showing royalty. Secondly, these six seals are outlined exactly by Jesus in His end times description of Matthew 24. There, Christ showed us the Antichrist would be revealed first. We will look at this in greater detail when we reach the sixth seal. Third, the rider here was GIVEN a crown, showing the Antichrist is only allowed to have power for a short time.

The answer to who is being conquered can be none other than the saints of the Living God. We will see this happening throughout the book of Revelation, although that is not the focus of the book. One example comes from Revelation 12 where we see a dragon with seven crowns on his head flung to the earth. In verse nine we are told this dragon is Satan. Then, in verse 17 we see the devil going to "make war" against the saints, although the saints are protected by God.

When the second seal was opened, John saw a fiery red horse. (See Zech 1:8; 6:2). This vision brought about war, and peace was taken from the earth. This will very likely be an outcome of the Antichrist's conquest. Therefore, the first seal brought forth the Antichrist and the second seal brought war.

It is interesting to see that Zecheriah saw the same thing as we are seeing here in the seal judgments. We read, "During the night I had a vision-- and there before me was a man riding a red horse! He was standing among the myrtle trees in a ravine. Behind him were red, brown and white horses. I asked, 'What are these, my lord?' The angel who was talking with me answered, 'I will show you what they are.' Then the man standing among the myrtle trees explained, 'They are the ones the LORD has sent to go throughout the earth'" (Zec 1:8-10). In later chapters Zecheriah also wrote, "The first chariot had red horses, the second black, the third white, and the fourth dappled--all of them powerful. I asked the angel who was speaking to me, 'What are these, my lord?' The angel answered me, 'These are the four spirits of heaven, going out from standing in the presence of the Lord of the whole world'" (Zec 6:2-5). The angel clearly tells us what these horses are, and as we continue through these seals in Revelation you will see the same colored horses.

Rev 6:5 When the Lamb opened the third seal, I heard the third living creature say, "Come!" I looked, and there before me was a black horse! Its rider was holding a pair of scales in his hand. 6:6 Then I heard what sounded like a voice among the four living creatures, saying, "A quart of wheat for a day's wages, and three quarts of barley for a day's wages, and do not damage the oil and the wine!" 6:7 When the Lamb opened the fourth seal, I heard the voice of the fourth living creature say, "Come!" 6:8 I looked, and there before me was a pale horse! Its rider was named Death, and Hades was following close behind him. They were given power over a

fourth of the earth to kill by sword, famine and plague, and by the wild beasts of the earth.

The third seal was opened and a black horse appeared with its rider holding a pair of scales. These scales are used to measure food, not mans' sin, as understood from the voice of the four living creatures. Wheat and barley, a necessity in times of famine, costs an entire day's wages. However, oil and wine are plentiful since they are not the coveted items when food is scarce. Famine is a logical consequence of the war that began after the second seal was opened. These may very well be the days God was describing to Ezekiel when He said, "Son of man, I will cut off the supply of food in Jerusalem. The people will eat rationed food in anxiety and drink rationed water in despair, for food and water will be scarce. They will be appalled at the sight of each other and will waste away because of their sin" (Ezek 4:17). Ezekiel's prophecies not only foretold of the coming destruction of Jerusalem by the Babylonian army, but also of end times as clearly pointed out many times (Ezek14:12ff; 37; 39; 40-48). The Old Testament prophets often spoke of these dual prophecies.

Then, the fourth seal was opened and a pale horse with a rider called Death came riding forth. Behind it, Hades followed. The paleness reminds us of the pale color of a dead body. Hades has the same meaning as the Hebrew *Sheol*, the "place of the dead." Again, the expected progression is seen. The Antichrist was revealed and brought war, which brought famine, which brought death. Famine not only brings death through lack of food, but often greed increases and people kill one another. Diseases run rampant and plagues begin. This may be why verse eight tells us that one-fourth of the earth dies by sword, famine, plague, and wild beasts. This is the same warning God gave Ezekiel, "I will send **famine** and **wild beasts** against you, and they will leave you childless. **Plague** and bloodshed will sweep through you, and I will bring the **sword** against you. I the LORD have spoken" (Ezek 5:17). Almost the same precaution was repeated later when God said, "For this is what the Sovereign LORD says: How much worse will it be when I send against Jerusalem My four dreadful judgments--**sword and famine and wild beasts and plague**--to kill its men and their animals" (Ezek 14:21)! Ezekiel chapter seven seems to have told us where these events would take place, "Outside is the sword, inside are plague and famine; those in the country will die by the sword, and those in the city will be devoured by famine and plague" (Ezek 7:15, see also Jer 15:2-3, Hos 13:14). This pale horse was called "dappled" in Zecheriah 6:3.

Now that the fourth seal has been opened, one can expect to see a change in theme or direction for the next two seals. It is more easily seen using the outline in the back of the book, but we will examine this further at the end of the sixth seal.

Rev 6:9 When he opened the fifth seal, I saw under the altar the souls of those who had been slain because of the word of God and the testimony they had maintained. 6:10 They called out in a loud voice, "How long, Sovereign Lord, holy and true, until you judge the inhabitants of the earth and avenge our blood?" 6:11 Then each of them was given a white

robe, and they were told to wait a little longer, until the number of their fellow servants and brothers who were to be killed as they had been was completed. 6:12 I watched as he opened the sixth seal. There was a great earthquake. The sun turned black like sackcloth made of goat hair, the whole moon turned blood red, 6:13 and the stars in the sky fell to earth, as late figs drop from a fig tree when shaken by a strong wind. 6:14 The sky receded like a scroll, rolling up, and every mountain and island was removed from its place.

The fifth seal was opened and John saw the souls of the Christian martyrs crying out for God to avenge their blood. It is important to realize they did not die defending their lives but were killed for the Word of God. Paul wrote, "Do not take revenge, my friends, but leave room for God's wrath, for it is written: 'It is Mine to avenge; I will repay,' says the Lord" (Rom 12:19). Also, these saints were under the altar. This is significant because in the Old Testament sacrifices the blood of the animal was poured out under the altar (Lev 4:7; Ex 29:12). These saints sacrificed their lives for the sake of Christ.

As a result of their faith the saints are rewarded with a white robe. We know this to be the "righteous acts" they did according to Revelation 19:8. They are also told that God's time to avenge has not yet come because there are more saints that must yet be martyred as they were. Apparently God is allowing those who are doing the killing to have their sins reach their full measure as He did with the Ammorites (Gen 15:16). It seems the rest of the saints to be killed will soon be in heaven, as we will see in Revelation 20:4.

The sixth seal was opened and a great earthquake removed mountains and hills from their places. In addition, the sun stopped giving its light, the moon turned red, the stars fell from the sky, and the sky itself was rolled up. One would think such a sign would cause even the most rabid atheist to become a Bible believing Christian, but it doesn't work that way. This very day had been prophesied about thousands of years earlier in many different instances. Some of these passages follow:

- Joel 2:30-32 "I will show wonders in the heavens and on the earth, blood and fire and billows of smoke. The sun will be turned to darkness and the moon to blood before the coming of the great and dreadful day of the LORD. And everyone who calls on the name of the LORD will be saved; for on Mount Zion and in Jerusalem there will be deliverance, as the LORD has said, among the survivors whom the LORD calls."
- Zec 14:4-8 "On that day His feet will stand on the Mount of Olives, east of Jerusalem, and the Mount of Olives will be split in two from east to west, forming a great valley, with half of the mountain moving north and half moving south. You will flee by My mountain valley, for it will extend to Azel. You will flee as you fled from the earthquake in the days of Uzziah king of Judah. Then the LORD my God will come, and all the holy ones with Him. On that day there will be no light, no cold or frost. It will be a unique day, without daytime or nighttime--a day known to the LORD. When

evening comes, there will be light. On that day living water will flow out from Jerusalem."

- Isa 13:9-13 "See, the day of the LORD is coming --a cruel day, with wrath and fierce anger-- to make the land desolate and destroy the sinners within it. The stars of heaven and their constellations will not show their light. The rising sun will be darkened and the moon will not give its light. I will punish the world for its evil, the wicked for their sins. I will put an end to the arrogance of the haughty and will humble the pride of the ruthless. I will make man scarcer than pure gold, more rare than the gold of Ophir. Therefore I will make the heavens tremble; and the earth will shake from its place at the wrath of the LORD Almighty, in the day of His burning anger."
- Hag 2:6-7 "This is what the LORD Almighty says: 'In a little while I will once more shake the heavens and the earth, the sea and the dry land. I will shake all nations, and the desired of all nations will come, and I will fill this house with glory,' says the LORD Almighty."
- Isa 34:4 "All the stars of the heavens will be dissolved and the sky rolled up like a scroll; all the starry host will fall like withered leaves from the vine, like shriveled figs from the fig tree."
- Mat 24:29-30 "Immediately after the distress of those days 'the sun will be darkened, and the moon will not give its light; the stars will fall from the sky, and the heavenly bodies will be shaken.' At that time the sign of the Son of Man will appear in the sky, and all the nations of the earth will mourn. They will see the Son of Man coming on the clouds of the sky, with power and great glory."

The sixth seal was clearly foretold and should be no surprise for the believer. However, it should be noted that another interpretation is possible. Rather than being interpreted literaly, many of the above verses are said to be used in symbolic ways. For example, the passage in Isaiah 34:4 was talking of the destruction of Edom, yet this never literally happened. Instead, it was "lights out" for that country, and its rulers fell. Therefore, the Matthew passage could be referring to the fall of Jerusalem in 70 AD when its stars fell. However, it is most likely that these passages were symbolic, but they will still be literally fulfilled in the future.

Rev 6:15 Then the kings of the earth, the princes, the generals, the rich, the mighty, and every slave and every free man hid in caves and among the rocks of the mountains. 6:16 They called to the mountains and the rocks, "Fall on us and hide us from the face of him who sits on the throne and from the wrath of the Lamb! 6:17 For the great day of their wrath has come, and who can stand?"

This day will be so dreadful for the unbeliever that even the powerful men of the earth will flee to the mountains and caves to hide. In desperation they will wish that the mountains would fall on them so they couldn't see the face of God on His throne. However, this is inescapable. We read in Romans, "'As surely as I live,' says the Lord, 'every knee will bow before Me; every tongue will confess to God.' So then, each of us will give an account of himself to God" (Rom 14:11-12). This day is also predicted by the Old and New Testament prophets. In Isaiah we read, "Go into the rocks, hide in the ground from dread of the LORD and the splendor of His majesty" (Isa 2:10)! Jesus gave this warning, "then let those who are in Judea flee to the mountains" (Mat 24:16). Even Hosea wrote, "Then they will say to the mountains, 'Cover us!' and to the hills, 'Fall on us" (Hosea 10:8)! But once again, even this terrible fear brings forth no repentance, but instead, an even harder heart as we will see in 9:20, and 16:9, 11, 21. In reference to the fall of Jerusalem, historians record that the Christians saw the Roman armies coming and they escaped death when they fled to the Judean hills.

    This discussion of the seals would not be complete without taking a serious look at Matthew 24. Because of its importance a large portion of it is quoted below. As one reads this section it is easy to identify the six seals of Revelation (in order) within the Matthew text. Verses three through twenty-eight have often been interpreted as being fulfilled at the 70 AD destruction of Jerusalem by Rome. Verses 29 to the end of the chapter have been thought to predict end time events. This may or may not be a complete interpretation for a number of reasons. Matthew states in verse 21 that the distress will be worse than ever has been or will be again. First of all, it is hard to imagine that the destruction of Jerusalem fits this type of distress, although Josephus records amazing tragedies and even says that this distress had been unequaled in Jewish history. However, Daniel 12:1 tells us, "There will be a time of distress such as has not happened from the beginning of nations until then. . . Multitudes who sleep in the dust of the earth will awake: some to everlasting life, others to shame and everlasting contempt. Daniel seems to be saying that this time of distress isn't 70 AD but rather at the resurrection. However, 70 AD could have certainly foreshadowed this day. Secondly, the abomination of desolation spoken of by Daniel is mentioned in verse 15. Has this happened? Daniel seems to be referring to end times. One possible interpretation of the Daniel passage points to the Moslem Mosque being that "abomination" that caused literal desolation of the Temple, however, this again could simply foreshadow a greater abomination. In a sense, the Mosque is a blessing of God. If it weren't there today, the Jews would be sacrificing animals for their sins. Because the Temple can only be built on Mount Moriah, the very place the Mosque sits, it must first be removed before the Temple could be built. As long as the Mosque is there, the Jews cannot diminish the ultimate Sacrifice; Jesus Christ. Third, Jesus is answering a question that referred to the end times. The question becomes, end of what? This is not to say that Jerusalem's fall did not fulfill end time events, but rather that it is possible that they only typified a greater fulfillment to come. Luke's parallel account of the above Matthew 24 events is worded this way, "When you see Jerusalem being *surrounded by armies*, you will know that its desolation is near. Then let those who are in Judea flee to the mountains, let those in the city get out, and let those in the country not enter the city" (Luke 21:20-21). This seems to suggest that the Roman armies surrounding the city could be what is being described. There are many passages that we will later be looking at that show Jerusalem may again be surrounded by armies, however, it doesn't seem that anyone will be fleeing, because God will protect us at that time. Simply put, the various views on Revelation may not be all wrong or all right, but because of God's orderly blueprint of history many of these interpretations may have truth in them. Each interpretation fulfills what is prophesied, but only in part.

Before going through Matthew we must review the seal judgments. Then, as you read through Matthew, note the almost identical descriptions in the same chronological order.

7 SEALS
1) White horse- Antichrist revealed.
2) Red horse- war.
3) Black horse- famine.
4) Pale horse- sword, famine, plague, and wild beasts.
5) Saints in heaven have been persecuted and slain.
6) Sun and moon were darkened. Stars fell from the sky. Men hid from God as He appeared.
7) Seven trumpets are blown.

Mat 24:3 "As Jesus was sitting on the Mount of Olives, the disciples came to him privately. 'Tell us,' they said, '**when will this happen, and what will be the sign of your coming and of the end of the age?**' 24:4 Jesus answered: '**Watch out that no one deceives you. 24:5 For many will come in My name, claiming, 'I am the Christ, ' and will deceive many.** [Seal #1] 24:6 You will hear of **wars and rumors of wars,** [Seal # 2] but see to it that you are not alarmed. Such things must happen, but the end is still to come. 24:7 Nation will rise against nation, and kingdom against kingdom. There will **be famines and earthquakes in various places. 24:8 All these are the beginning of birth pains.** [Seal # 3 and 4] 24:9 Then you will be handed over to be **persecuted and put to death [Seal #5]**, and you will be hated by all nations because of Me. 24:10 At that time many will turn away from the faith and will betray and hate each other, 24:11 and many false prophets will appear and deceive many people. 24:12 Because of the increase of wickedness, the love of most will grow cold, 24:13 but he who stands firm to the end will be saved. 24:14 And this Gospel of the kingdom will be preached in the whole world as a testimony to all nations, and then the end will come. 24:15 **So [This word implies the speaker is reviewing what has been talked about so far]** when you see standing in the holy place **'the abomination that causes desolation,'** spoken of through the prophet Daniel--let the reader understand-- 24:16 then let those who are in Judea flee to the mountains. 24:17 Let no one on the roof of his house go down to take anything out of the house. 24:18 Let no one in the field go back to get his cloak. 24:19 How dreadful it will be in those days for pregnant women and nursing mothers! 24:20 Pray that your flight will not take place in winter or on the Sabbath. 24:21 **For then there will be great distress, unequaled from the beginning of the world until now--and**

never to be equaled again. 24:22 If those days had not been cut short, no one would survive, but for the sake of the elect those days will be shortened. 24:23 At that time if anyone says to you, 'Look, here is the Christ!' or, 'There he is!' do not believe it. 24:24 For false Christs and false prophets will appear and **perform great signs and miracles** to deceive even the elect--if that were possible. 24:25 See, I have told you ahead of time. 24:26 So if anyone tells you, 'There he is, out in the desert,' do not go out; or, 'Here he is, in the inner rooms,' do not believe it. 24:27 For as lightning that comes from the east is visible even in the west, so will be the coming of the Son of Man. 24:28 Wherever there is a carcass, there the vultures will gather. 24:29 **Immediately after the distress of those days [in other words, after the fifth seal] the sun will be darkened, and the moon will not give its light; the stars will fall from the sky, and the heavenly bodies will be shaken. [Seal #6]** 24:30 At that time the sign of the **Son of Man will appear in the sky**, and all the nations of the earth will mourn. They will see the Son of Man coming on the clouds of the sky, with power and great glory. 24:31 And He will **send His angels with a loud trumpet call [Seal # 7 when trumpets begin to blow],** and they will gather His elect from the four winds, from one end of the heavens to the other. 24:32 Now learn this lesson from the fig tree: As soon as its twigs get tender and its leaves come out, you know that summer is near. 24:33 Even so, when you see all these things, you know that it is near, right at the door. 24:34 I tell you the truth, **this generation will certainly not pass away until all these things have happened."**[The generation that sees the seals being opened, therefore, it seems the seals will not go on beyond one generation]. However, some believe that this generation was the one alive during the days of Christ and that the seal judgments have already taken place.

At the start of this book we discussed the patterns displayed in any of the series of sevens. Each seven can be split with the first four following one theme, the next two another, and the third a rest or break from whatever event is being described. Let us again examine the seal judgments and see how this pattern is displayed.

7 SEALS

First 4 dealt with horses.
1) White horse- Antichrist revealed.
2) Red horse- war.
3) Black horse- famine.
4) Pale horse- sword, famine, plague, and wild beasts.

Next 2 followed another theme.
5) **Saints in heaven had been persecuted and slain.**
6) **Sun and moon were darkened. Stars fell from the sky. Men hid from God as He appeared.**

Last one had nothing to do with the seals. Seals rested! Commercial break between 6th and 7th is chapter 7.
7) The seven trumpets will blow.

CHAPTER 7

Rev 7:1 After this I saw four angels standing at the four corners of the earth, holding back the four winds of the earth to prevent any wind from blowing on the land or on the sea or on any tree. 7:2 Then I saw another angel coming up from the east, having the seal of the living God. He called out in a loud voice to the four angels who had been given power to harm the land and the sea: 7:3 "Do not harm the land or the sea or the trees until we put a seal on the foreheads of the servants of our God."

Chapter seven is our commercial break between the sixth and seventh seal. As mentioned earlier, between each of the sixth and seventh events, whether seals, trumpets or vials, there is an interlude or some type of break before the seventh one begins. Understanding this will help in following the flow of Revelation.

John saw four angels standing at the four corners of the earth; north, east, west, and south. The job of these angels was to keep the four winds from blowing anywhere on earth. These four winds are reserved for destruction and judgment for the earth and its evil inhabitants during the last days when they will "harm the land and sea" (v. 2). We see this image in Jeremiah: "I will bring against Elam the four winds from the four quarters of the heavens; I will scatter them to the four winds" (Jer 49:36). Daniel gives further insight showing that these winds may have a large part to do with the coming of the false prophet and/or Antichrist: "In my vision at night I looked, and there before me were the four winds of heaven churning up the great sea. Four great beasts, each different from the others, came up out of the sea" (Dan 7:2-3). This vision of Daniel is closely connected to his other visions in which the four great kingdoms were talked about. The fourth and final one was Rome, from which the Antichrist is to come. Matthew also uses this language to show the "elect" will be gathered from all parts of the world: "And He will send His angels with a loud trumpet call, and they will gather His elect from the four winds, from one end of the heavens to the other" (Mat 24:31). This passage in Matthew seems to refer to the blowing of the seventh trumpet, not the events discussed here, however, it does show the four winds as representing the whole earth.

Next, an angel from the east came with the seal of the Living God. This statement proclaimed the Easter theme, "He is Risen." Death has no mastery over Him because He is living. The angels of the four winds were instructed not to begin their destruction UNTIL certain servants of God were sealed. Ezekiel recorded this event when he wrote of his vision when the angels were instructed to, "go throughout the city of Jerusalem and put a mark on the foreheads of those who grieve and lament over all the detestable things that are done in it" (Ezek 9:4). Here the mark was the Hebrew letter, *Taw*. This was written as an X or perhaps even more significantly as a cross (+). This could be the sealing of the Holy Spirit spoke of in Ephesians: "And do not grieve the Holy Spirit of God, with whom you were sealed for the day of redemption" (Eph 4:30). Speaking of Christ, John wrote, "Do not work for food that spoils, but for food that endures to eternal life, which the Son of Man will give you. On Him God the Father has placed His seal of approval" (John 6:27). Since circumcision was replaced by baptism (Col 2:11-12), the book of Romans clearly tells us we are sealed through baptism: "And he received the sign of circumcision, a seal of the righteousness that he had by faith while he was still uncircumcised" (Rom 4:11). Also in Corinthians we read, "Now it is God who makes both us and you stand firm in Christ. He anointed us, set His seal of ownership on us, and put His Spirit in our hearts as a deposit, guaranteeing what is to come" (2 Cor 1:21-22).

Who these servants are will be discussed in the next section. However, we must remember that all believers are sealed and have God's seal of approval and protection. In chapter nine we will see some creatures of God's wrath that will not be allowed to harm anyone with the seal; in other words, any Christian.

Rev 7:4 Then I heard the number of those who were sealed: 144,000 from all the tribes of Israel. 7:5 From the tribe of Judah 12,000 were sealed, from the tribe of Reuben 12,000, from the tribe of Gad 12,000 7:6 from the tribe of Asher 12,000, from the tribe of Naphtali 12,000, from the tribe of Manasseh 12,000, 7:7 from the tribe of Simeon 12,000, from the tribe of Levi 12,000, from the tribe of Issachar 12,000, 7:8 from the tribe of Zebulun 12,000, from the tribe of Joseph 12,000, from the tribe of Benjamin 12,000.

John was now told that those who were sealed were from the tribes of Israel, 12,000 from each one. There are four main opinions regarding these 144,000: 1) 144,000 literal Israelites. 2) 144,000 literal Christians regardless of Israelite blood. 3) 144,000 simply representing a symbolic number of all Jewish Christians. 4) 144,000 simply representing a symbolic number for all Christian believers regardless of Jewish descent. There are no easy answers to any of these opinions, but as stated in the introduction, we are going to let the Bible speak for itself. We have no indication that these numbers were symbolically representing a different number. They are indeed symbolic, but perhaps literal at the same time. For example, the seven days of creation were seven literal, twenty-four hour days, but they were symbolic of completeness. Jesus was in the grave three literal days too, symbolizing completeness. A wedding ring symbolizes unity yet it remains a ring. Just because something has symbolic meaning doesn't mean it isn't literal. When things are to be taken figuratively in the book of Revelation, they are often explained for us. In chapter one, John was told that the stars in God's hand *represented* angels and the lampstands *represented* churches (1:19). The same type of explanations were given and will be given in many other places as well. In 11:8, John is even told that the great city is "figuratively" called Sodom. With the number 144,000 no such indications are given. This is not to say that it couldn't be figurative, however, nothing but presuppositions would lead us to think so.

That leads us to the question of who these 144,000 are: Jewish Christians or any Christians? The reason some believe they could be Christians of all nationalities stems from Romans where we read: "Nor because they are his descendants are they all Abraham's children. On the contrary, 'It is through Isaac that your offspring will be reckoned.' In other words, it is not the natural children who are God's children, but *it is the children of the promise who are regarded as Abraham's offspring*" (Rom 9:7-8). Also speaking of the Gentiles Paul wrote, "If some of the branches have been broken off, and you, though a *wild olive shoot, have been grafted in among the others* and now share in the nourishing sap from the olive root, do not boast over those branches. If you do, consider this: You do not support the root, but the root supports you" (Rom 11:17-18). In Peter we read that the Gentiles are, "*a chosen people, a royal priesthood, a holy nation,* a people belonging to God, that you may declare the praises of Him who called you out of darkness into His wonderful light. Once you were not a people, but now you are the people of God; once you had not received mercy, but now you have received mercy" (1 Pet 2:9). Likewise in the Old Testament this was said of Israel, "Now if you obey Me fully and keep My covenant, then out of all nations you will be My treasured possession. Although the whole earth is Mine, you will be for Me a *kingdom of priests and a holy nation.* These are the words you are to speak to the Israelites" (Exo 19:5-6). Scripturally, we cannot deny that the Gentile believers have been grafted into God's family as the offspring of Abraham. However, Scripturally there still remains a distinction between Jew and Gentile believers. The above Romans passage continues, "You will say then, 'Branches were broken off so that I could be grafted in.' Granted. But they were broken off because of unbelief, and you stand by faith. Do not be arrogant, but be afraid. For if God did not spare the natural branches, He will not spare you either. Consider therefore the kindness and sternness of God: sternness to those who fell, but kindness to you, provided that you continue in His kindness. Otherwise, you also will be cut off. And if they do not persist in unbelief, they will be grafted in, for God is able to graft them in again" (Rom 11:19-23). Note that God not only says He can graft the Jews into the church again, but that He will do it. Even more to the point a couple of verses later Paul wrote, "I do not want you to be ignorant of this **mystery,** brothers, so that you *may not be conceited*: Israel has experienced a hardening in part **until** the *full number of the Gentiles has come in.* And so **all Israel will be saved**, as it is written: 'The deliverer will come from Zion; He will turn godlessness away from *Jacob*. [It is interesting to note the word "Jacob" is used and not Israel. Non-Jewish believers are spiritual Israel but not spiritual Jacob.] And this is My **covenant with them** when I take away their sins.' As far as the gospel is concerned, **they** are enemies on your account; but as far as election is concerned, **they** are loved on account of the patriarchs" (Rom 11:25-27). From these verses there can be no question that God views the Jewish believers as His chosen race. This is not to say Gentile believers are any less important or less saved, however, God's promise to the Jews still stands. God does not break His covenants. Could these 144,000 be a literal number that symbolically represents all of Israel? This view will be further supported when we see that the next section specifically mentions Christian people who are of every nation, language, and tribe. God seems to make an intentional separation of Jews and Gentiles, back to back, in verses seven through ten in Revelation. It is also important to realize the 144,000 people were on earth and the multitude coming up in verse nine will be in heaven. Perhaps the reason for 144,000 people, is that these are a chosen few who will serve a purpose on earth during the end times. We will see these 144,000 later at the throne of God in heaven in chapter 14. The fact that verse nine will also mention "the tribe" may indicate Jewish believers are included there as well, just not among the 144,000. The following are a few of many other verses that may indicate a Jewish revival at the end times:

- "In that day the Lord will reach out His hand a second time to reclaim the remnant that is left of His people from Assyria, from Lower Egypt, from Upper Egypt, from Cush, from Elam, from Babylonia, from Hamath and from the islands of the sea. He will raise a banner for the nations and gather the exiles of Israel; He will assemble the scattered people of Judah from the *four quarters of the earth*" (Isa 11:11-12). *Keep in mind that here in chapter seven the angels are coming from the four corners of the earth.*
- "' In that day,' declares the LORD Almighty, 'I will break the yoke off their necks and will tear off their bonds; no longer will foreigners enslave them. Instead, they will serve the LORD their God and David their king, whom I will raise up for them. So do not fear, O Jacob My servant; do not be dismayed, O Israel,' declares the LORD. 'I will surely save you out of a distant place, your descendants from the land of their exile. Jacob will again have peace and security, and no one will make him afraid'" (Jer 30:8-10).
- "I will take the Israelites out of the nations where they have gone. I will gather them from all around and bring them back into their own land. I will make them one nation in the land, on the mountains of Israel. There will be one king over all of them and they will never again be two nations or be divided into two kingdoms. They will no longer defile themselves with their idols and vile images or with any of their offenses, for I will save them from all their sinful backsliding, and I will cleanse them. They will be My people, and I will be their God. My servant David will be king over them, and they will all have one shepherd. They will follow My laws and be careful to keep My decrees. They will live in the land I gave to My servant Jacob, the land where your fathers lived. They and their children and their children's children will live there forever, and David My servant will be their prince forever. I will make a covenant of peace with them; it will be an *everlasting* covenant. I will establish them and increase their numbers, and I will put My *sanctuary among them forever*. My dwelling place will be with them; I will be their God, and they will be My people. Then the nations will know that I the LORD make Israel holy, when My sanctuary is among them forever" (Ezek 37:21-28).
- "For the Israelites will live many days without king or prince, *without sacrifice* or sacred stones, without ephod or idol. Afterward the Israelites will return and seek the LORD their God and David their king. They will come trembling to the LORD and to His blessings *in the last days*" (Hosea 3:4-5).
- "'The days are coming,' declares the LORD, 'when men will no longer say, 'As surely as the LORD lives, who brought the Israelites up out of Egypt,' but they will say, 'As surely as the LORD lives, who brought the Israelites

up out of the land of the north and out of all the countries where He had banished them.' For I will restore them to the land I gave their forefathers'" (Jer 16:15-16).

- "As for you, O house of Israel, this is what the Sovereign LORD says: Go and serve your idols, every one of you! But afterward you will surely listen to Me and no longer profane My holy name with your gifts and idols. For on My holy mountain, the high mountain of Israel, declares the Sovereign LORD, there in the land the entire house of Israel will serve Me, and there I will accept them. There I will require your offerings and your choice gifts, along with all your holy sacrifices. I will accept you as fragrant incense when I bring you out from the nations and gather you from the countries where you have been scattered, and I will show Myself holy among you in the sight of the nations" (Ezek 20:39-41).
- "For I will be like a lion to Ephraim, like a great lion to Judah. I will tear them to pieces and go away; I will carry them off, with no one to rescue them. Then *I will go back to My place until they admit their guilt.* And they will seek My face; in their misery they will earnestly seek Me. Come, let us return to the LORD. He has torn us to pieces but He will heal us; He has injured us but He will bind up our wounds. After *two days* He will revive us; on the *third day* He will restore us, that we may live in His presence" (Hosea 5:14-6:2).

Another interesting fact is seen in the listed tribes. In Genesis, Joseph received a double portion of the inheritance and his two sons, Ephraim and Manasseh, became tribes. Though Manasseh remains here, Ephraim is missing and was replaced by Joseph. This was predicted by Hosea: "Ephraim will be laid waste *on the day of reckoning.* Among the tribes of Israel I proclaim what is certain" (Hosea 5:9).

Also in Genesis, Levi was not considered one of the tribes of Israel, but was scattered throughout the other 12 tribes in 48 towns to serve as priests. Here in Revelation, Levi was included. Who did he replace? The tribe of Dan is missing in Revelation. In Genesis 49:17 he was called a serpent. We also see some of Dan's idol worship described in Judges 18:30 and 1 Kings 12:29. Though not conclusive, it is possible that Dan's leadership in sin excluded him from the prize.

Rev 7:9 After this I looked and there before me was a great multitude that no one could count, from every nation, tribe, people and language, standing before the throne and in front of the Lamb. They were wearing white robes and were holding palm branches in their hands. 7:10 And they cried out in a loud voice: "Salvation belongs to our God, who sits on the throne, and to the Lamb."

After John saw the 144,000 he looked up to see a multitude of people beyond number. They were people of all nations and blood lines standing before the throne of God in heaven. We know that these are saints, yet for some reason they have been listed separately from the 144,000 above. Both groups were seen standing before the throne (7:9,14:3) in heaven. We see that John uses the same terminology to describe everyone, regardless of race, in 5:9, 11:9, 13:7, and 14:6. In 10:11 and 17:15 they are used as well, however, the word *tribe* is left out for some unknown reason.

The multitude were wearing white robes. In 3:4 we saw that anyone who overcame the sins of the flesh through faith in Christ's blood were to be dressed in white and walk with God. In 19:8, at the great wedding banquet of the Lamb, the bride (church) was given white linen to wear as a symbol of righteousness.

The multitude also held palm branches in their hands while they praised God and acknowledged His authority to reign and His power to save. In the Old Testament we see that palm branches were used for the Feast of Tabernacles (also called Feast of Booths) and was a celebration of God's deliverance. We read in Leviticus, "On the first day you are to take choice fruit from the trees, and palm fronds, leafy branches and poplars, and rejoice before the LORD your God for seven days. Celebrate this as a festival to the LORD for seven days each year" (Lev 23:40-41). During Jesus triumphant entry into Jerusalem the crowd seemed to realize that this feast was a celebration for the Messiah when He came: "many of the Jews were going over to Jesus and putting their faith in Him. The next day the great crowd that had come for the Feast heard that Jesus was on His way to Jerusalem. They took palm branches and went out to meet Him, shouting, 'Hosanna! Blessed is He who comes in the name of the Lord! Blessed is the King of Israel'" (John 12:11-13)! Therefore, the multitude in Revelation are praising God for His deliverance through their salvation. This is even more significant when we will see in verse 14 that these are the saints who have been brought out of the great tribulation, of which we will discuss in verse 14. Also keep in mind that we are seeing a large number of saints in heaven but these cannot be all of the saints because the seventh trumpet has not yet blown. It isn't until the final trumpet sounds that all believers enter heaven (1 Cor 15:52). At this point, the seventh seal, which ushers in the trumpets, has not yet been broken.

Rev 7:11 All the angels were standing around the throne and around the elders and the four living creatures. They fell down on their faces before the throne and worshipped God, 7:12 saying: "Amen! Praise and glory and wisdom and thanks and honor and power and strength be to our God for ever and ever. Amen!"

In verses 11 and 12 John saw the four living creatures, the elders, and all the angels around the throne. Where was the multitude? It is possible, as suggested in 4:4, that the elders represented the saints and the disciples. Therefore, the angels may have been surrounding the great multitude who stand before the throne. Keep in mind the multitude were in heaven and the 144,000 were still on earth.

All of the angels that surround the throne, elders and cherubim fall prostrate and worship. The previous four-fold (5:13) doxology is now complete as it here became seven-fold: 1) praise 2) glory 3) wisdom 4) thanks 5) honor 6) power 7) strength.

Rev 7:13 Then one of the elders asked me, "These in white robes-- who are they, and where did they come from?" 7:14 I answered, "Sir, you know." And he said, "These are they who have come out of the great tribulation; they have washed their robes and made them white in the blood of the Lamb. 7:15 Therefore, "they are before the throne of God and serve him day and night in his temple; and he who sits on the throne will spread his tent over them. 7:16 Never again will they hunger; never again will they thirst. The sun will not beat upon them, nor any scorching heat. 7:17 For the Lamb at the center of the throne will be their shepherd; he will lead them to springs of living water. And God will wipe away every tear from their eyes."

John was now told who these people were; the saints that came out of the tribulation. They were killed because of their belief and testimony of Christ (12:11). As already noted, their white robes represent the righteous acts of the saints (19:8). Does that mean we can earn our white robes through our "acts" or deeds? By no means! Note that the way their robes became white was not through their acts, but rather through Christ's act on the cross. It was through the blood of the Lamb that the saints became clothed in white. Through Christ's blood, all of our acts become righteous ones because anything unrighteous is forgiven and forgotten. John wrote, "But if we walk in the light, as He is in the light, we have fellowship with one another, and the blood of Jesus, His Son, purifies us from all sin" (1 John 1:7).

What is this great tribulation from which these people come? These are those days spoken of in Matthew that are reserved for the end times: "For then there will be great distress, unequaled from the beginning of the world until now--and never to be equaled again. If those days had not been cut short, no one would survive, but for the sake of the elect those days will be shortened. At that time if anyone says to you, 'Look, here is the Christ!' or, 'There he is!' do not believe it. For false Christs and false prophets will appear and perform great signs and miracles to deceive even the elect--if that were possible. See, I have told you ahead of time" (Mat 24:21-25). Daniel also spoke of these days as a time between the Antichrist and the seventh trumpet: "At that time Michael, the great prince who protects your people, will arise. There will be a time of distress such as has not happened from the beginning of nations until then. But at that time your people--everyone whose name is found written in the book--will be delivered. *Multitudes* who sleep in the dust of the earth will awake: some to everlasting life, others to shame and everlasting contempt" (Dan 12:1-2).

Some believe the tribulation started with the early church. Though those terrible times of persecution may have foreshadowed the great tribulation, the time discussed here is to be "short" and a time of distress "unequaled" in all of time. Also, as already discussed with the sixth seal, Matthew 24 is discussing the times of the seals, not before. This tribulation may be a three and one-half year time after the three and one-half years of the two witnesses, of whom we will discuss in chapter 11. Also see 12:15-17.

These saints are serving God at His throne and in His temple. It is interesting that in all 16 times the word for temple is used in Revelation, it always is in reference to the Most Holy Place of the temple. This was the place in which God dwelled in the Old Testament tabernacle or temple. Later on in this book we will take a closer look at some of the intricate patterns and symbolisms seen within the Old Testament Tabernacle. In short, every part of the Old Testament Temple foreshadowed something that is in heaven. Just as the priest foreshadowed the redeemed man, the temple foreshadowed the home of that man. Therefore, we see clear evidence that the saints are in heaven with God.

It is here in heaven that they are protected from all harm and danger with complete peace and joy by the great Shepherd. There are many promises fulfilled here in these last verses of chapter seven, which we will list separately.

- Serve God before His throne (v. 15): "No longer will there be any curse. The throne of God and of the Lamb will be in the city, and His servants will serve Him" (Rev 22:3).
- God's tent spread over them (v. 15): "Then the LORD will create over all of Mount Zion and over those who assemble there a cloud of smoke by day and a glow of flaming fire by night; over all the glory will be a canopy. It will be a shelter and shade from the heat of the day, and a refuge and hiding place from the storm and rain" (Isa 4:5-6). "And I heard a loud voice from the throne saying, 'Now the dwelling of God is with men, and He will live with them. They will be His people, and God Himself will be with them and be their God'" (Rev 21:3).
- Never be hungry or thirsty (v. 16): "Then Jesus declared, 'I am the bread of life. He who comes to Me will never go hungry, and he who believes in Me will never be thirsty'" (John 6:35).
- The sun will not hurt them (v. 16): "They will neither hunger nor thirst, nor will the desert heat or the sun beat upon them. He who has compassion on them will guide them and lead them beside springs of water" (Isa 49:10).
- The Lamb is their Shepherd (v. 17): "May the God of peace, who through the blood of the eternal covenant brought back from the dead our Lord Jesus, that great Shepherd of the sheep" (Heb 13:20). "I am the good shepherd. The good shepherd lays down His life for the sheep" (John 10:11).
- Wipe away all tears (v. 17): "He will swallow up death forever. The Sovereign LORD will wipe away the tears from all faces; He will remove the disgrace of His people from all the earth. The LORD has spoken" (Isa 25:8). "And the ransomed of the LORD will return. They will enter Zion with singing; everlasting joy will crown their heads. Gladness and joy will overtake them, and sorrow and sighing will flee away" (Isa 35:10). "I will rejoice over Jerusalem and take delight in My people; the sound of weeping and of crying will be heard in it no more" (Isa 65:19). "He will wipe every

tear from their eyes. There will be no more death or mourning or crying or pain, for the old order of things has passed away" (Rev 21:4).

There can be no doubt that the location of these saints is in heaven with Christ!

CHAPTER 8

Rev 8:1 When he opened the seventh seal, there was silence in heaven for about half an hour. 8:2 And I saw the seven angels who stand before God, and to them were given seven trumpets. 8:3 Another angel, who had a golden censer, came and stood at the altar. He was given much incense to offer, with the prayers of all the saints, on the golden altar before the throne. 8:4 The smoke of the incense, together with the prayers of the saints, went up before God from the angel's hand. 8:5 Then the angel took the censer, filled it with fire from the altar, and hurled it on the earth; and there came peals of thunder, rumblings, flashes of lightning and an earthquake.

Chapter eight can be outlined as silence (v.1), preparation (v. 2), prayer (v. 3-5), and punishment (v. 6-13). We will see the seventh seal opened up, which brings forth the seven trumpet judgments. Only the first four trumpets will be seen in chapter eight, making another break between the 4th and 5th event. However, since chapter breaks are man made, this is not an inspired pattern. There will be a break, but the chapter position does not qualify.

Just as the seventh day of Creation brought rest, the seventh seal ushered in a period of silence to prepare us for God's wrath. During this period seven angels were given seven trumpets. These were the angels seen in 7:2 that were commanded to withhold their punishment until the 144,000 had been sealed and protected. With each trumpet that is blown, a judgment will take place, just as with each seal that was opened. In Old Testament times, trumpets were used to warn or give signals of a coming event, usually war. Therefore, these seven trumpets will not only announce God's righteous judgment, but also warn us of the bowl judgments coming soon in chapter 16.

Also during this period of silence, another angel, besides the seven who were given trumpets, came and stood under the altar to offer incense of prayers to God at His golden altar. Do not think that this angel had these prayers because someone prayed to him. The angel had these prayers because someone GAVE them to him to offer to God, who sat on the throne (v. 3). Though the text says incense and prayers were given to this angel, the Greek implies that the incense was the prayers. This is supported back in 5:8 where we saw the four living creatures and the elders were bowing down and had golden bowls of incense which, "were the prayers of the saints."

The golden altar on which these prayers were offered in heaven was foreshadowed in the Old Testament tabernacle in the Most Holy Place: "Make an altar of acacia wood for burning incense. . . . Overlay the top and all the sides and the horns with pure gold, and make a gold molding around it. . . . Put the altar in front of the curtain that is before the ark of the Testimony--before the atonement cover that is over the Testimony--where I will meet with you. . . [Aaron] must burn again when he lights the lamps at twilight so incense will burn regularly before the LORD for the generations to come. Do not offer on this altar any other incense or any burnt offering or grain offering, and do not pour a drink offering on it" (Ex 30:1-9). We therefore see that in Aaron's days these fragrant offerings represented the prayers of God's people. The smoke would thus carry these prayers to God. Even the psalmist understood incense to represent prayers rising: "May my prayer be set before You like incense; may the lifting up of my hands be like the evening sacrifice" (Psa 141:2). We will continue to see this altar as we go through Revelation. It is important to remember that it was located in the Most Holy Place by the ark of the Testimony, which was representative of God's presence in Old Testament times.

After the prayers went up before God the angel filled the sensor that was in his hand with fire from the altar and poured it out upon the earth. It is possible that this action was in response or an answer to the saints prayers just offered by the angel. In any case, the pouring out of fire brought thunder, lightning and a great earthquake. We saw a similar view of thunder and lightning before God's throne in 4:5. In chapter four we saw the courtroom being seated and thus a judgment was about to take place. Again, we see that this is not a peaceful return of our Lord. He is to bring wrath for the final destruction of the ungodly.

Section 3 (Revelation 8:6-11:19) The Trumpets

Rev 8:6 Then the seven angels who had the seven trumpets prepared to sound them. 8:7 The first angel sounded his trumpet, and there came hail and fire mixed with blood, and it was hurled down upon the earth. A third of the earth was burned up, a third of the trees were burned up, and all the green grass was burned up.

When the first angel sounded his trumpet there came hail and fire mixed with blood. When it was hurled upon the earth, a third of the earth, whether green or brown, was burned up. In addition, all the green grass was burned. Speaking of end times Ezekiel wrote, "I will execute judgment upon [Gog] with plague and bloodshed; I will pour down torrents of rain, hailstones and burning sulfur on him and on his troops and on the many nations with him. And so I will show My greatness and My holiness, and I will make Myself known in the sight of many nations. Then they will know that I am the LORD" (Ezek 38:22-23). It is also interesting to see that many of the plagues God is bringing forth will mirror the plagues brought upon Egypt. In Moses's day hail destroyed their crops and stripped every green tree. Though fire was not involved, the plague was to "show you My power and that My Name might be proclaimed in all the earth" (Ex 9:16).

Rev 8:8 The second angel sounded his trumpet, and something like a huge mountain, all ablaze, was thrown into the sea. A third of the sea turned into blood, 8:9 a third of the living creatures in the sea died, and a third of the ships were destroyed.

The second angel blew his trumpet and a third of the sea turned into blood destroying a third of the ships and killing a third of the animals in the water. This came about by what could be a meteor or comet falling into the oceans. However, it could certainly be something unknown as well. We must be careful in limiting God's power to only what is in the realm of our experience today. God does often use the scientific laws of nature and the world around us for His judgments, but there are many events in Old Testament times that cannot be explained with our current understanding of scientific principles.

Some believe these trumpet judgments are identical to the bowl judgments yet to come. However, this is not justifiable Scripturally for many reasons, most of which we will discuss when we get to the bowl judgments. For now just be aware that only 1/3 of the earth, sea, etc. is affected. In the bowl judgments, however, the remaining 2/3 will be destroyed so that there is total annihilation.

Once again, the plagues of Egypt were mirrored as water was turned into blood (Ex 7:20-21).

Rev 8:10 The third angel sounded his trumpet, and a great star, blazing like a torch, fell from the sky on a third of the rivers and on the springs of water-- 8:11 the name of the star is Wormwood. A third of the waters turned bitter, and many people died from the waters that had become bitter.

When the third trumpet sounded a great blazing star fell on the earth and affected one-third of all the fresh water. The star was named Wormwood, which means *bitter*, because it made the fresh water undrinkable. In fact, many who tried to drink it, died. Mark wrote of a day that seems to be referring more to the sixth seal or fourth trumpet, but the third trumpet would also fit when he said, "the stars will fall from the sky, and the heavenly bodies will be shaken."

A similar event of bitter water was foretold by Jeremiah: "Therefore, this is what the LORD Almighty, the God of Israel, says: 'See, I will make this people eat bitter food and drink poisoned water'" (Jer 9:15, see also 23:15). Also, during the Egyptian plagues the freshwater was undrinkable because it turned to blood.

Thanks to Hollywood, one can visualize the attitude the United States or any other country would have to such an event. Movies such as *Armageddon* or *Deep Impact* have glorified our scientific knowledge and confidence thereof. It is believed that if we see a comet or asteroid coming towards the earth we can send astronauts to blow it up with nuclear explosions or deflect it off its Earth bound course. NASA is confident that such an event can be prevented. In fact, a few years ago they discovered an asteroid that was going to hit the Earth shortly after the year 2000. The scientists were telling us that by then we would certainly have the means to stop it and, therefore, we had no need to worry. It is almost as if we are being prepared for this shocking event. However, rather than seeing it as a Divine judgment, it may very well be seen as a NASA screwup. This is one event that no amount of scientific knowledge will be able to stop.

Remember, "pride goes before destruction, a haughty spirit before a fall" (Prov 16:18).

Rev 8:12 The fourth angel sounded his trumpet, and a third of the sun was struck, a third of the moon, and a third of the stars, so that a third of them turned dark. A third of the day was without light, and also a third of the night. 8:13 As I watched, I heard an eagle that was flying in midair call out in a loud voice: "Woe! Woe! Woe to the inhabitants of the earth, because of the trumpet blasts about to be sounded by the other three angels!"

The fourth trumpet brings forth a judgment upon the heavens. One-third of the sun, moon and stars are struck with darkness. As a result, one-third of the day is without light. This may indicate that this is a time period of darkness rather than a certain percentage of the sun or moon being darkened. Although some speculate this will be caused by an eclipse or the sun burning out, the fact is, we cannot say. More than likely it will be a Divine miracle of which no explanation outside of Scripture will be adequate. When this happens I am sure explanations will be given to unbelievers, but not adequate ones. I believe Ezekiel may give us the best understanding of how God will do this. Rather than the sun itself being darkened or the stars falling, there may be a covering that doesn't allow the sun, moon or starlight to shine through. A simple eclipse doesn't explain why the stars wouldn't be seen. However, Ezekiel explains, "When I snuff you out, I will cover the heavens and darken their stars; I will cover the sun with a cloud, and the moon will not give its light. All the shining lights in the heavens I will darken over you; I will bring darkness over your land, declares the Sovereign LORD" (Ezek 32:7-8). We again see the plagues of Egypt revisited when darkness covered the land for three days: "Then the LORD said to Moses, 'Stretch out your hand toward the sky so that darkness will spread over Egypt--darkness that can be felt'" (Ex 10:21). I am sure the darkness during these end times will be a darkness that can be felt in our innermost parts. It is also interesting that this darkness took place in Egypt just before the exodus out of slavery. Here too, this darkness is occurring just before our exodus out of this sin-filled world at the seventh trumpet.

As always, whether it be seals, trumpets or vials, the fourth event is separated from the fifth. Verse thirteen shows us this change in theme as an eagle (probably an angel) flies through the air warning the ungodly of the next three trumpet blasts. (Keep in mind the seventh trumpet blast is actually the seven vials being poured out). One interesting note about the eagle could be seen in Psalm 91 where we read, "He will cover you with His feathers, and under His wings you will find refuge; His faithfulness will be your shield and rampart. You will not fear the terror of night, nor the arrow that flies by day" (Psa 91:4-5). There can be no explanation other than God being that eagle. As we will discuss later in Revelation 12:14, the wings of an eagle (God) are given to protect the Lord's people. This predicts the same deliverance that the Israelites had during the Exodus (Ex 19:4). Therefore, in all cases the eagle points to God.

These three woes will be announced each time the next trumpet is about to blow (9:12, 11:14). Chapter nine, verse six shows us that these trumpet blasts will only affect the ungodly and is therefore nothing to concern ourselves with. However, with that said it is important for us to look outside ourselves. One of the wonderful messages of Revelation is that the time of the end is soon. For believers that is a great thing because that means our heaven is about to begin. Right now on earth, this is as bad as it gets for us. On the other hand, for the ungodly their heaven is now. The present earth is as good as it gets for them. Only hell fills their future. This should give us a sense of urgency to go out and preach the Gospel boldly to our friends and family who do not believe in Christ as their PERSONAL Savior. Sometimes it is easy to put off the great commission and wait for the "right" time. Revelation shows us that time is NOW. After all, aren't our loved ones worth it? We are told that nothing lasts forever. All the things we work for in life are just going to decay and perish. Your house, car, money and pets will all die and come to an end. But think about the children. They WILL live forever. It is important for us to realize this. Our children will live forever and ever; in either heaven or hell. We are also told that when we die we can take nothing with us. I guess that is true to a point, but what about our children? Maybe we can send them on ahead or wait for them there, but they can go to heaven with us. Is your love for them important and urgent enough not to put it off any longer? Is your love for your family deep enough to not compromise with the world? What is your priority in raising your children or living with your family? The Bible says, "Everything is permissible for me-- but not everything is beneficial" (1 Cor 6:12). We can watch the TV, spend our time in sports, games, jobs, recreation, etc., but what benefit is there in these things? These are not necessarily sinful or bad ways to spend time (although they can be), but why not shut off the TV to read the Bible, lead a Bible study, help others in the community while letting them know God's Word is your motivation, get involved in any sort of ministry where God's Word is shared, train your children in Godly things, etc.? These things have eternal benefits. I would rather my child watch a Christian video than Sesame Street. There isn't anything wrong with Sesame Street, but there really isn't an eternal benefit either. There are good Christian Bible programs that teach ABC's and numbers that also provide food for the spirit. Make your witness and parental responsibility urgent! After all, only God's Word can give us *wisdom* and *knowledge* (book smarts) without wisdom is only folly.

We will again do a quick recap of the first eight chapters to keep the flow of things and keep some order in our minds.

1. In chapter one we saw a basic introduction showing us who wrote this, how and from whom John received it, and what he saw while the message was given. We saw a description of a Judge (God) among His churches and holding the angels of those churches in His hands.
2. In chapter two we shifted back to earth to see the churches which God was watching over. They symbolized all churches throughout all of

time. Each church brought us closer to the present era with their attributes getting worse and worse until finally ending with Laodicea, a lukewarm church who rejected God as Creator.
3. In chapter three we continued through those seven churches.
4. In chapter four we shifted back to heaven and returned to the Judge who was taking His seat on the throne to judge those churches. Around Him were the angels, saints and disciples praising Him.
5. In chapter five we saw Christ with God, having a scroll or deed to the earth while the praises continued. He is now ready to open the scroll so that the earth and its inhabitants can be judged by God's verdict.
6. Chapter six described six seal judgments as the scrolls were opened.
7. Chapter seven was our commercial break or interlude between the sixth and seventh seal. Here the 144,000 were sealed by God in order to be protected by the judgments affecting the people on earth. We also saw a great multitude of saints from all nations praising God in heaven for their deliverance.
8. Chapter eight showed the seventh seal opened which brought forth the blowing of the first four trumpets.

CHAPTER 9

Rev 9:1 The fifth angel sounded his trumpet, and I saw a star that had fallen from the sky to the earth. The star was given the key to the shaft of the Abyss. 9:2 When he opened the Abyss, smoke rose from it like the smoke from a gigantic furnace. The sun and sky were darkened by the smoke from the Abyss. 9:3 And out of the smoke locusts came down upon the earth and were given power like that of scorpions of the earth. 9:4 They were told not to harm the grass of the earth or any plant or tree, but only those people who did not have the seal of God on their foreheads.

Chapter nine continues the trumpet judgments of chapter eight. When the fifth trumpet sounded John saw a star that had fallen to earth. This was no ordinary star since it was given a key to the Abyss. Note that the star *had* fallen, indicating at some point in the past. Biblically speaking, this star must be Satan. In the book of Luke Jesus said, "The seventy-two returned with joy and said, 'Lord, even the demons submit to us in your name.' He replied, 'I saw Satan fall like lightning from heaven. I have given you authority to trample on snakes and scorpions and to overcome all the power of the enemy; nothing will harm you'" (Luke 10:17-19). In Isaiah we read of Satan's fall from his heavenly position: "How you have fallen from heaven, O morning star, son of the dawn! *You have been cast down to the earth,* you who once laid low the nations! You said in your heart, 'I will ascend to heaven; I will raise my throne above the stars of God; I will sit enthroned on the mount of assembly, on the utmost heights of the sacred mountain. I will ascend above the tops of the clouds; I will make myself like the Most High.' But you are brought down to the grave, to the depths of the pit" (Isa 14:12-15).

We will again see an angel having the key to the Abyss in 20:1, however, then it will be a good angel, not the fallen one. The star here was *given* the key to the Abyss, showing he does not have control over it. Who gave Satan the key? God! When God was speaking at the beginning of Revelation He said, "I am the Living One; I was dead, and behold I am alive for ever and ever! And I hold the keys of death and Hades" (Rev 1:18).

What is this Abyss? Scripture gives us a lot of indirect information about it, but we are still left with unanswered questions. It doesn't seem to be the final hell which is described as the lake of fire (Rev 20:14-15), but that doesn't necessarily mean that the two couldn't be speaking of the same thing. In either case, God holds the key to the Abyss and no one can get out without God allowing it. The following are some things we do know about the Abyss:

- Not all demons currently reside there. The demon legion was roaming the earth freely and begged Jesus not to send them there: "And they begged Him repeatedly not to order them to go into the Abyss" (Luke 8:31).
- It is a dark place used to retain fallen angels: "And the angels who did not keep their positions of authority but abandoned their own home--these *He*

has kept in darkness, bound with everlasting chains for judgment on the great Day" (Jude 1:6).
- Jesus controls the Abyss (Rev 1:18).
- If the spiritual prison is the Abyss then Jesus announced His victory over death there: "For Christ died for sins once for all, the righteous for the unrighteous, to bring you to God. He was put to death in the body but made alive by the Spirit, through whom also He went and preached [Greek word for preach can also mean proclaim or announce] to the spirits in prison who disobeyed long ago when God waited patiently in the days of Noah while the ark was being built" (1 Pet 3:18-20).

When the Abyss was opened smoke rose up like from a gigantic furnace, probably much like it did at Sodom and Gomorrah in appearance (Gen 19:28, see also Ex 19:18). However, this smoke was much different in that some type of locusts came out of it and went down upon the earth. These were not ordinary locusts as we will see. It is very possible that they were demons of some sort. In any case, they were given power like that of a scorpion from God to torment the unbelievers on the earth.

Ordinary locusts devour every green thing in their path. In fact, great famines have occurred as a result of locusts. But these locusts were instructed not to harm anything green because they have one purpose only; to punish the wicked who had not been sealed by God in chapter seven. As mentioned there, all Christians have been sealed by the Holy Spirit and will be protected from these creatures.

The fifth trumpet woe of locusts reminds us of the Egyptian plague of locusts (Ex 10:1-20). The Israelites were kept from these plagues while only the land of Egypt was affected. The same Divine protection will be given at the end of time.

Joel saw locusts as part of God's end time judgments. After describing the devastation of the locusts he wrote, "Alas for that day! For *the day of the LORD* is near; it will come like destruction from the Almighty. Has not the food been cut off before our very eyes-- joy and gladness from the house of our God?" (Joel 1:15-16).

Rev 9:5 They were not given power to kill them, but only to torture them for five months. And the agony they suffered was like that of the sting of a scorpion when it strikes a man. 9:6 During those days men will seek death, but will not find it; they will long to die, but death will elude them.

The scorpions were not allowed to bring about death, only a five month period of pain. We can only speculate as to why the period of five months. The judgment waters of Noah's Flood remained steady for five months (Gen 8:10). Some have also suggested this is the period of time that the danger of locusts threatened crops during the early spring and summer. I tend to think Noah's Flood comes closer to the true reason for the five months, but at this point it remains a mystery.

The sting of the locust is like that of a scorpion. So painful are these stings that men will seek death but will not be able to die. Therefore, neither the locusts nor the men themselves were given the power to kill. Jeremiah wrote of God's judgments; "Wherever I banish them, all the survivors of this evil nation will prefer death to life, declares the LORD Almighty" (Jer 8:3). I think the desire for death goes far beyond anything we can imagine because, in this case, death could not happen. No matter how hard one would try, only further pain and torment would come about. Suicide was impossible. This makes no sense to us, but we need to remember that God gives life. Death is merely the taking away of the soul to another place. Life goes on forever, whether good or bad, it is just a matter of what situation it goes on in. Heaven or hell? Our life is not our own even today. Suicide doesn't "kill" you, it only removes you from your earthly tent. During these five months the spirit of the man was not allowed to leave the body of flesh. Nothing but the seal of God kept this torment from occurring.

When one considers the torment brought about by these creatures, Christian persecution doesn't seem bad at all. Many of us wonder if we would be able to stand up under persecution and not deny our Lord. One can either temporarily suffer for good and be rewarded, or he can suffer for evil knowing that his present pains are as good as his life is going to get. Actually, Christian persecution shouldn't be bad anyway, that is, if our focus is right. Through Christ we can have the power to overcome most selfish desires. Peter writes, "he who has suffered in his body is done with sin" (1 Pet 4:1). What a deep truth. When one can surrender his all to God, he is done with sin. Think of how many sins we fall into as a result of our concern for self. Whether it be hunger, escape from pain, being tired, lazy, sexual desires needing fulfillment, or need of attention, it all comes back to me, me, me. When one is able to surrender all these aspects of our life to God, allowing ourselves to suffer hunger or lack of sleep, etc., it keeps our focus on God and, in a sense, we are done with sin. Obviously we don't ever stop sinning because of our sinful nature, but we certainly lead a sanctified life through the Spirit of God and the forgiveness of Christ. I have found that fasting is such a blessing because it helps me to be aware of my*self*. The first time I fasted I was surprised at how many times my attention was directed toward myself. The blessings came when each time those desires of myself appeared, I immediately directed my thoughts to God and looked to Him for comfort rather than to food, etc. It made me realize how many fleshly desires take our focus off Christ. But suffering allows us to redirect our thoughts to God for deliverance. If you have not set aside a day for prayer and fasting, I would encourage you to do so, not as an experiment or for personal health, but as a day dedicated to the Lord. I believe you will see what I am talking about. We will discuss this sanctified life further on the section about saints.

As I said, being able to suffer takes one's focus off self and puts it on Christ. I have wondered how much physical suffering Christ really had. Don't get me wrong, He did suffer physically, however, we sometimes tend to focus on this aspect more than His resurrection. What I mean is this: how often do we think of the cross rather than the empty tomb. I know Christ suffered, but I believe more so *emotionally* rather than physically. He took upon all of our sins and thus was "forsaken" by God. That would be more emotional and spiritual torment than I could ever imagine. I believe emotional torment is far worse than physical suffering. Did Christ suffer physically? Our natural response is absolutely, without a doubt because He had nails driven through His hands. How can that not be physical torture? Psalm 22 clearly shows Christ felt physical pain, however, I don't believe it was to the extent we normally have in our minds. Why? If any of you have shot a gun that really packs a kick you may be able to relate to this. If you are shooting at an inanimate object it is sometimes difficult to pull the trigger because you know the kick is coming and you know you will feel it. However, when the same gun is taken out hunting, a bird or deer may jump out and you can shoot and shoot (In my case, usually many times without getting anything) without feeling a thing. Sometimes in fact, you can come home with bruises on your shoulder the size of a softball. A kick that leaves a bruise should hurt, but it doesn't. Why? Your focus was somewhere else. I have even known people who have had the gun's scope cut open their eyebrow, yet not realize it. Again, when our focus is taken off of self and put somewhere else, physical pain can be lessened.

    I believe that Christ's focus on the cross was on us, and more importantly, the Father. Therefore, yes, Christ did suffer, but perhaps not to the extent one might think physically. Why is this important? Because when we look at Paul, he was beaten for the name of Christ many times, yet he found it pure joy and an honor to suffer for the LORD. Today, someone who would do such a thing would be considered a lunatic. But Paul's focus was not on himself, it was on Christ. After Paul was flogged in Acts 16:23 (no typical easy beating), he was singing songs in prison. Most people would be moaning and groaning, but not Paul. His focus was not on the flesh, but on the Spirit. There may come a time when our faith will have to stand the test of persecution. Where will your focus be? Even if persecution is not an issue, how much joy would fill our hearts if our daily focus was on Christ, not our jobs, family or problems that occur in our lives? Again, where is your focus? If it isn't on Christ, this can be a dangerous and perhaps painful answer.

    Rev 9:7 The locusts looked like horses prepared for battle. On their heads they wore something like crowns of gold, and their faces resembled human faces. 9:8 Their hair was like women's hair, and their teeth were like lions' teeth. 9:9 They had breastplates like breastplates of iron, and the sound of their wings was like the thundering of many horses and chariots rushing into battle. 9:10 They had tails and stings like scorpions, and in their tails they had power to torment people for five months. 9:11 They had as king over them the angel of the Abyss, whose name in Hebrew is Abaddon, and in Greek, Apollyon. 9:12 The first woe is past; two other woes are yet to come.

    The description of these locusts is enough to put holy fear in almost anyone's heart; anyone but the unbeliever that is. Even after such terrific pain as described in verses five and six, these ungodly men will still refuse to follow God (see v. 20).

The locusts looked like horses going into battle; proud, strong and intent on winning. Job gives a good description of a horse with qualities that fit the focus of these locusts: "Do you give the horse his *strength* or clothe his neck with a flowing mane? Do you make him *leap like a locust, striking terror* with his proud snorting? He paws fiercely, rejoicing in his strength, and charges into the fray. *He laughs at fear, afraid of nothing*; he does not shy away from the sword. The quiver rattles against his side, along with the flashing spear and lance. In frenzied excitement he eats up the ground; he cannot stand still when the trumpet sounds. *At the blast of the trumpet* he snorts, 'Aha!' He catches the scent of battle from afar, the shout of commanders and the battle cry" (Job 39:19-25). It may be significant to note that the sounding of a trumpet was mentioned. It is at the sound of the fifth trumpet that these locusts take upon the attitude described by Job.

The locusts also had the appearance of a man on their faces and wore something like a gold crown. The fact that it was "something" like a crown may indicate that a part of the locust's natural body gave the appearance of a victor's crown. After all, these locusts will be victorious with the purpose they were given. The human faces may symbolize their intelligence and understanding of their purpose. Also, having human faces may make the torture that much more infuriating and personal. Demons seem to be a logical explanation as to what these locusts may be. If this is the case, the demons were given power to do what they love to do, possess and torture the souls of men.

The locusts also had hair like a woman, teeth like a lion, and breastplates of iron. The hair could look like a horse's mane, however, I believe John would probably have described it that way if it were so. The lion's teeth show power and the ability to destroy and wound. The iron breastplate shows their protection and power as well. These creatures will inflict injury on others, but will not be able to be killed themselves. All these descriptions show that the locusts will be powerful and ready for battle, for they are an army from the Lord. Joel, while describing the locusts he saw in his vision, recorded, "A nation has invaded my land, powerful and without number; it has the *teeth of a lion, the fangs of a lioness*" (Joel 1:6). In the next chapter, Joel went on to describe the locusts further: "They have the *appearance of horses*; they gallop along like cavalry. With a *noise like that of chariots* they leap over the mountain tops, like a crackling fire consuming stubble, *like a mighty army drawn up for battle*. At the sight of them, nations are in anguish; *every face turns pale*. They charge like warriors; they scale walls like soldiers. They all march in line, not swerving from their course. They do not jostle each other; each marches straight ahead. They plunge through defenses without breaking ranks. They rush upon the city; they run along the wall. They climb into the houses; *like thieves* they enter through the windows. *Before them the earth shakes, the sky trembles, the sun and moon are darkened, and the stars no longer shine.* The LORD thunders at the head of His army; His forces are beyond number, and mighty are those who obey His command. The day of the LORD is great; it is dreadful. Who can endure it" (Joel 2:4-11)?

Joel was obviously describing what we see here in Revelation. He saw locusts like horses with their wings making noises like chariots going to battle. They brought anguish and fear. They could not be hidden from because they enter the houses. Perhaps even more significant, "before them" the earth shook, and the sun, moon and stars were darkened. The locusts came at the fifth trumpet. The fourth trumpet brought about the sun, moon and stars being darkened.

Though God allows this army of demons to come, their king is Satan himself, the angel of the Abyss who carries the name Abaddon or Apollyon. Both names mean "destroyer," embodying the very nature of Satan. The fact that he is king over the locusts and that these locusts came up out of the smoke from the Abyss further supports the idea that the locusts are demons.

At the end of the fourth trumpet the inhabitants of the earth were warned of the three final trumpet woes. Verse 12 again warns of the next two woes coming. The message seems to be: "If you thought the scorpions were bad, just wait until you see what happens next!"

Rev 9:13 The sixth angel sounded his trumpet, and I heard a voice coming from the horns of the golden altar that is before God. 9:14 It said to the sixth angel who had the trumpet, "Release the four angels who are bound at the great river Euphrates." 9:15 And the four angels who had been kept ready for this very hour and day and month and year were released to kill a third of mankind. 9:16 The number of the mounted troops was two hundred million. I heard their number.

The sixth trumpet began with a voice coming from the golden altar of incense before God's throne. In 8:3 we saw an angel offering incense (prayers of saints that God gave him) on this altar. Therefore, the voice could be coming from this angel.

It is also significant that the voice comes from the horns of this altar. In Old Testament times, if one was facing judgment, he could grab on to the horns to look for mercy (1 Kings 1:50-51). Amos tells us that a time was coming when mercy would not be shown: "On the day I punish Israel for her sins, I will destroy the altars of Bethel; the horns of the altar will be cut off and fall to the ground" (Amos 3:14). Now the altar is in heaven where mercy resides.

The voice instructed the sixth angel in charge of the sixth trumpet to release four evil angels from the Euphrates River. The angels have to be evil because they are "bound." Further, just as we saw the angel of the Abyss was king over the locusts, now these angels are in charge of the destroying horsemen.

The Euphrates River has been an important river historically and spiritually. Though it came out of the Garden of Eden in paradise, it was from Eden that sin first came. Likewise, the Euphrates River was centered in Babylon, the mother of harlots and the root of post-Flood sin. Historically, it ran a distance of about 1,700 miles and served as a boundary between Israel (God's people) and Assyria and Babylon (Israel's enemies. See Is 8:5-8). Here in Revelation, the Euphrates also seems to be a dividing point between the good and the bad. In 16:12 we will see this river play an important part in the preparation for the Armageddon battle. Isaiah wrote of this future event: "The LORD will dry up the gulf of the Egyptian sea; with a scorching wind He will sweep His hand over the Euphrates River. He will break it up into seven streams so that men can cross over in sandals. There will be a highway for the remnant of His people that is left from Assyria, as there was for Israel when they came up from Egypt. In that day you will say: 'I will praise You, O LORD. Although You were angry with me, Your anger has turned away and You have comforted me. Surely God is my salvation; I will trust and not be afraid. The LORD, the LORD, is my strength and my song; He has become my salvation.' With joy you will draw water from the wells of salvation. In that day you will say: 'Give thanks to the LORD, call on His name; make known among the nations what He has done, and proclaim that His name is exalted'" (Isa 11:15-12:4).

    The angels who had been bound at the Euphrates were kept there for this very purpose. History is not a collection of coincidences, it all plays a part of God's big plan, ending with what we read about in Revelation. There not only is a set year, month and day, but a predetermined hour that this will take place. These angels lead out the army of horses to kill one-third of the ungodly people. In 6:8 we saw the Pale horse (4th seal) kill one-fourth of the wicked men on earth. Together, with the one-third here in chapter nine, that is just over one-half of all unbelievers destroyed.

    The number of riders and horses given to John was 200 million. Either this represents an incalculable number or it was a literal number. In either case, the message was the same. God was allowing vast numbers of demons to have open season on the ungodly.

Rev 9:17 The horses and riders I saw in my vision looked like this: Their breastplates were fiery red, dark blue, and yellow as sulfur. The heads of the horses resembled the heads of lions, and out of their mouths came fire, smoke and sulfur. 9:18 A third of mankind was killed by the three plagues of fire, smoke and sulfur that came out of their mouths. 9:19 The power of the horses was in their mouths and in their tails; for their tails were like snakes, having heads with which they inflict injury. 9:20 The rest of mankind that were not killed by these plagues still did not repent of the work of their hands; they did not stop worshipping demons, and idols of gold, silver, bronze, stone and wood--idols that cannot see or hear or walk. 9:21 Nor did they repent of their murders, their magic arts, their sexual immorality or their thefts.

    John's description of these horses reminds us of the locusts brought about by the fifth trumpet. Both went after the wicked men of the earth, although the locusts were only allowed to harm and not kill. Both resembled lions, had power in their tails, and were fitted with breastplates.

    The breastplates of the riders were red, blue, and yellow. This may correspond with the fact that fire (red), smoke (blue), and sulfur (yellow) came out of their mouths. The horses' heads resembled lions, which again showed the power and strength of these demonic beings.

The power of these creatures was seen in their colors because it is the fire, smoke and sulfur which kills one-third of the ungodly people. The power to kill came from their mouths, also the place from which the proclamation of the plagues comes. However, the power to harm came from their tails that were like the heads of snakes. With these tails, the beasts would torture people much like the locusts did.

With all of this pain and suffering, one would think that the remaining inhabitants would repent and turn to God, but they don't. In fact, not only do they refuse to worship God, but they continue worshipping demons and idols, not realizing that it was the demons that just tormented them. They blame God for the events going on rather than taking the blame themselves and recognizing Satan's role in their suffering.

One need not look too far to see the same type of things happening today. Children murder students and teachers in the schools while presidents and counselors explain away why these tragedies occur. Their solutions bring forth more programs, counselors, metal detectors, etc., but God's Word is never sought. All the while, they refuse to see their own hand in this evil because God, His Word, prayer, and His Spirit have been kept out of the schools. In fact, I don't believe it will be long until the Christians (and indirectly, God) will be blamed for the problems in our society.

During the days of Lot, the angels came to warn Lot and his family to get out of Sodom. Almost an entire night had passed before the angels had to actually grab their hands and guide them out of the city. Lot's wife looked back and became a pillar of salt. Her main sin was that she looked back, longing for what she was losing. It is hard to understand how one can long for such a lifestyle. It was only the night before that all the men of the town were threatening to kill her husband, yet she desired to stay. The same will be the case at the end. People will be blinded to the evil that fills their very being. They will not repent because they don't want to stop what they are doing.

Verses 20-21 show us that murder, sex, drugs, and the worship of anything but God continued to persist. The word for magic arts is *pharmakon,* from which we get our word pharmacy. Often times drugs were used in these magical arts showing that drugs will continue to prevail right up to the end.

In the days shortly after Christ ascended, Paul went to Ephesus. After preaching God's Word to them, "a number who had practiced sorcery brought their scrolls together and burned them publicly. When they calculated the value of the scrolls, the total came to fifty thousand drachmas [one drachma was worth a day's wages]. In this way the Word of the Lord spread widely and grew in power" (Acts 19:19-20). Yet even physical suffering will not keep these wicked men from practicing sorcery in the end times. In fact, they will curse God (16:21) on account of their pain. Once a heart is hardened, it is too late, repentance cannot come about. A hardened heart means God's hand of grace has been withdrawn and, therefore, man does not have the capability to repent anymore. That is why Jesus said, "No one can come to Me unless the Father who sent Me draws him, and I will raise him up at the last day" (John 6:44). Again, our job as a Christian should be that much more urgent when we realize that the opportunity for friends and family to believe won't be here forever.

7 TRUMPETS

First 4 dealt with   1) 1/3 of the earth burned.
1/3 destruction's   2) 1/3 of the salt water turned to blood.
of physical earth.   3) 1/3 of the fresh water turned bitter.
                        4) 1/3 of the heavens darkened.

Next 2 followed   **5) Locusts torture man for 5 months.**
theme of torture   **6) Horses and riders kill and torture.**
for the ungodly.

Last one had   7) The seven vials will be opened.
nothing to do
with the trumpets.
Trumpets rested!
Commercial break between
6th and 7th is 10:1-11:14.

CHAPTER 10

Rev 10:1 Then I saw another mighty angel coming down from heaven. He was robed in a cloud, with a rainbow above his head; his face was like the sun, and his legs were like fiery pillars. 10:2 He was holding a little scroll, which lay open in his hand. He planted his right foot on the sea and his left foot on the land, 10:3 and he gave a loud shout like the roar of a lion. When he shouted, the voices of the seven thunders spoke. 10:4 And when the seven thunders spoke, I was about to write; but I heard a voice from heaven say, "Seal up what the seven thunders have said and do not write it down."

Now we tune in for the commercial break or interlude between the sixth and seventh trumpet. Our attention is turned to heaven where John saw an Angel that can be none other than Christ Himself. In my book on Genesis, I have shown many Old Testament examples of Christ appearing as the Angel of the Lord. We know this because the angels are worshipped, and at times, even called the Lord (One Angel at Sodom and Gomorrah). Here is a New Testament example of the same type of appearance by Christ.

The angel referred to in Revelation was robed in a cloud, had a face like the sun, legs like fiery pillars, and had a rainbow above His head. All of these descriptions were given and explained in chapters one and four (see 1:12-16 and 4:2-6). For further Scriptural support of these descriptions of Christ, see Mat 17:2, Luke 1:78, Mal 4:2, Ezek 1:28, Rev 1:15-16, 5:2, 18:1, and 17:2-5. In addition, we see the Angel was holding an open scroll in His hand. In chapter 5 verses 5-9, we saw Christ was given the scroll which represented a deed to the earth. It was sealed with seven seals that were opened in chapters six and seven. Now the scroll lays open because all seven seals have been opened.

This scene is describing Christ's return just prior to our coming ascension with Christ in the clouds at the seventh trumpet which will be blown after this commercial break. The Psalmist wrote, "The LORD says to My Lord: 'Sit at My right hand <u>until</u> I make Your enemies a footstool for Your feet'" (Psa 110:1). Until now, Christ has been reigning at the right hand of God just as Stephen saw before going to join Him (Acts 7), but the time has come when all the enemies of Christ are defeated and, therefore, He is coming back! John saw Christ putting one foot on the land and one foot on the sea as if He was claiming ownership of the entire earth. The scroll, or deed to the earth, was in His hand and, therefore, there is no question as to who the rightful owner (Creator) is. In Matthew 22:33 Christ told us the parable of the Tenants. The owner of a vineyard (God) had gone away. As the harvest approached (but wasn't ready) he sent some servants to be ready to gather the fruit. However, the servants the owner had left in charge of the vineyard (Jews and people of the earth) killed the servants he sent to collect the rent (prophets and Christians). He sent more servants, but they too, were killed. Finally, the owner sent his son (Jesus), but they killed him as well. Christ ended the parable asking, "when the owner of the vineyard comes, what will he do to those tenants?" The answer Christ got was, "'He will bring those wretches to a wretched end,' they replied 'and he will rent the vineyard to other tenants, who will give him his share of the crop at harvest time'" (Mat 21:40-41). The harvest time has now come in Revelation and God is coming to bring the tenants He left in charge of this earth to their wretched end. The open scroll showed His judgments upon the people of the earth. It should be noted that this parable also pointed to the destruction of Jerusalem in 70 AD. In Matthew 21:43-45 it states, "'Therefore I tell you that the kingdom of God will be taken away from you and given to a people who will produce its fruit. He who falls on this Stone will be broken to pieces, but he on whom It falls will be crushed.' When the chief priests and the Pharisees heard Jesus' parables, *they knew He was talking about them*." The Pharisees understood that this parable was referring to their destruction, however, as the theme throughout Revelation has been, Jesus' words serve as a dual prophecy of both 70 AD and end time events.

John also heard our Lord give a loud shout, like that of a lion's roar. This sounds much like what Hosea prophesied, "They will follow the LORD; He will roar like a lion. When He roars, His children will come trembling from the west" (Hosea 11:10). Joel said, "The LORD will roar from Zion and thunder from Jerusalem; the earth and the sky will tremble. But the LORD will be a refuge for His people, a stronghold for the people of Israel" (Joel 3:16). This roar shows God's judgment, not His mercy. In Proverbs we read, "A king's rage is like the roar of a lion, but his favor is like dew on the grass" (Prov 19:12). The King of kings is about to show His full rage and wrath when the seventh trumpet blows. At that time the believers will be caught up in the air with Christ and the non-believers will have seven vial judgments of God's wrath poured out on them.

Verse four leaves us hanging with John being instructed to seal up the words the seven thunders utter. Their message will only be revealed when this event occurs. What are these seven thunders? Psalms may give us a clue by indicating that the seven thunders are simply God's voice: "The voice of the LORD is over the waters; the God of glory *thunders*, the LORD thunders over the mighty waters [1]. The voice of the LORD is powerful [2]; the voice of the LORD is majestic [3]. The voice of the LORD breaks the cedars [4]; the LORD breaks in pieces the cedars of Lebanon. He makes Lebanon skip like a calf, Sirion like a young wild ox. The voice of the LORD strikes with flashes of lightning [5]. The voice of the LORD shakes the desert [6]; the LORD shakes the Desert of Kadesh. The voice of the LORD twists the oaks and strips the forests bare [7]. And in His temple all cry, 'Glory!' The LORD sits enthroned over the flood; the LORD is enthroned as King forever" (Psa 29:3-10). Here we see seven descriptions of God's voice thundering and, therefore, the seven thunders may be God powerfully declaring His judgment.

John's command to refrain from writing down the message of the thunder is similar to Daniel who was told not to write down the words on the scroll: "But you, Daniel, close up and seal the words of the scroll until the time of the end. Many will go here and there to increase knowledge" (Dan 12:4; see also Dan 8:26). It is very possible that Daniel heard what was going to happen when the seals were opened, however, he was not allowed to tell anyone. Now in Revelation, this mystery has been made known, but another mystery has been added.

Rev 10:5 Then the angel I had seen standing on the sea and on the land raised his right hand to heaven. 10:6 And he swore by him who lives for ever and ever, who created the heavens and all that is in them, the earth and all that is in it, and the sea and all that is in it, and said, "There will be no more delay! 10:7 But in the days when the seventh angel is about to sound his trumpet, the mystery of God will be accomplished, just as he announced to his servants the prophets."

The same Angel John just saw raised His hand towards heaven and swore by the eternal God that there would be no more delay, the end has come. Earlier, the saints were told to be patient and wait for other martyrs to be slain as they had been (6:10). That time is now completed and God's saints will be delivered. Daniel wrote, "At that time Michael, the great prince who protects Your people, will arise. There will be a time of distress such as has not happened from the beginning of nations until then. But at that time Your people--everyone whose name is found written in the book--will be delivered" (Dan 12:1). Just before Daniel was told to seal up the words of the scroll, he was told God's judgment day would take place after the saints had been persecuted for three and one-half years: "The man clothed in linen, who was above the waters of the river, lifted His right hand and His left hand toward heaven, and I heard Him swear by Him who lives forever, saying, 'It will be for a time, times and half a time. When the power of the holy people has been finally broken, all these things will be completed'" (Dan 12:7).

The angel not only swore by the Name of the eternal God, but also the One who created the entire universe. (See Gen 14:22, Ex 6:8, Num 14:30, Ps 115:15, and 146:6). Again, this shows God's right to do what He is about to do; judge His creation by redeeming and rejecting.

Verse seven points out that the seventh trumpet is about to sound. In the brief time before it blows, the mystery of God will be completed, just as it has been said since time began. These verses are outlined exactly by Matthew's account of the end times where we see God will appear in the sky just before the seventh trumpet sounds. "At that time the sign of the Son of Man will appear in the sky, and all the nations of the earth will mourn. They will see the Son of Man coming on the clouds of the sky, with power and great glory. And He will send His angels with a loud trumpet call, and they will gather His elect from the four winds, from one end of the heavens to the other" (Mat 24:30-31). Also, because of Thessalonians, it is possible that the angel that blows this trumpet could be either Gabriel or Michael, the only archangels mentioned in Scripture: "For the Lord Himself will come down from heaven, with a loud command, with the voice of the archangel and with the trumpet call of God, and the dead in Christ will rise first" (1 Th 4:16).

The mystery which is completed seems to be the salvation of all believers, including Gentiles, through the marvelous plan God laid out *before* the creation of the world (Eph 1:4, 1 Pet 1:20). Understanding this, one must wonder if the whole span of time, as we know it, has had the purpose of luring Satan into his final and eternal doom. Before Creation, God had it in His plan to have man fall and thus, need a Savior. By death, man was cursed and Satan made proud, but by death, man was cured and Satan was destroyed. Only through the mysterious plan of Christ did God make man (John 1:1), sealing Satan's doom eternally and welcoming all believers into heaven. Some verses describing this mystery follow:

- ". . . that is, the mystery made known to me by revelation, as I have already written briefly. In reading this, then, you will be able to understand my insight into the mystery of Christ, which was not made known to men in other generations as it has now been revealed by the Spirit to God's holy apostles and prophets. *This mystery is that through the gospel the Gentiles are heirs together with Israel, members together of one body, and sharers together in the promise in Christ Jesus*" (Eph 3:3-7).
- "Now to Him who is able to establish you by my gospel and the proclamation of Jesus Christ, according to the revelation of the mystery hidden for long ages past, but now revealed and made known through the prophetic writings by the command of the eternal God, so that all nations might believe and obey Him-- to the only wise God be glory forever through Jesus Christ! Amen" (Rom 16:25-27).
- "I do not want you to be ignorant of this mystery, brothers, so that you may not be conceited: Israel has experienced a hardening in part *until* the full number of the Gentiles has come in" (Rom 11:25).
- "And He made known to us the mystery of His will according to His good pleasure, which He purposed in Christ, to be put into effect when the times will have reached their fulfillment--to bring all things in heaven and on earth together under one head, even Christ" (Eph 1:9-10).
- "I have become its servant by the commission God gave me to present to you the Word of God in its fullness-- the mystery that has been kept hidden for ages and generations, but is now disclosed to the saints" (Col 1:25-26).
- ". . . in order that they may know the mystery of God, namely, Christ" (Col 2:2).

It is also interesting to note that if you examine these verses carefully, you will see that God almost always refers to the Gentile's welcome into the Gospel as a mystery that has been hidden for ages. It is no accident, therefore, that the mystery of God is fulfilled at the blowing of the seventh trumpet. We see Jesus tell the disciples that the end (seventh trumpet) cannot come until all the world has heard the message of Christ: "And this gospel of the kingdom will be preached in the whole world as a testimony to all nations, and then the end will come" (Mat 24:14). If the mystery is to bring Gentiles into the church and the end cannot come until all nations (Gentiles included) have had the Gospel preached to them, the seventh trumpet cannot blow until the full number of the Gentiles comes in. That is why Romans stated, "I do not want you to be ignorant of this mystery, brothers, so that you may not be conceited: Israel has experienced a hardening in part *until* the full number of the Gentiles has come in" (Rom 11:25). As verse seven states, the trumpet is about to sound when the mystery is accomplished.

Rev 10:8 Then the voice that I had heard from heaven spoke to me once more: "Go, take the scroll that lies open in the hand of the angel who is standing on the sea and on the land." 10:9 So I went to the angel and asked him to give me the little scroll. He said to me, "Take it and eat it. It will turn your stomach sour, but in your mouth it will be as sweet as honey." 10:10 I took the little scroll from the angel's hand and ate it. It tasted as sweet as honey in my mouth, but when I had eaten it, my stomach turned sour. 10:11 Then I was told, "You must prophesy again about many peoples, nations, languages and kings."

The same voice which earlier had thundered, now only "spoke" to John. Rather than judgment, John received mercy. The voice told John to go and take the scroll that was in the hand of the Angel. When he did, the Angel told him to eat the scroll, but also warned him that though it would taste sweet, it would also turn his stomach bitter. John did what he was told and it did taste sweet, but it turned sour in his stomach.

Knowing that the contents of the scroll were the seal judgments makes this message more understandable. We know that the scroll contained God's Word, which is a delight for man. Jeremiah wrote, "When Your words came, I ate them; they were my joy and my heart's delight, for I bear your name, O LORD God Almighty" (Jer 15:16). We also know that these particular words were that of judgment and warning. The psalmist records, "The ordinances of the LORD are sure and altogether righteous. They are more precious than gold, than much pure gold; they are sweeter than honey, than honey from the comb. By them is your servant warned; in keeping them there is great reward" (Psa 19:9-11). Just before being lifted up to heaven where he could see the cherubim, Ezekiel went through a process almost identical to what John was doing here. In fact, if these events are the same, we have a better understanding of what John was doing and why he was told to eat the scroll. Ezekiel was told, "open your mouth and eat what I give you. Then I looked, and I saw a hand stretched out to me. In it was a scroll, which He unrolled before me. On both sides of it were written words of lament and *mourning and woe*. And He said to me, 'Son of man, eat what is before you, eat this scroll; then go and speak to the house of Israel.' So I opened my mouth, and He gave me the scroll to eat. Then He said to me, 'Son of man, eat this scroll I am giving you and fill your stomach with it.' So I ate it, and it tasted as sweet as honey in my mouth. He then said to me: 'Son of man, go now to the house of Israel and *speak My words to them*'" (Ezek 2:8-3:4).

Ezekiel's vision tells us the words on the scroll were that of lament and woe. The first six seals opened brought many reasons for lamenting and mourning. The seventh seal brought forth the trumpets which even caused an angel to say, "Woe! Woe! Woe to the inhabitants of the earth, because of the trumpet blasts about to be sounded" (Rev 8:13). We also see Ezekiel was to take the words written on the scroll and eat them. Why? So that he could go and preach them to Israel. Therefore, the act of eating symbolized taking them upon the lips and tongue so that they could be spoken. Words of judgment are sweet for the unbeliever who is shown mercy because we were told God would avenge our blood and persecution (Heb 10:30, Rom 12:19, Rev 6:10). Our deliverance is the good, sweet news, however, at the same time, these judgments can be bitter in the stomach when fully digested. Many of our friends and family will be the ones being judged. After all, Jesus said to "Love your enemies and pray for those who persecute you" (Mat 5:44).

Just as Ezekiel went to prophesy to Israel, John was instructed to do the same *again* (v.11). However, he was not told to prophesy "against" Israel, rather to prophesy "about" many people, nations, languages and kings. Again, we see the bitter sweetness of the seals. John would not only prophesy *about* the ungodly and their destruction, but also *about* the deliverance of the saints and the fulfillment of God's plan. Part of this message will be revealed in chapter eleven as our commercial break continues.

CHAPTER 11

Rev 11:1 I was given a reed like a measuring rod and was told, "Go and measure the temple of God and the altar, and count the worshipers there. 11:2 But exclude the outer court; do not measure it, because it has been given to the Gentiles. They will trample on the holy city for 42 months.

Chapter eleven, verses one through fifteen is a very important part of our interlude. This section is not something to just stick into a chronological timeline because it covers a period of time. They may very well span a number of seals or trumpet judgments. If nothing else, later chapters of Revelation will certainly be fulfilled sometime during the time explained in these verses.

It began by John being given a measuring rod to measure the temple of God and to count the worshippers within it. Ezekiel was involved in a similar experience: "He took me there, and I saw a man whose appearance was like bronze; He was standing in the gateway with a linen cord and a measuring rod in His hand. The Man said to me, 'Son of man, look with your eyes and hear with your ears and pay attention to everything I am going to show you, for that is why you have been brought here. Tell the house of Israel everything you see'" (Ezek 40:3-4).

In Ezekiel's vision the angels measured the outer court (Ezek 40:17-20), but here John was told to exclude the area reserved for the Gentiles. Perhaps this exclusion has something to do with the purpose in measurement. Zechariah also saw a similar measuring done: "Then I looked up--and there before me was a man with a measuring line in his hand! I asked, 'Where are you going?' He answered me, 'To measure Jerusalem, to find out how wide and how long it is.' Then the angel who was speaking to me left, and another angel came to meet him and said to him: 'Run, tell that young man, "Jerusalem will be a city without walls because of the great number of men and livestock in it. And I Myself will be a wall of fire around it," declares the LORD, 'and I will be its glory within'" (Zec 2:1-5). Zechariah seems to be talking about a holy city of worshippers being protected by God. Later in Revelation we see the new Jerusalem, which comes out of heaven, being measured. Therefore, it may be that the measuring done in these verses is to prepare a place of protection for the godly people; the church.

The Gentiles were given the outer court to trample on for 42 months, or 3 1/2 years. This period of time is very significant in that it has been prophesied about for thousands of years in very specific terms. It has been called a time, times and half a time (Dan 7:25, 12:7, Rev 12:14), 42 months (Rev 11:2), and 1,260 days (Rev 12:6; keep in mind the Jews use a 360 day per year calendar). Regarding this period Luke wrote, "They will fall by the sword and will be taken as prisoners to all the nations. Jerusalem will be trampled on by the Gentiles until the times of the Gentiles are fulfilled" (Luke 21:24). As seen with the angel's measurement of the temple of God, perhaps this is a period of time when we are protected, "The woman fled into the desert to a place prepared for her by God, where she might be taken care of for 1,260 days" (Rev 12:6). A few verses later it also states, "The woman was given the two wings of a great eagle, so that she might fly to the place prepared for her in the desert, where she would be taken care of for a time, times and half a time [a time is one, times is two and half a time is one-half and thus, 3 1/2 years], out of the serpent's reach" (Rev 12:14).

To fully understand this 3 1/2 year time period one must realize that there are seven years of tribulation. The first 3 1/2 seem to be the time of the two witnesses which will be discussed in 11:3ff. The second 3 1/2 years is a time when the Antichrist will persecute the saints and set up the abomination which causes desolation. Daniel described these 3 1/2 years as the split in the final "70th week" before the end came: "He [Antichrist] will confirm a covenant with many for one 'seven.' **In the middle of the 'seven'** he will put an end to sacrifice and offering. And on a wing of the temple he will *set up an abomination that causes desolation,* until the end that is decreed is poured out on him" (Dan 9:27). Even Matthew spoke of this time, "So when you see standing in the holy place *'the abomination that causes desolation,' spoken of through the prophet Daniel*--let the reader understand--then let those who are in Judea flee to the mountains" (Mat 24:15-16, see also Mark 13:14). Daniel spoke of this period as a time when the Antichrist would "speak against the Most High and oppress His saints and try to change the set times and the laws. The saints will be handed over to him for a time, times and half a time [3 1/2 years]. But the court [God's judgment day] will sit, and his power will be taken away and completely destroyed forever" (Dan 7:25-26). Even in Revelation we see a 3 1/2 year period in which the Antichrist will go after the saints: "The beast was given a mouth to utter proud words and blasphemies and to exercise his authority for forty-two months" (Rev 13:5).

Some believe the three year reign of Antioches Epiphenes (168-165 BC) was the fulfillment of this event. Antioches persecuted the Jews and forbade worship in the temple. He even desecrated the altar of God by burning a pig on it. However, Antioches can only foreshadow the end of the 3 1/2 year tribulation with the Antichrist. Matthew and Mark were certainly not talking about Antioches, nor is John here in Revelation. Perhaps Daniel alluded to Antioches, but only as a dual prophecy which would end at the time spoken of here in Revelation.

Rev 11:3 And I will give power to my two witnesses, and they will prophesy for 1,260 days, clothed in sackcloth." 11:4 These are the two olive trees and the two lampstands that stand before the Lord of the earth. 11:5 If anyone tries to harm them, fire comes from their mouths and devours their enemies. This is how anyone who wants to harm them must die. 11:6 These men have power to shut up the sky so that it will not rain during the time they are prophesying; and they have power to turn the waters into blood and to strike the earth with every kind of plague as often as they want.

John was told that God was going to give two witnesses power to prophesy for 3 1/2 years. Their message would be one of repentance since they were clothed in sackcloth (see Gen 37:34, Ne 9:1, Joel 1:13 and John 3:5 for other examples of sackcloth being used for repentance).

Zecheriah asked the same question many do today, who are these two witnesses? We read in Zechariah: "Then I asked the angel, 'What are these two olive trees on the right and the left of the lampstand?' Again I asked him, 'What are these two olive branches beside the two gold pipes that pour out golden oil?' He replied, 'Do you not know what these are?' 'No, my lord,' I said. So he said, *'These are the two who are anointed to serve the Lord* of all the earth'" (Zec 4:11-14). From these verses we know that God has two chosen men who serve Him. Here in verse four they are said to be the two olive trees and the two lampstands, the exact thing Zechariah was inquiring about.

Do we know who these two servants of God are by name? Probably! In Jesus' day, it was an accepted fact that Elijah would return before the Lord did. The Jews got this understanding from the last verses of the Old Testament where it predicts, "See, I will send you the prophet Elijah before that great and dreadful day of the LORD comes" (Mal 4:5). On the Mount of Transfiguration Moses and Elijah had appeared to meet with Christ. The disciples knew who they were without being introduced, just as it will be for us in heaven. When coming down the mountain with Jesus the disciples asked Him, "'Why then do the teachers of the law say that Elijah must come first?' Jesus replied, 'To be sure, Elijah comes **and will restore** all things. **But** I tell you, Elijah **has already come**, and they did not recognize him, but have done to him everything they wished. In the same way the Son of Man is going to suffer at their hands.' Then the disciples understood that He was talking to them about John the Baptist" (Mat 17:10-13). In a sense, Elijah did come at the transfiguration, but he didn't restore all things. Because of these verses in Matthew some believe that John the Baptist fulfilled the prophecy of Malachi. However, that is not what Jesus said. Jesus gave a dual prophecy again when He said that Elijah will come (future tense), but he has also already come (past tense). Scripture tells us that the disciples knew John the Baptist was the one that had already come, but who could the one that "will come" be other than Elijah? John the Baptist only came in the spirit of Elijah, bringing a message of repentance through his baptism of water. John the Baptist denied being Elijah: "They asked him, 'Then who are you? Are you Elijah?' He said, 'I am not.' 'Are you the Prophet?' He answered, 'No'" (John 1:21). Therefore, we have an indication that one of these two witnesses is Elijah. Further support of this will be given in the verses ahead.

Another reason some believe Elijah to be one of the witnesses is because of Hebrews where it says man is destined to die only once (Heb 9:27). Elijah never died in the Old Testament because he was taken to heaven alive in a fiery chariot (2 Kings 2:11). However, this argument may not be a valid one. What do you do with Enoch (Gen 5:24, Heb 11:5)? What about Lazarus (John 11) or the many other people who were raised from the dead? I believe the Scriptures indicated man was to die once as a general rule, but God is not bound by these rules. Perhaps more of a spiritual death was meant. As Christians, we are dead to our trespasses and our old Adam is destroyed. On the other hand, the ungodly will have an eternal spiritual death in hell. In any case, it seems to be a weak argument to use this for evidence supporting Elijah as a witness.

Before we move on into other evidences of Elijah as a witness, let us examine who the other witness may be. Most would agree that it is Moses. After all, it was Moses and Elijah who appeared to Christ on the Mount of Transfiguration. They were "standing" before God and serving Him just as the two olive trees were to do.

The belief that both witnesses are Elijah and Moses is supported in the miracles that these two witnesses perform. If anyone tries to harm them, fire comes from their mouths and devours their enemies. When Elijah walked the earth, fire from heaven protected him from King Ahab: "Elijah answered the captain, 'If I am a man of God, may fire come down from heaven and consume you and your fifty men!' Then fire fell from heaven and consumed the captain and his men" (2 Ki 1:10). Likewise, while challenging the prophets of Baal on Mount Carmel, Elijah called upon the Lord, "'Answer me, O LORD, answer me, so these people will know that You, O LORD, are God, and that You are turning their hearts back again.' Then the fire of the LORD fell and burned up the sacrifice, the wood, the stones and the soil, and also licked up the water in the trench" (1 Ki 18:37-38). In Revelation, God's fire will come from the mouths of these two witnesses, and this may be alluded to in Jeremiah: "Therefore this is what the LORD God Almighty says: 'Because the people have spoken these words, I will make My words in your mouth a fire and these people the wood it consumes'" (Jer 5:14). The fire coming from the servants of God is in sharp contrast to the demons on the horses killing with fire in 9:17-18.

The witnesses will also have power to keep it from raining during the time of their prophesying. Verse three told us their time of prophesying would be 3 1/2 years. Again, this is something Elijah did while on earth: "Elijah was a man just like us. He prayed earnestly that it would not rain, and it did not rain on the land for three and a half years" (James 5:17). See also 1 Kings 17:1 and Luke 4:25-26.

If the fire and rain are not enough, Moses and Elijah could also turn water into blood. This miracle is something Moses was well acquainted with during the Israelite deliverance from Egypt (Ex 7:17). Now it will be used for the deliverance of all people, and just as Pharaoh refused to listen, so too will the ungodly of these days.

In addition to blood, *any* plague they wish and as often as they wish, can be brought upon the earth from God. It will not be surprising if many of them mimic those of the Egyptian plagues.

Another interesting point regarding the death of Moses, is that for some unknown reason, Moses' body was the only one ever mentioned in Scripture that Satan wanted control of. Jude recorded, "But even the archangel Michael, when he was disputing with the devil about the body of Moses, did not dare to bring a slanderous accusation against him, but said, 'The Lord rebuke you'" (Jude 1:9)! Perhaps Satan knew God's plan for Moses and wanted to keep that from happening.

Not only is the purpose of these two witnesses to preach repentance, but also to make Christ's return sure. In Old and New Testament times, the law required two witnesses before anyone could be pronounced guilty. Even the book of Hebrews shows this practice: "Anyone who rejected the law of Moses died without mercy on the testimony of two or three witnesses" (Heb 10:28). Here, the law is followed and these two witnesses make the judgment of the wicked sure.

It is interesting to note that often times when Jesus was on earth, two angels appeared. While Jesus ascended "they were looking intently up into the sky as He was going, when suddenly two men dressed in white stood beside them" (Acts 1:10). When the garden tomb was discovered empty, "they were wondering about this, suddenly two men in clothes that gleamed like lightning stood beside them" (Luke 24:4). Could these two men have been Moses and Elijah since they were anointed to serve the Lord of all the earth? It is possible, but not for certain.

Rev 11:7 Now when they have finished their testimony, the beast that comes up from the Abyss will attack them, and overpower and kill them. 11:8 Their bodies will lie in the street of the great city, which is figuratively called Sodom and Egypt, where also their Lord was crucified. 11:9 For three and a half days men from every people, tribe, language and nation will gaze on their bodies and refuse them burial. 11:10 The inhabitants of the earth will gloat over them and will celebrate by sending each other gifts, because these two prophets had tormented those who live on the earth.

Once the witnesses finish their work of preaching, they have one final part in God's plan here on earth. No one could kill these two witnesses without being killed themselves. However, a beast which came up out of the Abyss was able to get the job done. This beast is the Antichrist as we will see in chapter 13. We see the first reference to the Antichrist in Daniel, "As I watched, this horn was waging war against the saints and defeating them" (Dan 7:21, see Rev 13:1,7). It seems that his ability to kill the two witnesses will have a large part in his gaining followers.

The witnesses were hated by the wicked men of the earth. So much so, that when the witnesses were killed, they denied them burial to disgrace their bodies. Their bodies laid in the streets of Jerusalem where Christ was crucified. Jerusalem is called Sodom and Egypt here in Revelation. As earlier mentioned, if something is to be taken figuratively, we are often told, just as we are here. The purpose in calling the Holy City by this name is to show its complete depravity. In Jeremiah we see the same name attached to Jerusalem, "And among the prophets of Jerusalem I have seen something horrible: They commit adultery and live a lie. They strengthen the hands of evildoers, so that no one turns from his wickedness. They are all like Sodom to Me; the people of Jerusalem are like Gomorrah" (Jer 23:14, see also Ezek 16:46 and Isa 1:9). While Sodom represented the moral corruption, Egypt may have represented their slavery to sin.

Three and one-half days after their death, the two witnesses will be mocked and defiled. The whole world will look on, which is not impossible in the days of satellites, Internet, and television. Past destructions of Jerusalem foreshadowed an event like this. The Psalmist recorded, "They have given the dead bodies of your servants as food to the birds of the air, the flesh of Your saints to the beasts of the earth. They have poured out blood like water all around Jerusalem, and there is no one to bury the dead" (Psa 79:2-3).

The people will gloat over them and celebrate by sending gifts to one another because of their deliverance from these two men. We saw a similar custom in the book of Esther after the Jews were delivered from Haman's evil plot. "That is why rural Jews--those living in villages--observe the fourteenth of the month of Adar as a day of joy and feasting, a day for giving presents to each other.. . as the time when the Jews got relief from their enemies, and as the month when their sorrow was turned into joy and their mourning into a day of celebration. He wrote them to observe the days as days of feasting and joy and giving presents of food to one another and gifts to the poor" (Est 9:19,22). In the last days the people will again believe they have been delivered from evil, not realizing they are walking right into it.

The reason the two witnesses were hated was seen in verse ten; the two witnesses tormented the people. The witnesses preached a doctrine of intolerance and repentance, not something that goes over well in a very lukewarm, tolerant and unrepentant society. The plagues and fire that came from their commands also infuriated the wicked men. Rather than repent, they became more angry and insolent and looked for someone to deliver them from these men. The Antichrist was that deliverer who lead them away from THE Deliverer.

Rev 11:11 But after the three and a half days a breath of life from God entered them, and they stood on their feet, and terror struck those who saw them. 11:12 Then they heard a loud voice from heaven saying to them, "Come up here." And they went up to heaven in a cloud, while their enemies looked on.

After the three and one-half days of their bodies laying in the streets, God gave the witnesses life again. This bodily resurrection reminds us of Ezekiel's prophecy about the valley of dry bones. Although not the same event as the witnesses, perhaps a similar scene for those watching: "'This is what the Sovereign LORD says to these bones: I will make breath enter you, and you will come to life. I will attach tendons to you and make flesh come upon you and cover you with skin; I will put breath in you, and you will come to life. Then you will know that I am the LORD.' So I prophesied as I was commanded. And as I was prophesying, there was a noise, a rattling sound, and the bones came together, bone to bone. I looked, and tendons and flesh appeared on them and skin covered them, but there was no breath in them. Then He said to me, 'Prophesy to the breath; prophesy, son of man, and say to it, "This is what the Sovereign LORD says: Come from the four winds, O breath, and breathe into these slain, that they may live."' So I prophesied as He commanded me, and breath entered them; they came to life and stood up on their feet--a vast army" (Ezek 37:5-10). As they stood up on their feet, the world was filled with terror, not only because of the miraculous resurrection, but also because of the voice that came out of heaven and called the witnesses up. As in Christ's ascension (Acts 1:9), these two men went up in a cloud while their enemies gazed at them. This may also foreshadow our resurrection when, "After that, we who are still alive *and are left* will be caught up together *with them* in the clouds to meet the Lord in the air. And so we will be with the Lord forever" (1 Th 4:17).

    One would think this heavenly sign would be proof enough that the witnesses had Divine support, but it doesn't work that way. Even at Christ's death, there was an earthquake, darkness loomed over the city, and some of the dead arose and went out to meet those in town. Yet even these miracles did not make believers out of the inhabitants of Jerusalem. Miracles don't bring faith, the Holy Spirit brings it. We are reminded of the Pharisees of Jesus' day when they came to Jesus asking Him to show them a sign that He was the Messiah. Christ would not give them one because He knew it would make no difference to a hardened heart. We read in Matthew, "'Teacher, we want to see a miraculous sign from You.' He answered, 'A wicked and adulterous generation asks for a miraculous sign! But none will be given it except the sign of the prophet Jonah. For as Jonah was three days and three nights in the belly of a huge fish, so the Son of Man will be three days and three nights in the heart of the earth. The men of Nineveh will stand up at the judgment with this generation and condemn it; for they repented at the preaching of Jonah, and now one greater than Jonah is here'" (Mat 12:39-41).

Rev 11:13 At that very hour there was a severe earthquake and a tenth of the city collapsed. Seven thousand people were killed in the earthquake, and the survivors were terrified and gave glory to the God of heaven. 11:14 The second woe has passed; the third woe is coming soon.

    Just as at Christ's death, the resurrection of these two witnesses brought a severe earthquake. So powerful was this earthquake that a tenth of the city was destroyed and 7,000 wicked people in that city were killed. Ezekiel had warned of such a day, "In My zeal and fiery wrath I declare that at that time there shall be a great earthquake in the land of Israel" (Ezek 38:19).

    Those who survived may have been Christian already because they gave glory to God. However, it is probably more reasonable that the glory given to God is not out of repentance, but out of realization that God is in heaven. Knowing God exists and actually having a personal walk with Him are two separate things, ending in two separate results. As James stated, "You believe that there is one God. Good! Even the demons believe that--and shudder" (James 2:19).

    Earlier in 8:13 we saw an angel warning us about the last three trumpets, or the last three woes. In 9:12 we saw the first woe passed with the locusts having a sting like that of scorpions (5th trumpet). Now we see the second woe has passed with the horsemen and their snake-like tails (6th trumpet), Now we have the conclusion of our interlude before the third and final woe takes place (7th trumpet bringing on 7 vial judgments).

Rev 11:15 The seventh angel sounded his trumpet, and there were loud voices in heaven, which said: "The kingdom of the world has become the kingdom of our Lord and of his Christ, and he will reign for ever and ever."

The commercial break between the sixth and seventh trumpet has ended. The seventh angel blew his trumpet and loud voices began to praise God, acknowledging that the world has become the kingdom of God forever.

The seventh trumpet is the single most important event in Revelation for a Christian. It is at this time that all believers will be caught up in the air to meet Christ face to face in our heavenly home. Paul wrote, "Listen, I tell you a mystery: We will not all sleep, but we will all be changed-- in a flash, in the twinkling of an eye, *at the last trumpet*. For the trumpet will sound, the dead will be raised imperishable, and we will be changed. For the perishable must clothe itself with the imperishable, and the mortal with immortality. When the perishable has been clothed with the imperishable, and the mortal with immortality, then the saying that is written will come true: 'Death has been swallowed up in victory'" (1 Cor 15:51-54). The final trumpet call brings about our heavenly reign with Christ. Our old perishable bodies will be changed into something new; something imperishable. Our sinful flesh will no longer be sinful and mortality will disappear. However, the people who are still living at the time of the seventh trumpet must wait a few seconds until all the people who have died previously are raised up from the dead. We read, "For the Lord Himself will come down from heaven, with a loud command, with the voice of the archangel and with the **trumpet call of God**, and the dead in Christ will rise first. *After that*, we who are still alive and are left will be caught up together with them in the clouds to meet the Lord in the air. And so we will be with the Lord forever" (1 Th 4:16-17). Even Isaiah wrote of this day, "In that day the LORD will thresh from the flowing Euphrates to the Wadi of Egypt, and you, O Israelites, will be gathered up one by one. And in that day a great **trumpet will sound**" (Isa 27:12). Jesus spoke of this day in Matthew as a day that followed the seal judgments, "And He will send His angels with *a loud* **trumpet call**, and they will gather His elect from the four winds, from one end of the heavens to the other" (Mat 24:31).

Some believe that the battle of Jericho foreshadowed this event. To get the full effect of this, however, we must go back and look at the entire Old Testament patterns to see how they fit into our lives today. We often tend to look at the Bible as 66 books filled with many Sunday School stories to teach a lesson and to point us to Christ. This is true, but within these stories lies a deeper understanding of God's plan.

Shortly after the creation of the world, man fell into sin and thus had a need for the Savior. The world became wicked, causing God to destroy every living creature except eight people and the animals spared in the Ark. Soon after the Ark landed, people began to settle again at Babel where God once more intervened and scattered people around the world. Once people were scattered, God chose a nation to be blessed, and that nation would descend through Abraham. Abraham was given the promise of many offspring and a promised child. Now as one thinks about this story, he must let his mind go beyond the face value of what is being said. Abraham meaning (*father of many nations*), may represent God, our Father. Isaac, the promised son, will then represent Christ, the Son of God.

Not long after the birth of Isaac, Abraham was told to offer Isaac as a sacrifice. Though Isaac was spared, the parallels between Christ and Isaac are astounding. Indeed Isaac was a "type" of Christ foreshadowing what was to come. We read, "The promises were spoken to Abraham and to his seed. The Scripture does not say 'and to seeds,' meaning many people, but 'and to your seed,' meaning one person, who is Christ" (Gal 3:16). Let us look at the similarities. "Father" Abraham was about to show his love to God by offering his "one and only son" (Gen 22:2; Heb 11:17) as a sacrifice, but "This is how God showed His love among us: He sent His one and only Son into the world that we might live through Him" (1 John 4:9). Isaac carried his own wood on his back (Gen 22:6) and Christ, carried His own cross (John 19:17). Genesis 22:6 shows Isaac and his father went on together as did God the Father and God the Son. Isaac willingly went up the hill just as Christ laid down His own life (John 10:17). Isaac was about to be crucified on Mount Moriah. This is where the Dome of the Rock is today and where the old Temple of Solomon was. It is here that many sacrifices were to be made years later in the Temple (2 Chronicles 3:1), all foreshadowing the Sacrifice to come; Christ, our Savior, who would die not far from here. In Hebrews we read how "figuratively speaking, [Abraham] did receive Isaac back from death" (Heb 11:19). Once Abraham set out to go to Mount Moriah, his son was "figuratively" dead until God saved him. Note in Genesis 22:4, it took three days to get to the mountain just as Christ was dead three days and rose again thereafter. This, too, must also foreshadow the resurrection. Both took long journeys away from home. Isaac spoke up to his father (22:7), just as Jesus spoke up to His Father many times in prayer (Luke 4:42; 6:12; Mat 26:36). Isaac was the promised son as was Jesus the promised Messiah. Isaac was bound (v. 9) as was Jesus (Mat 27:2). Isaac was conceived and born miraculously as was Jesus (Luke 1:35). Isaac was given a name by God before birth (Gen 17:19) as was Christ (Mat 1:21).

On the way up the hill, Isaac asked his father where the sacrifice was. Abraham responded with, "God will provide." What a deep truth lies within this statement. Though the LORD does provide a ram in place of Isaac (22:13), the Lamb that WILL BE provided was yet to come. Christ was our Passover Lamb, which is why when John saw Jesus coming he said, "Look, the Lamb of God, who takes away the sin of the world" (John 1:29)! These are just a few examples of the many times Christ is found in the Old Testament. What a beautiful picture of God's love for us that was provided near that very mountain.

We also see from Galatians that Abraham's wife, Sarah, represented the New Covenant while, Hagar, his servant, represented the Old Covenant. Isaac (Sarah's son), therefore represents Christ, and Ishmael (Hagar's son), represents the law of Mount Sinai: "Abraham had two sons, one by the slave woman and the other by the free woman. His son by the slave woman was born in the ordinary way; but his son by the free woman was born as the result of a promise. These things may be taken figuratively, for the women represent two covenants.

One covenant is from Mount Sinai and bears children who are to be slaves: This is Hagar. Now Hagar stands for Mount Sinai in Arabia and corresponds to the present city of Jerusalem, because she is in slavery with her children. But the Jerusalem that is above is free, and she is our mother. For it is written: 'Be glad, O barren woman, who bears no children; break forth and cry aloud, you who have no labor pains; because more are the children of the desolate woman than of her who has a husband.' Now you, brothers, like Isaac, are children of promise" (Gal 4:22-28). As Hagar was a slave woman, she represents the law of Mt. Sinai where she dwelt and also the earthly Jerusalem. Ishmael, the offspring of the slave woman, is natural or ordinary just as the law is naturally in our hearts and, therefore, we become slaves to the law (Rom 2:15). Isaac was born by a promise and he represents freedom of the law. Sarah, likewise, represents the new Jerusalem of heaven (Rev 3:12; 21:2), of which all believers are to receive since we are "children of the promise."

Isaac then leads us to Jacob who takes us to Joseph. Joseph then brings the Israelites to Egypt where they become slaves for 400 years. This slavery represents our daily bondage to sin in the flesh. We, like the Israelites, needed a Savior. Enter Moses, who could represent the Spirit of God who leads us to that Savior. Though Isaac was a type of Christ, we must remember that Christ is coming again, but this time in full glory.

Through a number of events, Moses leads us out of bondage where we are brought into the "glorious freedom of the children of God" (Rom 8:21). How was this done? Through the crossing of the Red Sea which, for us, is Baptism. The Red Sea crossing did in fact point to Baptism wherein we become God's children through the Holy Spirit and the Word. We read, "They all passed through the sea. They were all baptized into Moses in the cloud and in the sea" (1 Cor 10:1-2). Israel's deliverance from bondage symbolizes our deliverance through baptism.

Once the Israelites crossed the Red Sea the Promised Land was in sight, but they were unable to enter right away. We, too, after becoming children of God, have heaven in our focus as we, "rejoice in the hope of the glory of God" (Rom 5:2).

Next came the 40 years of wilderness wanderings. This represents our life. The goal of the Israelites was to get into the promised land just as our goal is to get to our promised land - heaven. While in the desert they ate manna from heaven and drank water from the Rock. This clearly represents our communion with Christ today. Paul writes, "They all ate the same spiritual food and drank the same spiritual drink; for they drank from the spiritual rock that accompanied them, and that rock was Christ. Nevertheless, God was not pleased with most of them; their bodies were scattered over the desert. Now these things occurred as examples to keep us from setting our hearts on evil things as they did" (1 Cor 10:3-6). Regarding the manna we read in John, "Your forefathers ate the manna in the desert, yet they died. But here is the Bread that comes down from heaven, which a man may eat and not die. I am the living Bread that came down from heaven. If anyone eats of this Bread, he will live forever. This Bread is My flesh, which I will give for the life of the world" (John 6:49-51).

Just as the Israelites struggled through the 40 years of desert wandering, our lives are full of trials and temptations all with the goal of strengthening our faith and building our trust in the LORD. In addition, when the Israelites complained God sent the poisonous snakes to bite them. "Then when anyone was bitten by a snake and looked at the bronze snake, he lived" (Num 21:9). This was the only way to be saved. Likewise, "Let us fix our eyes on Jesus, the Author and Perfecter of our faith, who for the joy set before Him endured the cross" (Heb 12:2). I find it ironic that when reading the stories of the wilderness wanderings we are often judgmental of the Israelites for their non-belief. One need only look at our lives to see the same pattern. God blesses and we take it for granted. Troubles come. We complain rather than trust in God's deliverance.

Just as the Israelites had the Ten Commandments, we have a law today. Though it is not the law that motivates us to do good, it still applies for all who willingly do evil. We read in Romans, "For we maintain that a man is justified by faith apart from observing the law. Is God the God of Jews only? Is he not the God of Gentiles too? Yes, of Gentiles too, since there is only one God, who will justify the circumcised by faith and the uncircumcised through that same faith. Do we, then, nullify the law by this faith? Not at all! Rather, we uphold the law" (Rom 3:28-31). And, "through Christ Jesus the law of the Spirit of life set me free from the law of sin and death. For what the law was powerless to do in that it was weakened by the sinful nature, God did by sending His own Son in the likeness of sinful man to be a sin offering. And so He condemned sin in sinful man, in order that the righteous requirements of the law might be fully met in us, who do not live according to the sinful nature but according to the Spirit" (Rom 8:2-4).

The Israelites also had the ark of the covenant with them in the wilderness. This ark represented God's presence among them. We also have God's presence among, and in us today. "Whoever eats My flesh and drinks My blood remains in Me, and I in him. Just as the living Father sent Me and I live because of the Father, so the one who feeds on Me will live because of Me" (John 6:56-57).

Many other parallels can be found connecting the 40 years of wandering to our daily lives, but for the sake of room we must move on.

Finally, at the end of the 40 years, they crossed the Jordan River. Jericho was the first city destroyed and thus the first official entrance into the promised land. Jericho fell only after the seventh trumpet had blown. This, too, is when we will finally inherit our promised land. "Listen, I tell you a mystery: We will not all sleep, but we will all be changed-- in a flash, in the twinkling of an eye, at the last trumpet. For the trumpet will sound, the dead will be raised imperishable, and we will be changed" (1 Cor 15:51-52). We read in Revelation 10:7 "But in the days when the seventh angel is about to sound his trumpet, the mystery of God will be accomplished, just as He announced to His servants the prophets."

Once in the promised land, Israel reigned with David as their king just as we shall reign with Christ, our King.

We see how God's plan serves as a model for our lives today. God (Abraham) is the father of all nations. He gave His one and only son, Jesus (Isaac) to die for us. Though we were born into sin (slavery in Egypt) God provided a deliverer, the Holy Spirit (Moses) who leads us out of bondage through Baptism (Red Sea). After this we see the promised land ahead, (Joshua and Caleb spying out the promised land), but we must go through our lives (40 years in desert) keeping the faith. Christ gives us a law of righteousness (Ten Commandments) and lives in us (Ark of the covenant) through the sacraments. All who look to Him (Bronze snake) shall be saved. When the seventh trumpet blows (Jericho) we will enter the eternal paradise and we will reign with Christ (Promised Land and the Heavenly United Kingdom) eternally. So for now, "if we hope for what we do not yet have we wait for it patiently" (Rom 8:25).

After the trumpet sounded, the angel told John that the kingdom of the world was now the kingdom of God. Christ has had dominion over all His creation throughout all of time, "Your kingdom is an everlasting kingdom, and Your dominion endures through all generations" (Psa 145:13). However, though Christ is in control, Satan has been cast down to the earth (Rev 12:10, Ezek 20:34-38, 22:18-22) and the kingdom of God has not yet *fully* begun. We know that though Satan, the prince of the world, roams on this earth, he may not do so with complete freedom: "Now is the time for judgment on this world; now *the prince of this world will be driven out*. But I, when I am lifted up from the earth, will draw all men to Myself" (John 12:31-32); and "When He [Holy Spirit] comes, He will convict the world of guilt in regard to sin and righteousness and judgment: in regard to sin, because men do not believe in Me; in regard to righteousness, because I am going to the Father, where you can see Me no longer; and in regard to judgment, *because the prince of this world now stands condemned*" (John 16:8-11). Though Satan is condemned and has been driven out of this world, this only is in reference to his ability to roam freely throughout the universe, as we will discuss in chapter 12. But the earth is still Satan's playground until the seventh trumpet blows. That is why we are warned, "Be self-controlled and alert. Your enemy the devil prowls around like a roaring lion looking for someone to devour" (1 Pet 5:8).

God's kingdom begins when Satan will be cast into the pits of hell. There are many verses referring to this glorious day as one that will be eternal, where the saints rule, and Mount Zion will be its center. A few of these verses follow:

- "In the time of those kings, the God of heaven will set up a kingdom that will never be destroyed, nor will it be left to another people. It will crush all those kingdoms and bring them to an end, but it will itself endure forever" (Dan 2:44).
- "His dominion is an everlasting dominion that will not pass away, and His kingdom is one that will never be destroyed" (Dan 7:14).
- "Then the sovereignty, power and greatness of the kingdoms under the whole heaven will be handed over to the saints, the people of the Most High. His kingdom will be an everlasting kingdom, and all rulers will worship and obey Him" (Dan 7:27).

- "I will make the lame a remnant, those driven away a strong nation. The LORD will rule over them in Mount Zion from that day and forever" (Micah 4:7).
- "The LORD will be king over the whole earth. On that day there will be one LORD, and His name the only name" (Zec 14:9).
- "and He will reign over the house of Jacob forever; His kingdom will never end" (Luke 1:33).

Rev 11:16 And the twenty-four elders, who were seated on their thrones before God, fell on their faces and worshipped God, 11:17 saying: "We give thanks to you, Lord God Almighty, the One who is and who was, because you have taken your great power and have begun to reign. 11:18 The nations were angry; and your wrath has come. The time has come for judging the dead, and for rewarding your servants the prophets and your saints and those who reverence your name, both small and great-- and for destroying those who destroy the earth."

This is the day spoken of in 10:7 when the mystery of God is accomplished. The 24 elders we saw in 4:4 and 5:8 fell down prostrate to worship God on His throne. Their praise gives us a beautiful message. First of all, they are giving thanks. As the Psalmist said, "that my heart may sing to You and not be silent. O LORD my God, I will give you thanks forever" (Psa 30:12).

Second, they are giving thanks to the One who is and who was. Notice anything missing? No longer is Christ called the "One who is to come" as in 1:4 and 1:8. Christ has come at the sound of the 7th trumpet and His kingdom "has begun" as stated in verse 17. What an awesome day it will be when we will no longer think of Christ's coming in a future tense.

The nations refused to repent of their evil deeds and instead blamed God for their torments and problems. Therefore, their time of judgment had come. We will see and discuss this judgment of the wicked and the rewarding of the saints in greater detail in 14:14-20 and 20:1.

Rev 11:19 Then God's temple in heaven was opened, and within his temple was seen the ark of his covenant. And there came flashes of lightning, rumblings, peals of thunder, an earthquake and a great hailstorm.

Verse 19 is a key verse in showing the timing of the bowl judgments. As mentioned earlier, the seventh church was the time period that the seven seals were opened. The seventh seal brought about the seven trumpets. The seventh trumpet also brings about seven vial judgments. After all, the seventh trumpet just issued in God's kingdom and we were told that the saints would be rewarded and the wicked punished. The bowl or vial judgments deliver this punishment. The key word in verse 19 is "then," showing after the seventh trumpet blew. What happens after the seventh trumpet?

1. God's Temple is opened.
2. Ark of the covenant is seen in the Temple showing God's presence.
3. Lightning, rumblings and peals of thunder.
4. An earthquake and hailstorm.

This is important when we compare the above list to Revelation 15:5 and 16:18-19. In 15:5 we will see that the seven angels who are going to pour out these bowl or vial judgments upon the earth are given the bowls by one of the four living creatures. Verse five says John looked and saw 1) heaven or the tabernacle opened. Why was it opened? So the angels could come out to pour out the bowl judgments. John also saw 2) God's presence filled the tabernacle with smoke (v. 8). Then chapter 16 goes and describes the seven bowl judgments until verse 18 where we see immediately after the seventh bowl was poured out, 3) lightning, rumblings and thunder occurred and, 4) a severe earthquake (v. 18) and hail (v. 21). The exact same things were seen after the seventh trumpet blew. Therefore, it seems that 11:19 is focused more on the saints when discussing the seventh trumpet. John is telling us that we will go to heaven and the world will be judged. He doesn't bother going into the details of the judgment, but rather says, "Then" (after the seventh trumpet) heaven will be opened (so the angels can pour out their bowl judgments), and after they are poured out, the lightning, thunder, earthquake and hail will take place. In 11:19 we have from A to Z skipping the in-between. In 15:5 through 16:21 we have from A to Z with all the details.

One other interesting point is that the ark of the covenant is seen in heaven. There are all kinds of arguments and theories as to where the ark of the covenant went. It seems that it is no longer on earth, because God took it to heaven. We see in Jeremiah, "'In those days, when your numbers have increased greatly in the land,' declares the LORD, 'men will no longer say, "The ark of the covenant of the LORD." It will never enter their minds or be remembered; it will not be missed, nor will another one be made. At that time they will call Jerusalem The Throne of the LORD, and all nations will gather in Jerusalem to honor the Name of the LORD'" (Jer 3:16-17). The ark of the covenant was kept in the Most Holy Place of the Tabernacle (2 Chron 5:7), which was symbolic of heaven and God's presence, therefore, it makes sense that it should remain in heaven.

AN IMPORTANT NOTE ABOUT THE TEMPLE AND THE MOST HOLY PLACE REFERRED TO IN REVELATION MANY TIMES

Virtually everything in the Old Testament Temple pointed to Christ. The reason for this is clearly mentioned later in Revelation where we read, "I did not see a temple in the city, because the Lord God Almighty and the Lamb are its temple" (Rev 21:22). When we examine the Old Testament Temple we see that there was only one gate that a person could enter, and it was on the east side. Likewise, Christ is the "Way," and the "Door" of our salvation. Jesus said, "I am the gate; whoever enters through Me will be saved. He will come in and go out, and find pasture" (John 10:9). Just as the Garden of Eden had its gate on the eastern side only, according to the Jewish faith, Christ is to return through the Eastern Gate of Jerusalem (Sometimes called the Golden Gate).

Once through the gate, or literally coming in through Christ, there stood a brazen altar on which daily sacrifices were made. In order to get to the Most Holy Place, which represented heaven, one had to first make a sacrifice to atone for their sins. Hebrews states, "He did not enter by means of the blood of goats and calves; but He entered the Most Holy Place once for all by His own blood, having obtained eternal redemption" (Heb 9:12). On this altar, as well, were four horns. Horns have symbolized power throughout the Scriptures (Deut 33:17, Ps 75:10). Yet in Romans we read, "I am not ashamed of the gospel, *because it is the power* of God for the salvation of everyone who believes" (Rom 1:16). It was Christ who gave us the power of salvation through His sacrifice on the cross. Without going through the altar there was no way to enter the Most Holy Place. Likewise, without going through the cross, we have no access to heaven. This altar speaks of mans' justification through Christ.

After the sacrifice, one went to the washing laver. As the altar represented justification, the laver represents sanctification. The priests would wash their hands and feet many times daily to keep themselves pure. This symbolizes our pure service for Christ with our hands and our daily walk with Him. When Jesus was going to wash Peter's feet in John 13, Peter rejected this gift at first: "'No,' said Peter, 'You shall never wash my feet.' Jesus answered, 'Unless I wash you, you have no part with Me'" (John 13:8). Peter then responded wisely, "'Then, Lord,' Simon Peter replied, 'not just my feet but my hands and my head as well'" (John 13:9)! But Jesus said, "A person who has had a bath needs only to wash his feet; his whole body is clean" (John 13:10) By this, Jesus meant that if our walk with Christ is pure through His power, our whole body is righteous. To put it another way, "faith without works is dead" (James 2:17). If we say we have faith, but do not have works, you probably don't have faith. The clean feet represented a sanctified life in Christ.

Moving further into the Holy Place was the Show Bread which represented our fellowship with Christ. Christ is the "Bread of Life" upon which we commune today, and will commune with forever. Jesus said Himself, "For the bread of God is He who comes down from heaven and gives life to the world.... I am the bread of life. He who comes to Me will never go hungry, and he who believes in Me will never be thirsty" (John 6:33,35). This is also why we read in Revelation, "To him who overcomes, I will give some of the hidden Manna" (Rev 2:17).

Also in the Holy Place were the candlesticks, representing Christ as the Light of the world. It is Christ who is our Lamp that lights our path through life: "Your word is a lamp to my feet and a light for my path" (Psa 119:105). And as Christ said, "I have come into the world as a light, so that no one who believes in Me should stay in darkness" (John 12:46).

Finally, the altar of incense was also in the Holy Place. The incense represented our prayer and worship. In Revelation we see this explained with the elders: "Each one had a harp and they were holding golden bowls full of incense, which are the prayers of the saints" (Rev 5:8). Christ is our Mediator. We do not need a priest to pray for us anymore. Therefore, we do not need to pray to saints or anyone else. In Hebrews it tells us that this altar of incense was in the Most Holy Place (Heb 9:3). It wasn't there in the Old Testament, but now that Christ has risen, He entered the Most Holy Place and we now pray directly to Him in His Most Holy Place. The veil that separated the Most Holy Place from the Holy Place was rent in two when Christ died on the cross, showing us that we now have free access to the Most Holy Place through Christ, our High Priest. As we read in Psalms, "May my prayer be set before you like incense" (Psa 141:2). Prayer without faith is pointless. The position of this altar of incense is important. One had to first go through the sacrifice (Christ) to get to the incense. Prayer is for the believer. Even in Christ's prayer for His followers He said, "I pray for them. I am not praying for the world, but for those you have given Me, for they are Yours" (John 17:9). Prayer without first going through the bloody altar is unacceptable.

It should also be mentioned that from the outside, the temple looked rather drab and unattractive. It wasn't until one reached the inside that things appeared beautiful and priceless. Likewise, from the outside Christ may appear to be nothing more than a good man to many unbelievers. It isn't until one enters through the altar of sacrifice (cross) that Christ's true beauty, joy and peace are experienced, and it isn't until one enters the Most Holy Place (representing heaven) that the tremendous climax is reached.

As every human being is body, soul and spirit, the temple was represented by three parts as well. The body was like the outer court area, which was the only visible place. It was the place of sacrifice. As Paul states, "Therefore, I urge you, brothers, in view of God's mercy, to offer your bodies as living sacrifices, holy and pleasing to God--this is your spiritual act of worship" (Rom 12:1). The soul may be represented by the Holy Place, which was the place of worship. It was there that the priests had fellowship with Christ at the table of the Show Bread and walked in the light of the golden candlestick, worshipping and praying at the altar or incense. The soul is our seat of emotions and fellowship. Finally, the utmost adoration was behind the veil in the Most Holy Place. It was here that the priest had to enter with God ALONE and approach His throne, or Mercy Seat. As we read in Hebrews, "Let us then approach the throne of grace with confidence, so that we may receive mercy and find grace to help us in our time of need" (Heb 4:16). Have you found time to spend with God one on One lately? It is here that we find the greatest joy and blessings of Christianity; the bloody Mercy Seat. The life is in the Blood and we go to that Blood for our peace and salvation, as we shall see in a closer examination of the Most Holy Place.

Furthest into the Temple was the Most Holy Place that housed the Ark and the cherubim. As we have discussed earlier in Revelation, the cherubim always guard God's throne, His Mercy Seat. Keeping in mind that the entire Temple was a model of heaven, there is much significance with the Ark being mentioned in Revelation. We also see blood mentioned many times in Revelation as well. In fact, the saints were said to overcome evil by the Blood of the Lamb (12:11), and were to wash their robes in it, making them white by that Blood (7:14). The blood and the Ark of the Covenant go hand in hand. There are three "arks" mentioned in Scripture: 1) Noah's Ark, 2) Basket Moses was put in, and 3) the Ark of the Covenant.

God gave these instructions to Noah before building the Ark, "So make yourself an ark of cypress wood; make rooms in it and coat it with pitch inside and out" (Gen 6:14). The word translated "pitch" is the same word for "atonement." Literally translated it could read, "atone (*kaphar* – verb) it with atonement (*kophar* – noun) inside and out." Atonement meant, "to cover." The pitch was the "atonement" of the ark to keep the judgment waters out. Likewise, the pitch that covered Moses' "ark" was an atonement, or covering for Moses. This is exactly what the blood atonement of all the Old Testament sacrifices did as well. The blood of the animals could not take away our sins, but only cover them. Once a year the high priest would enter the Most Holy Place and pour blood upon the mercy seat that rested on top of the Ark of the Covenant. That blood foreshadowed the Blood of our High Priest to come, as Hebrews puts it, "But when this Priest had offered for all time one sacrifice for sins, He sat down at the right hand of God [and, therefore, rested because His work was done]. Since that time He waits for His enemies to be made into His footstool, because by *one* sacrifice, He has made perfect *forever* those who are being made holy" (Heb 10:12-14). It is interesting that in any culture of any time, people have been shedding blood to atone for sins. Missionaries will tell you that no tribe in the world has not attempted to appease their gods for wrongs they have done. Atheism is a modern term, because you will find no atheists among pagans and savages. Everyone, by nature, knows he is sinful and looks for an atonement, but Christ is the only true atonement that has been made.

The blood that was poured out on the Mercy Seat was our covering before Christ. Inside the Ark of the Covenant were the Ten Commandments; God's law. It was through this law that we were condemned: "When the commandment came, sin sprang to life and I died. I found that the very commandment that was intended to bring life actually brought death" (Rom 7:9-10). Something or Someone needed to cover this law for us. This Ark of the Covenant pointed to that Someone; Christ Jesus, our Lord. In 1 Samuel 6:19 the Ark of the Lord was being returned by the Philistines who had captured it in war. Some Israelites looked in the Ark, probably innocently, to see if the Philistines had put anything in or had taken anything out. However, God struck them dead! For just a moment they peered in on the law of God *without the blood* to cover it, and judgment fell upon them. If we remove the blood from God's throne, His Mercy Seat, it becomes a throne of judgment. That is why the saints wash their robes in the Blood of the Lamb. That is how we "overcome" the evils of this world. Paul tells us about Christ: "God presented Him as a sacrifice of atonement, through faith in His blood" (Rom 3:25). The Word for atonement here is *hilasterion*, and is literally translated, "Mercy Seat" in some translations. This word only appears one other time in Hebrews where it says, "Above the ark were the cherubim of the Glory, overshadowing the *atonement cover*" (Heb 9:5). It is through Christ's Blood that He becomes our Mercy Seat.

There are many more things that could be discussed regarding the temple, even to its finest details. For more information on this you may look to my book on Exodus.

CHAPTER 12

Section 4 (Revelation 12:1-14:20) Opposing Kingdoms

Rev 12:1 A great and wondrous sign appeared in heaven: a woman clothed with the sun, with the moon under her feet and a crown of twelve stars on her head. 12:2 She was pregnant and cried out in pain as she was about to give birth.

Chapter twelve is going to depart from our chronological timeline by going all the way back to Satan's fall.

John saw a "sign" in heaven so that it is to be taken figuratively. By taking things in context one is able to see exactly what is being signaled. A woman clothed with the sun was seen. Some try to say that the woman is Christ, but Christ wouldn't give birth to Himself in verse five. Others try to say the woman is Mary since Christ comes from her in verse five. However, verse 14 talks about two wings being given to the woman and the earth helping her. Also, the dragon will make war against the rest of her offspring in v. 17. None of this makes any sense for Mary. The only logical explanation is that the woman is Israel, as we will see throughout this chapter. In verse one we see that she was clothed with the sun. The sun represents God. She also had the moon under her feet and a crown of twelve stars on her head. Genesis makes it clear that this is Israel. When Joseph was young he had two dreams telling that his brothers and father would bow down before him: "'Listen,' he said, 'I had another dream, and this time the sun and moon and eleven stars were bowing down to me.' When he told his father as well as his brothers, his father rebuked him and said, 'What is this dream you had? Will your mother and I and your brothers actually come and bow down to the ground before you'" (Gen 37:9-10)? Joseph's father, Jacob, was the father of 12 sons who became the tribes of Israel. In Joseph's dream the stars represented his brothers (since Joseph had the dream, that is why there were only 11 stars) or the tribes of Israel. Later, Joseph's dream comes true and he recognizes it as being fulfilled (Gen 42:9).

Verse two tells us that the woman was about to give birth. Again, this supports the woman as being Israel since Christ comes from Israel, from the tribe of Judah. Regarding the Jewish race, Romans states, "Theirs are the patriarchs, and from them is traced the human ancestry of Christ" (Rom 9:5). Note also that the woman cannot be the bride of Christ or the church. The church did not give birth to Christ, rather Christ gave birth to the church. The Messiah comes out of Israel and, therefore, the woman must be Israel.

Rev 12:3 Then another sign appeared in heaven: an enormous red dragon with seven heads and ten horns and seven crowns on his heads. 12:4 His tail swept a third of the stars out of the sky and flung them to the earth.

The dragon stood in front of the woman who was about to give birth, so that he might devour her child the moment it was born. 12:5 She gave birth to a son, a male child, who will rule all the nations with an iron scepter. And her child was snatched up to God and to his throne.

Then John saw a red dragon (Satan v. 9) with seven heads, seven crowns and ten horns. As usual when something is symbolic we are told what they represent. To understand this we need to look at other beasts that appear in Scripture with the same type of descriptions.

- Daniel 7:7,20 - A fourth beast with **ten horns**. Verse 24 tells us the ten horns are kings.
- Revelation 17:3,7,9,12 has a beast with **ten horns and seven heads**. Verse 12 tells us the ten horns are ten kings. Verse 9 tells us the heads are seven hills.
- Revelation 13:1 shows a beast coming out of the sea with **ten horns, seven heads and ten crowns**. It seems it is the same beast in Revelation 17:3.

The dragon in our verses being discussed, is closely connected to the beasts discussed above. It is the Antichrist who is described by Daniel and John in the above verses, but Satan is the dragon described here (v. 9). It is Satan that gives the Antichrist his power. Therefore, the ten horns and heads should be interpreted as they are for us in chapter 17, as kings and hills. The kings will be under Satan's power and they will rule on the city of seven hills. More will be discussed later in chapter 13, as this dragon will play an important role.

Verse four shows Satan had flung a third of the stars out of the sky down to the earth. It is generally accepted that these are not physical stars, but rather fallen angels. It seems that when Satan fell he took a third of the angels with him. After all, Satan was one of the chief angels (cherubs) before his pride brought him to his destruction. In Matthew we have reference to Satan's angels: "Then He will say to those on His left, 'Depart from Me, you who are cursed, into the eternal fire prepared for the devil and his angels'" (Mat 25:41). We read of Satan's fall in Isaiah, "How you have fallen from heaven, O morning star, son of the dawn! You have been cast down to the earth, you who once laid low the nations! You said in your heart, 'I will ascend to heaven; I will raise my throne above the stars of God; I will sit enthroned on the mount of assembly, on the utmost heights of the sacred mountain. I will ascend above the tops of the clouds; I will make myself like the Most High.' But you are brought down to the grave, to the depths of the pit" (Isa 14:12-15). Ezekiel also writes, "Through your widespread trade you were filled with violence, and you sinned. So I drove you in disgrace from the mount of God, and I expelled you, O guardian cherub, from among the fiery stones. Your heart became proud on account of your beauty, and you corrupted your wisdom because of your splendor. So I threw you to the earth" (Ezek 28:16-17). When speaking of the little horn, which is the Antichrist, (Satan's tool to do his work) Daniel also refers to the stars being thrown down: "It grew until it reached the host of the heavens, and it threw some of the starry host down to the earth and *trampled on them*. It set itself up to be as great as the Prince of the host; it took away the daily sacrifice from Him, and the place of His sanctuary was brought low" (Dan 8:10-11). Therefore, these angels were not cast out of heaven because they wanted to be, rather because they, too, must have disobeyed God. Satan apparently tramples on them as chief over them.

The first item on the dragon's agenda is to wait for Israel (woman) to give birth to Jesus (woman's child). It is not surprising then, that when Christ was born one of the first things that happened was Herod gave the orders to kill all male babies two years old or younger (Mat 2:16).

The woman did give birth to a male child who would rule all the nations with an iron scepter. No clearer description of Christ could have been given. In Psalms, Christ is predicted to, "rule them with an iron scepter; You will dash them to pieces like pottery" (Psa 2:9). In Revelation 2:27 the same prediction was said of Christ at His second coming. This iron scepter is often representative of a king's power. Christ's power is in His Word. That, too, is elaborated on in chapter nineteen where we read of Christ, "Out of His mouth comes a sharp sword with which to strike down the nations. He will rule them with an iron scepter" (Rev 19:15). Christ will not technically rule with the iron scepter until His return. The one He will rule over is the dragon, or Satan and his followers. That is precisely why the dragon waited for the child to be born; to try to destroy Him. God would not allow that to happen and Satan's attempt through Herod failed.

After Christ's death, of which Satan knew was his own death, God raised Him from the dead and seated Him on His right hand. The following verses make this sure:

- "After the Lord Jesus had spoken to them, He was taken up into heaven and He sat at the right hand of God" (Mark 16:19).
- "Exalted to the right hand of God, He has received from the Father the promised Holy Spirit and has poured out what you now see and hear" (Acts 2:33).
- "But Stephen, full of the Holy Spirit, looked up to heaven and saw the glory of God, and Jesus standing at the right hand of God" (Acts 7:55).
- "'Look,' he said, 'I see heaven open and the Son of Man standing at the right hand of God'" (Acts 7:56).
- "Who is He that condemns? Christ Jesus, who died--more than that, who was raised to life--is at the right hand of God and is also interceding for us" (Rom 8:34).
- "Since, then, you have been raised with Christ, set your hearts on things above, where Christ is seated at the right hand of God" (Col 3:1).
- "But when this Priest had offered for all time one sacrifice for sins, He sat down at the right hand of God" (Heb 10:12).

Rev 12:6 The woman fled into the desert to a place prepared for her by God, where she might be taken care of for 1,260 days. 12:7 And there was war in heaven. Michael and his angels fought against the dragon, and the dragon and his angels fought back. 12:8 But he was not strong

enough, and they lost their place in heaven. 12:9 The great dragon was hurled down--that ancient serpent called the devil, or Satan, who leads the whole world astray. He was hurled to the earth, and his angels with him.

The woman (Israel) fled into the desert to a place where she was protected by God for three and one-half years. So far we have seen a lot of history in only six verses. We started with God choosing the tribes of Israel. From there we saw Satan had been cast down out of heaven along with one-third of the angels. Then Jesus came through the line of Israel while Satan waited to destroy Him. When the devil failed at his attempt to kill Christ, he was angry because he knew this meant that he would be ruled with an iron scepter in the last days. Satan's power was destroyed. God raised Christ from the dead and brought Him to sit at the right hand of God. Now that Satan could not change the fact that he lost, he decided to go after God's chosen Israel because his time is short. For a period of three and one-half years he will be intent on destroying Israel and the saints, but will not be able to. After this three and one-half year period of protection, another three and one-half year period of persecution will take place. Daniel tells us that Satan would go after the saints using his servant, the Antichrist. However, after the second three and one-half years, Satan and his servants will be destroyed by the iron scepter: "He will speak against the Most High and oppress His saints and try to change the set times and the laws. The saints will be handed over to him for a time, times and half a time" (Dan 7:25). (See 11:1 for further explanation on the three and one-half years).

The woman fled to the desert, not describing a desolate place, but as a place of refuge and care. Hosea may have had this in mind when he wrote, "Therefore I am now going to allure her; I will lead her into the desert and speak tenderly to her" (Hosea 2:14).

Verse seven shows us that the battle is not here on earth as much as it is in heaven, in the spiritual realm.

There have been other times when the archangel, Michael, has fought against Satan: "But even the archangel Michael, when he was disputing with the devil about the body of Moses, did not dare to bring a slanderous accusation against him, but said, 'The Lord rebuke you!'" (Jude 1:9). However, Michael has been ready for this very day discussed here in verse seven. Daniel prophesied: "At that time Michael, the great prince who *protects Your people*, will arise. There will be a *time of distress such as has not happened from the beginning of nations until then*. But *at that time* your people--everyone whose name is found written in the book--will be delivered" (Dan 12:1). Here we see that Michael has been appointed to protect God's people in the last days when the time of distress comes upon the world (Mat 24:21).

Satan and his stars (angels) obviously lost their fight in the garden, on the cross, and at the end of time. It is interesting that they lost their place in heaven. In Job we see that Satan was able to approach the throne of God in heaven: "One day the angels came to present themselves before the LORD, and Satan also came with them. The LORD said to Satan, 'Where have you come from?' Satan answered the LORD, 'From roaming through the earth and going back and forth in it'" (Job 1:6-7). When Christ died and rose again, Satan lost his privilege to roam about the heavens because he was cast to earth. Satan can no longer accuse the saints of anything, because Christ's blood has made us clean and has washed away all of Satan's lies. Satan is called the accuser, and he even tried to accuse Joshua, the high priest (Zech 3:1). But those days are over for Jesus Himself said, "I saw Satan fall like lightning from heaven" (Luke 10:18). Just before His death Christ also stated, "Now is the time for judgment on this world; now the prince of this world will be driven out" (John 12:31). This means that Satan's kingdom was on earth, and though driven out of heaven, he roams the earth, and is still very active in many lives today. However, he does not have control anymore. Because of Christ he has been subdued. Our, "enemy the devil prowls around like a roaring lion looking for someone to devour" (1 Pet 5:8). Satan has not yet been cast out of the earth, but only heaven. His power is indeed limited, but not to be something mocked at either. That is why Jude wrote, "But even the archangel Michael, when he was disputing with the devil about the body of Moses, did not dare to bring a slanderous accusation against him, but said, 'The Lord rebuke you'" (Jude 1:9)! We must not take Satan and his power lightly, but go to God's Word for our protection and shield: "take up the shield of faith, with which you can extinguish all the flaming arrows of the evil one" (Eph 6:16). Though Satan cannot accuse us before God, he certainly is going after the saints to get them to deny their Shield (or at least get too busy to put it on).

A time is coming, however, when Satan will even lose his place on earth and will be cast into hell. Jesus will soon say "to those on His left, 'Depart from Me, you who are cursed, into the eternal fire prepared for the devil and his angels'" (Mat 25:41). But until that time, be aware, because Satan is going after the saints with the same vengeance he went after Christ in the wilderness, the garden, and the cross. He has asked to "sift us like wheat" (Luke 22:31, see also John 13:2 and 2 Cor 11:3). Always put on your armor of God.

Rev 12:10 Then I heard a loud voice in heaven say: "Now have come the salvation and the power and the kingdom of our God, and the authority of his Christ. For the accuser of our brothers, who accuses them before our God day and night, has been hurled down. 12:11 They overcame him by the blood of the Lamb and by the word of their testimony; they did not love their lives so much as to shrink from death. 12:12 Therefore rejoice, you heavens and you who dwell in them! But woe to the earth and the sea, because the devil has gone down to you! He is filled with fury, because he knows that his time is short."

After Satan had been hurled to the earth a voice from heaven proclaimed Christ's salvation. God's power, salvation and His kingdom were shown, and in effect when the accuser was cast down. Satan is indeed our accuser (Job 1:9-11, Zec 3:1). In fact, the word for Satan in the Hebrew is *accuser*. He continually tries to accuse us of sins before God. But after Christ's resurrection our slate is clean and Satan can accuse us no more.

It was only through Christ's blood and by His testimony that the saints (Rev 6:9, 7:14) were able to overcome the power of Satan. Even if confronted with death, Christ was never denied, thereby their strength never left. Jesus said, "If anyone comes to Me and does not hate his father and mother, his wife and children, his brothers and sisters--yes, even his own life--he cannot be My disciple" (Luke 14:26). As a result of the victory we have through Christ, all of heaven rejoices; especially since Satan is there no more. As the Psalmists said, "Let the heavens rejoice, let the earth be glad; let the sea resound, and all that is in it" (Psa 96:11). It is because of our redemption that all of creation praises our Lord, "Sing for joy, O heavens, for the LORD has done this; shout aloud, O earth beneath. Burst into song, you mountains, you forests and all your trees, for the LORD has redeemed Jacob, He displays His glory in Israel" (Isa 44:23, see also Isa 49:13). But God also deserves praise because of our deliverance and Satan's destruction, "Rejoice over her, O heaven! Rejoice, saints and apostles and prophets! God has judged her for the way she treated you" (Rev 18:20).

However, because Satan had been cast down to the earth, a woe is given to its inhabitants. Satan knows his time is short and, therefore, he is filled with fury. He is going after the saints in full force (see Rev 8:13).

Rev 12:13 When the dragon saw that he had been hurled to the earth, he pursued the woman who had given birth to the male child. 12:14 The woman was given the two wings of a great eagle, so that she might fly to the place prepared for her in the desert, where she would be taken care of for a time, times and half a time, out of the serpent's reach. 12:15 Then from his mouth the serpent spewed water like a river, to overtake the woman and sweep her away with the torrent. 12:16 But the earth helped the woman by opening its mouth and swallowing the river that the dragon had spewed out of his mouth. 12:17 Then the dragon was enraged at the woman and went off to make war against the rest of her offspring--those who obey God's commandments and hold to the testimony of Jesus.

Once Satan had been cast to the earth he went after God's chosen people (woman), however, God protected them by giving them wings of an eagle to fly away to a special place prepared just for them. This will take place during the first 3 and 1/2 years of the seven year tribulation. Though the woman goes to a desert, it is her deliverance, much like the Exodus was for the Israelites. However, even a desert can be made fruitful with God's providence. Hosea explains, "Therefore I am now going to allure her; I will lead her into the desert and speak tenderly to her. There I will give her back her vineyards, and will make the Valley of Achor a door of hope. There she will sing as in the days of her youth, as in the day she came up *out of Egypt*. . . . you will call Me 'my husband'; you will no longer call Me 'my master.' I will remove the names of the Baals from her lips; no longer will their names be invoked. In that day I will make a covenant for them with the beasts of the field and the birds of the air and the creatures that move along the ground. Bow and sword and battle I will abolish from the land, so that all may lie down in safety. I will betroth you to Me forever; I will betroth you in righteousness and justice, in love and compassion" (Hosea 2:14-19).

The eagle's wings also alludes to the Exodus out of slavery in Egypt. God told the Israelites, "You yourselves have seen what I did to Egypt, and how *I carried you on eagles' wings* and brought you to Myself" (Exo 19:4). Once more symbolism is explained using the rest of the Scriptures. We discussed the eagle further in Revelation 8:13.

It seems that Egypt is continually alluded to in chapter 13. Perhaps Jeremiah was seeing a foreshadowing of this day, "'However, the days are coming,' declares the LORD, 'when men will no longer say, As surely as the LORD lives, who brought the Israelites up out of Egypt' but they will say, 'As surely as the LORD lives, who brought the Israelites up out of the land of the north and out of all the countries where He had banished them'" (Jer 16:14-15).

Though the woman is out of Satan's reach, he will spew water like a river to flood her out. However, God will help the woman by opening up the earth to take in the water. Using the Old Testament as our guide, the flood seems to represent an army or enemy of God's people. Jeremiah recorded, "This is what the LORD says: 'See how the waters are rising in the north; they will become an *overflowing torrent*. They will overflow the land and everything in it, the towns and those who live in them. The people will cry out; all who dwell in the land will wail at the sound of the hoofs of galloping steeds, at the noise of enemy chariots and the rumble of their wheels'" (Jer 47:2-3, see also Jer 46:8 and Dan 11:26). In addition, Satan tries to inundate us with temptations, disbelief, discouragement, and busyness in our bodies, minds and spirit. We fall into Satan's trap of being held in captivity by activity. He works hard to carry us away with the flood waters of life, but God will not let us go down providing we let God fight the fight for us. Remember, God *gives* the "eagle wings" to the woman, we don't make them.

The waters being swallowed by the earth is similar to when Korah and his family were swallowed up by the earth for their rebellion, "and the earth opened its mouth and swallowed them, with their households and all Korah's men and all their possessions" (Num 16:32, see also Exo 15:12).

Verse 17 shows that when Satan realizes that he cannot be successful in going after the woman, he goes after the rest of her offspring. This offspring can be none other than all believers outside of blood Israel. Speaking about the Gentiles Paul wrote, "If the root is holy, so are the branches. If some of the branches have been broken off, and you, though *a wild olive shoot*, have been grafted in among the others and *now share* in the nourishing sap from the olive root" (Rom 11:16-17). Even more to the point Paul said, "In other words, it is not the natural children who are God's children, but it is the children of the promise who are regarded as Abraham's offspring" (Rom 9:8).

In verse seven we saw that the dragon was not only given power to make war against the saints, but also to *conquer* them. These saints will obey God's commands and hold to their testimony about Christ. They will not shrink from death (v. 11). Jesus Himself said, "If you love Me, you will obey what I command" (John 14:15). These are the same saints we saw in Revelation 6:9 and 7:14.

Once a Christian is obedient to God's Word, Satan seems to go after them all the more. Immediately after Christ was baptized and God gave His divine approval of Jesus' ministry, Satan tempted Him in the wilderness to try and stop Christ's ministry. Right after Peter confessed Christ to be the Rock of faith, Satan began sifting the disciples to keep that message from being spread. So, too, in our lives. Once we follow up on God's call, Satan is right there to do everything possible to prevent us from continuing. It seems that every time I have decided to take a call or try to expand the creation ministry, Satan throws all kinds of problems and road blocks at me. But God always prevails. A friend once told me, "God will always take responsibility for the consequences of our obedience." How true that is. God has never let me down and I know He never will. Where God's Word is preached, Satan will work overtime. He awaits to devour the woman's offspring when they become "children of the promise." However, just as the woman was, we, too, will be delivered. Wherever God's Word is preached, loved and obeyed, is a place that Satan must also flee from.

CHAPTER 13

Rev 13:1 And the dragon stood on the shore of the sea. And I saw a beast coming out of the sea. He had ten horns and seven heads, with ten crowns on his horns, and on each head a blasphemous name.

Chapter 13 identifies the evil trinity. Our Creator is God the Father, Christ the Son, and the Holy Spirit; three in one. Satan attempts to mimic God in every way possible to disguise himself as an angel of light. We were told plainly that the dragon we read about in chapter 12 was Satan. Now Satan waits on the sea-shore to call up one of his servants, the beast out of the sea; the Antichrist. In verse 11 we will see another beast come out of the earth, there it will be the False Prophet. Therefore, we have the dragon being the Antigod, the beast out of the sea being the Antichrist, and the beast out of the earth being the Anti-Holy Spirit. More on this line of thought will be discussed as we look into the following verses.

We know this beast is the Anitchrist because Daniel 7:3-17 describes the same scenario. Daniel saw four beasts coming out of the sea, each of which represented a world kingdom (7:3). The fourth one had ten horns (7:7) and a mouth that spoke boastfully (7:8). During the time of this beast's reign, God's judgment seat was seen in heaven as the courtroom was seated (7:9-10), much like what we saw in Revelation chapters one and four. The fourth beast was then captured and thrown into hell (7:11). The fact that it came out of the fourth kingdom also tells us that it came out of the Roman kingdom. In four separate visions, Daniel shows four kingdoms arising: Babylon, Medo-Persian, Greece, and Rome. For example, in Daniel's vision of the statue, the gold head was Babylon, the silver chest was the Medes and Persians, the bronze belly and thighs represented the Greeks, and the iron legs represented Rome. Interestingly, connected with the legs of the fourth kingdom, were feet with ten iron and clay mixed toes. The ten toes represented kings, just like the ten horns on the beast here in Revelation represented kings. Out of a mountain a huge stone was cut (but not by human hands) and it rolled down and smashed all the kingdoms of this statue. Once this was done the Rock (Jesus) grew and became an everlasting kingdom (God's heavenly kingdom). Daniel had the same story told in his vision of four beasts (7:1), which represented the same four kingdoms in the same order (winged lion, bear, leopard, and a different fourth beast that looked terrifying. It had part of all the above animal characteristics). Again Daniel saw a vision of a ram and a goat (Medo-Persian empire and the Greeks). Point being, the Antichrist came out of the fourth kingdom; Rome. This idea will also be continued in later verses.

The ten horns on the beast that John saw were ten kings (17:12). The seven heads were also kings and hills (17:9). Therefore, this beast would have other kings under his control and power. There would also be an additional seven kings who would rule on seven hills. Even to the present time, Rome has been known as the city of seven hills. True, other cities have also been known by that name, but none that exist in the fourth kingdom of Daniel's vision. Ancient Roman writers like Virgil, Martial, Cicero and others, all referred to Rome as the "city of seven hills."

The blasphemous names on the horns show that the Antichrist would speak boastfully against God. Daniel predicted this of the Antichrist as well, "The king will do as he pleases. He will exalt and magnify himself above every god and will say unheard-of things against the God of gods. He will be successful until the time of wrath is completed, for what has been determined must take place" (Dan 11:36). Another interesting connection between Rome and the Antichrist may be in the fact that the Roman kings used to be blasphemous as well. For example, Domitian, who persecuted the Christians (like the Antichrist will do) demanded to be called *Dominus et Deus noster*, meaning "Our Lord and God." In chapter 17 we will see a scarlet beast covered in blasphemous names (v. 3) having ten horns and seven heads (v. 7). Therefore, the beast that comes out of the sea here in Revelation 13 will be elaborated on further in chapter 17.

It is also important to note the different focus of the evil trinity. The dragon (Satan) is in charge of things and gives his power to the Antichrist and the False Prophet. The Antichrist (beast out of the sea) is political in nature, having kings under him, and the False Prophet (beast out of the earth) is religious in nature.

Rev 13:2 The beast I saw resembled a leopard, but had feet like those of a bear and a mouth like that of a lion. The dragon gave the beast his power and his throne and great authority. 13:3 One of the heads of the beast seemed to have had a fatal wound, but the fatal wound had been healed. The whole world was astonished and followed the beast. 13:4 Men worshipped the dragon because he had given authority to the beast, and they also worshipped the beast and asked, "Who is like the beast? Who can make war against him?"

This beast out of the sea represented a lion, leopard, and bear. These were the exact same beasts Daniel saw in his vision of the four beasts coming out of the sea (Dan 7:3). This shows that though the fourth beast reigned, other aspects or qualities of these other countries remained. Rome boasted about its ability to meld other cultures into its own. Many people think that an organization like the United Nations will play a part in the end times because of the number of kings (ten horns and seven heads) involved with the Antichrist. The fact that this beast also had qualities of other kingdoms may give support to this theory. (Remember in Daniel, Babylon, Medo-Persian and Greek empires were represented by the lion, bear and leopard).

Note it was Satan that gave the Antichrist his power and throne. However, this reign was doomed to destruction as the fifth bowl judgment will be poured out on the beast and his throne (16:10).

One of the heads (kings or hills) under the control of the beast had a near fatal wound, however, he was healed to the astonishment of the nations.

This should bring to mind Genesis 3:15 where it says that Satan would have his head crushed by Christ. (Keep in mind, ONLY unbelievers will be astonished as seen in 17:8). Perhaps it was the Antichrist who healed the king, because as a result, people followed the beast (Anitchrist) and worshipped Satan (dragon), who gave the beast his power. The Antichrist was worshipped because the dragon and the beasts are all part of the evil trinity; three in one. Just as Daniel said (7:8, 11, 20, 25; 11:36) the beast would set himself up as a god and the people would put their full trust in Satan and the Antichrist, perhaps not even realizing who they really were. Thessalonians states, "He will oppose and will exalt himself over everything that is called God or is worshipped, so that he sets himself up in God's temple, proclaiming himself to be God" (2 Th 2:4). The people believed that no one could make war against their leaders. The words of the people even echo blasphemy as they said "who is like the beast." In Exodus, this is what was said of God: "Who among the gods is like You, O LORD? Who is like You-- majestic in holiness, awesome in glory, working wonders" (Exo 15:11)?

Sometimes it is difficult to tell which part of the evil trinity is being discussed when we look back in Thessalonians, Daniel and other books because they are three in one. In 12:3 we saw Satan (dragon) had ten horns and seven crowns on its seven heads. In 13:1 we saw the Antichrist had ten horns and seven heads. In 17:7 the beast has the same ten horns and seven heads. Whether we talk about Satan, or the Antichrist through whom he displays his power, the blasphemy and persecution of God's people is their united intent. However, it is generally accepted that the book of Daniel and Thessalonians are talking about the Antichrist who displays Satan's power.

Rev 13:5 The beast was given a mouth to utter proud words and blasphemies and to exercise his authority for forty-two months. 13:6 He opened his mouth to blaspheme God, and to slander his name and his dwelling place and those who live in heaven. 13:7 He was given power to make war against the saints and to conquer them. And he was given authority over every tribe, people, language and nation.

The Antichrist was seen as one having charismatic speech, and yet, a blasphemer. As we saw in the preceding verses, there are many Scriptural references supporting this (Dan 7:8, 11, 20, 25; 11:36). The beast was given his authority by the dragon, who was only allowed to have his power because God gave it to him. The Antichrist will use that power for 42 months, or 3 and 1/2 years. We have seen this time period before (Dan 7:25, Rev 11:2, 12:6) and, therefore, we may have an indication that the time period discussed will take place during the preaching of the two witnesses in 11:2 where we read, "But exclude the outer court; do not measure it, because it has been given to the Gentiles. They will trample on the holy city for 42 months" (Rev 11:2).

We also saw that the Antichrist went after the saints to make war against them. We earlier saw the dragon went off to make war against the saints in 12:17 (see also Dan 7:7), showing the evil trinity and their common purpose.

In verses 5-7 we saw that power was "given" to the beast four times. This shows his subordinate role. It is really Satan who is behind the beast's actions.

Daniel described this as a time when "he will cause deceit to prosper, and he will consider himself superior. When they feel secure, *he will destroy many and take his stand against the Prince of princes.* Yet he will be destroyed, but not by human power" (Dan 8:25). The Antichrist will go after the saints for a period of 3 and 1/2 years, after an initial 3 and 1/2 year strengthening of his reign. Therefore, this must be the second half of the seven year tribulation.

Not only does the above quote from Daniel show the beast's blasphemous intentions against God and his hatred for the saints, but also his pride stemming from his superior (but temporary) power. Verse seven showed that he had authority over all the nations. He will indeed be a powerful political ruler. As we saw in chapter 11, all the inhabitants of the earth hated the two witnesses, but a beast came up out of the Abyss and delivered them from these two men. Perhaps this is how he gained his world-wide support.

To support that Revelation not only points to the end of time, but also to the end of Jerusalem in 70 AD, we see that from November of AD 64 to June of AD 68 is exactly 42 months. This is the time that Nero reigned in Rome. As we will see in Revelation 13:10, there is mention of "dying by the sword." Nero killed himself by sticking his own sword into his throat. Back in Revelation 13:3 we saw that one of the heads of the beast received a fatal wound that was healed. When Nero died in AD 68 there were four emperors who reigned in about one year's time (Galba, Otho, Vitellius, Vespasian). It seemed as if Rome had received a fatal wound and was about to die as the bordering countries began shaking loose from Rome. Ancient historians record this event this way: "This was the condition of the Roman state when Galba entered upon the year. It was to be for Galba his last, and for the state, almost the end" (Tacitus, Histories I.11). However, Seutonius recorded the revival of Rome this way: "The empire, for which a long time had been unsettled and drifting through the usurpation and violent death of three emperors, was at last taken in hand and given stability by the Flavian family" (Seutonius, Vespasian I). Josephus also commented on the unexpected revival of Rome: "So upon this confirmation of Vespasian's entire government, which was now settled, and upon the unexpected deliverance of the public affairs of the Romans from ruin. . ." (Josephus, Wars IV. 11.5). Therefore, one could say that Rome received a near fatal blow and recovered quickly to the astonishment of the nations.

Regarding the proud and blasphemous words, Nero saw himself as Apollo, the sun god. He was very proud and boastful of this blasphemous belief. In addition, as Caesar, he was considered to be divine by the state. All of these support Revelation as meaningful throughout history, but certainly not yet having been completely fulfilled today.

Rev 13:8 All inhabitants of the earth will worship the beast--all whose names have not been written in the book of life belonging to the Lamb that was slain from the creation of the world. 13:9 He who has an ear, let him hear. 13:10 If anyone is to go into captivity, into captivity he will go. If anyone is to be killed with the sword, with the sword he will be

killed. This calls for patient endurance and faithfulness on the part of the saints.

The whole population of unbelievers would love and worship the beast. However, those whose names were written in the Book of Life would refuse. To worship the beast meant to have their name taken out of the Book of Life (where all the names of those saved have been recorded). As John wrote earlier, "He who overcomes will, like them, be dressed in white. I will never blot out his name from the book of life, but will acknowledge his name before My Father and His angels" (Rev 3:5).

The Book of Life belongs to the Lamb (Jesus), because it is through Christ's blood that all names are written in the Book. It isn't until the free gift of the blood of Christ is rejected that one's name is blotted out. It is clear that the Lamb was Jesus, as John said in his Gospel, "the next day John saw Jesus coming toward him and said, 'Look, the Lamb of God, who takes away the sin of the world'" (John 1:29)!

It is also interesting that God's plan of salvation for each of us was written down before the creation of the world, even before the stars of heaven were placed. Matthew recorded, "Then the King will say to those on His right, 'Come, you who are blessed by My Father; take your inheritance, the kingdom prepared for you since the creation of the world'" (Mat 25:34). Paul also wrote, "For He chose us in Him before the creation of the world to be holy and blameless in His sight" (Eph 1:4, see also 1 Pet 1:20 and John 17:24).

Verses nine and ten closed by telling us to hear God's Word and to stop rejecting it. Anyone who has an open mind can hear God's message. It is only those who consciously refuse to listen to God that will not hear. Jeremiah warned, "'Hear this you foolish and senseless people, who have eyes but do not see, who have ears but do not hear: Should you not fear Me?' declares the LORD" (Jer 5:21-22). Ezekiel tells us why they could not hear, "They have eyes to see but do not see and ears to hear but do not hear, for they are a rebellious people" (Ezek 12:2). Jesus Himself testified to this: "He who belongs to God hears what God says. The reason you do not hear is that you do not belong to God" (John 8:47).

Verse ten shows that hearing God's Word is the only way to find protection. There will be nothing one can do to keep the events, preordained before the creation of the world, from taking place. If you will be taken captive or killed by the sword, that is what will happen. However, as a believer who hears God's voice, you will be taken care of. For those who do not hear God's voice, it will only get worse. The point being, we are all in God's hands. God is either a merciful Redeemer or a just Judge. Jeremiah showed a similar warning, "And if they ask you, 'Where shall we go?' tell them, 'This is what the LORD says: Those destined for death, to death; those for the sword, to the sword; those for starvation, to starvation; those for captivity, to captivity'" (Jer 15:2). Also, "He will come and attack Egypt, bringing death to those destined for death, captivity to those destined for captivity, and the sword to those destined for the sword" (Jer 43:11). It is obvious that man is NOT in control of his own destiny.

The events of this seven year tribulation will be terrible. As Jesus said, "For then there will be great distress, unequaled from the beginning of the world until now--and never to be equaled again. If those days had not been cut short, no one would survive, but for the sake of the elect those days will be shortened" (Mat 24:21). That is why these times will call for patient endurance and faithfulness for the saints. As Christians, this is not a time to be afraid of, but certainly a time to prepare for. How? By reading God's Word and partaking of His sacraments in order that power may dwell within you. Ephesians puts it so clearly, "Put on the full armor of God so that you can take your stand against the devil's schemes. For our struggle is not against flesh and blood, but against the rulers, against the authorities, against the powers of this dark world and against the spiritual forces of evil in the heavenly realms. Therefore put on the full armor of God, so that when the day of evil comes, you may be able to stand your ground" (Eph 6:11-13). Also, as the writer of Hebrews said, "We do not want you to become lazy, but to imitate those who through faith and patience *inherit what has been promised*" (Heb 6:12). May God bless you on your commitment to read His Word and know Him.

As a little side note. Have you ever asked yourself the question whether or not it is Christ you love, or the possiblity of getting to heaven? What if heaven was "hellish?" What if heaven consisted of a scarcity of food, dry and hot weather, hard labor, no entertainment, and a heavily over populated area? Each day, however, you could work side by side with Jesus. You also lived with Jesus and would come home after each long day of work to share an apartment with Him and eight other people, but you could spend those evenings talking with Jesus, and He would answer every question you had.

On the other hand, what if hell was "heavenly?" It was beautiful with flowing streams and green palm trees, mountains and pleasant aromas. What if there was no work and you could have any material possession or do anything you wanted? You could have plenty of friends, however, Jesus wasn't there, because He was in heaven. Where would you want to go? Sometimes this could be a hard question because it makes us ask ourselves whether we are in love with heaven or Jesus.

Consider it this way. Let's say your spouse was diagnosed with a disease and the doctors said the only way he/she could live was to move out into a secluded desert. Would you tell your spouse, "go on ahead, I think I will stay here and take care of the house and yard to make sure it doesn't get run down?" You would promise to call him/her every night before bed and before every meal. You would also agree to meet once a week on a hard park bench for one hour to visit. Would this be a desired marriage relationship? Certainly not! You would give up all you had to be with the one you love. Sometimes, however, this is exactly how we treat Christ. Rather than living *with* Him and building our relationship and knowing Him more, we simply pray before meals and bed, and once a week meet Him at church for a short time before going home to do our own things. We visit Christ when we should, as Scripture tells us, live with Him. We should love Christ as we love our spouse; desiring to know Him fully. Heaven is not a place as much as it is a marriage relationship. We read in John, "We know also that the Son of God has come and has given us understanding, *so that we may know Him* who is true. And we are **in** Him who is true--even in His Son Jesus Christ. He is the true God **and eternal life**" (1 John 5:20). Note that we are IN Christ and that Christ IS eternal life. Therefore, we don't inherit a place of eternal life, we fully inherit the person; Christ Jesus. As discussed in chapter three, we are being built into God's temple; Jesus. Did you know that for every verse that says Christ is in us, there are ten that say *we* are in Christ? Knowing we are IN Jesus on earth makes our daily relationship with Him "heavenly."

Rev 13:11 Then I saw another beast, coming out of the earth. He had two horns like a lamb, but he spoke like a dragon. 13:12 He exercised all the authority of the first beast on his behalf, and made the earth and its inhabitants worship the first beast, whose fatal wound had been healed. 13:13 And he performed great and miraculous signs, even causing fire to come down from heaven to earth in full view of men. 13:14 Because of the signs he was given power to do on behalf of the first beast, he deceived the inhabitants of the earth. He ordered them to set up an image in honor of the beast who was wounded by the sword and yet lived.

John saw another beast coming out of the earth rather than the sea. This beast had two horns like a lamb, but his looks were deceiving because in speech he was a dreadful dragon. One might say a wolf in sheep's clothing. Jesus warned us to, "Watch out for false prophets. They come to you in sheep's clothing, but inwardly they are ferocious wolves. By their fruit you will recognize them. Do people pick grapes from thornbushes, or figs from thistles" (Mat 7:15-16)? Even when Jesus was telling the disciples about these end times, He warned, "For false Christs and false prophets will appear and perform great signs and miracles to deceive even the elect--if that were possible. See, I have told you ahead of time" (Mat 24:24-25). This beast is known as the False Prophet (16:13) because he is religious in nature and leads people away from the Creator. As earlier mentioned, the False Prophet is the Anti-Holy Spirit. Just as the Holy Spirit brings us to Christ, who received His authority from the Father, the Anti-Holy Spirit (False Prophet or beast out of the earth) leads the unbelievers to worship the Antichrist (beast of out the sea), who received his authority from the Anti-God (Dragon or Satan).

The False Prophet got his power from the first beast, which ultimately comes from Satan. In Thessalonians we read, "The coming of the lawless one will be in accordance with the work of Satan displayed in all kinds of counterfeit miracles, signs and wonders, and in every sort of evil that deceives those who are perishing. They perish because they refused to love the truth and so be saved" (2 Th 2:9-10). This beast also demanded that everyone worship the first beast that came out of the sea. Woe to those who follow in this idolatry, as we see the fate of those who do: "A third angel followed them and said in a loud voice: 'If anyone worships the beast *and his image* [see v. 14] and receives his mark on the forehead or on the hand, he, too, will drink of the wine of God's fury, which has been poured full strength into the cup of His wrath. He will be tormented with burning sulfur in the presence of the holy angels and of the Lamb. And the smoke of their torment rises for ever and ever. There is no rest day or night for those who worship the beast and his image, or for anyone who receives the mark of his name.'" (Rev 14:9-11; see also 16:2, 19:20, and 20:4).

With Nero as a type of Antichrist, we can view this mark as a means of his exercising power and control. In Deuteronomy God said of His laws: "Tie them as *symbols* on your hands and bind them on your foreheads" (Deu 6:8). The Jews took this very literally and put tiny verses in boxes called phylacteries and then bound them to their foreheads. The forehead is the center of thought or symbolic of the mind. The seal of God was put on the foreheads of the saints and, as we discussed earlier, baptism also seals us (see chapter 7). God tells us in Corinthians, "We demolish arguments and every pretension that sets itself up against the knowledge of God, and *we take captive every thought* to make it obedient to Christ" (2 Cor 10:5). We are to seal our mind with Godly thoughts and obedience to them. Therefore, the mark of the beast could, in part, be a metaphor of Nero controlling what people did and thought.

To validate his authority the second beast was given power to do many miracles, even causing fire to come down from heaven, mimicking true prophets like Elijah or even God Himself (1 Kings 18:38, 2 Kings 1:10, Luke 9:54, Revelation 20:9). This is something Nero could not do. This power also comes from demons as John tells us in chapter 16: "Then I saw three evil spirits that looked like frogs; they came out of the mouth of the dragon, out of the mouth of the beast and out of the mouth of *the false prophet. They are spirits of demons* performing miraculous signs, and they go out to the kings of the whole world, to gather them for the battle on the great day of God Almighty" (Rev 16:13). I believe there are many "spirits of demons" today who lead many astray by so called miraculous visits from the dead, near death experiences (where Christ is not the focus), seances etc.. As John tells us, "Dear friends, do not believe every spirit, but test the spirits to see whether they are from God, because many false prophets have gone out into the world. This is how you can recognize the Spirit of God: Every spirit that acknowledges that Jesus Christ has come in the flesh is from God" (1 John 4:1-2).

Verse 14 tells us that to aid in the worship of the first beast (Antichrist) an image was set up in his honor. The above miracles were also used to validate the image's power and right to be worshipped. Even Moses warned, "If a prophet, or one who foretells by dreams, appears among you and announces to you a miraculous sign or wonder, and if the sign or wonder of which he has spoken takes place, and he says, 'Let us follow other gods' (gods you have not known) 'and let us worship them,' you must not listen to the words of that prophet or dreamer. The LORD your God is testing you to find out whether you love Him with all your heart and with all your soul" (Deu 13:1-3). Not only will this image be worshipped, but it will also serve as a sign for the believers: "So when you see standing in the holy place 'the abomination that causes desolation,' spoken of through the prophet Daniel--let the reader understand--" (Mat 24:15, Dan 3:1-11). Even Thessalonians tells us that this image will be set up in God's temple because it is part of the Antichrist's plan in calling himself a god: "He will oppose and will exalt himself over everything that is called God or is worshipped, so that he sets himself up in God's temple, proclaiming himself to be God" (2 Th 2:4).

The doom of both these beasts will be seen in 19:20 where they are cast into the fiery pits of hell.

Rev 13:15 He was given power to give breath to the image of the first beast, so that it could speak and cause all who refused to worship the image to be killed. 13:16 He also forced everyone, small and great, rich and poor, free and slave, to receive a mark on his right hand or on his forehead, 13:17 so that no one could buy or sell unless he had the mark, which is the name of the beast or the number of his name. 13:18 This calls for wisdom. If anyone has insight, let him calculate the number of the beast, for it is man's number. His number is 666.

Verse 15 tells us of an amazing miraculous sign given to this inanimate image. The False Prophet gave it breath to speak. This breath can be none other than demons from hell that come out of the mouth of all three parts of the evil trinity (Rev 16:13-14). No doubt the image will speak boastfully as we have already seen in many passages (Dan 7:8, 11, Rev 13:5). These verses remind us of a similar event in Daniel when Nebuchadnezzar had an image built and demanded worship of it. It seems that this foreshadowed the image of the Anitchrist. In both cases, if the image was not worshipped, fire would destroy you. Shadrach, Meshach and Abednego show us the true lesson to be learned. They refused to bow down to Nebuchadnezzar's image and chose the fiery furnace instead. Their words to the King show their faith in God: "O Nebuchadnezzar, we do not need to defend ourselves before you in this matter. If we are thrown into the blazing furnace, the God we serve is able to save us from it, and He will rescue us from your hand, O king. But even if He does not, we want you to know, O king, that we will not serve your gods or worship the image of gold you have set up" (Dan 3:16-18). As you know, God did save them from the fiery furnace and God was praised by the whole nation as a result.

The False Prophet and the Antichrist demand worship, as did Nebuchadnezzar. To ensure worship of the beast and his image you will be forced to take a mark on your forehead or right hand. This marking may imitate the seal of God put on the foreheads of the 144,000 in chapter seven. However, without this mark one will be unable to buy or sell the basic necessities of life, including food. This means that there will be no sign of a Christian business anywhere. One will not even be able to "fake it" because the mark of the beast will not even be imitated by a Bible believing man. So what will a Christian do during this time? We have seen many passages showing God's care and providence for us during these times, including God's seal in chapter seven. Even in Old Testament times we see many examples of God's deliverance through impossible situations (using human reason, that is). In the 40 year desert wandering there was no food for the Israelites, but God rained down manna from heaven (Exo 16:31-35) and water came out of the rocks (Exo 17:6). Elijah had no food so the ravens brought it to him (1 Ki 17:4). Also during Elijah's day, when the widow of Zarephath's oil and flour were almost out, God provided a continuos flow that did not end until the famine was over (1 Ki 17:14). Time and time again, God provides for His followers. I believe that if a time comes when we need water or food, God will provide for us. Like in Elijah's case, He may give us an address where food or water can be found (1 Ki 17:3). If not, maybe He will give the ravens our address. Whatever the case may be, "man does not live on bread alone, but on every Word that comes from the mouth of God" (Mat 4:4). One must be very careful as it is a common thing to see many people getting caught up in the interpreting of the mark of the beast, when in fact, Revelation focuses more on the Seal of God. Just as the High Priest wore a gold plate marked, "Holy to the Lord," we, too, are marked in a similar way. It is in this that we find our strength and encouragement.

Remember, nobody can force us to worship anything or any one, they can only threaten our lives. We, like Shadrach, Meshach and Abednego, must be like the saints in heaven who, "overcame him by the blood of the Lamb and by the Word of their testimony; they did not love their lives so much as to shrink from death" (Rev 12:11). If one thinks it through, either way you are going to die. Either at the hand of men, from whom God may deliver you, or from the hand of God, where there will be no deliverance, only eternal hell and damnation. Why put off getting to heaven by loving your lives more than God? The doom of those who take the mark of the beast is hell and eternal torment (Rev 14:9, 16:2, 19:20), but those who refuse to take it will live in heaven with God (Rev 15:2, 20:4).

The mark is described as the number of the beast's name; 666. It has been said that this number falls short of complete perfection. Since both three and seven have been used over and over in the Scriptures to show completeness and perfection, Satan is possibly shown here to fall short of perfection (7) three times (completely). It is also significant that in Old Testament times Solomon received 666 talents of gold a year (1 Kings 10:14; 2 Chron 9:13). Riches and power were the beginnings of his downfall, as God had clearly warned not to collect gold (1 Kings 10:14-25), horses (1 Kings 10:26-29), or many wives (1 Kings 11:1-8).

We read in Exodus, "For in six days the LORD made the heavens and the earth, the sea, and all that is in them, but He rested on the seventh day. Therefore the LORD blessed the Sabbath day and made it holy" (Exo 20:11). Here we see that if the six days finished creation, perfection or holiness would never have come. Likewise, this seventh Sabbath day rest still stands for the perfection we all wait for in heaven: "For if Joshua had given [the Israelites] rest, God would not have spoken later about another day. There remains, then, a Sabbath-rest for the people of God; for anyone who enters God's rest also rests from his own work, just as God did from His. Let us, therefore, make every effort to enter that rest, so that no one will fall by following their example of disobedience" (Heb 4:8-11). Satan will never enter that seventh, Sabbath day rest.

Mans' number is also 666. Without Christ we are mere men and can never enter that rest either. This also implies that the number will be understandable. There are many ideas floating around trying to pinpoint what this number may be. Some believe it is the Social Security number. Others believe it to be a Marc Card bearing on it, 666, which is issued by the armed forces. Still others think the tiny computer chip implants put in the neck of animals at many veterinary clinics today will someday be used for human beings. Another theory is that the number 666 is the sum total of all the letters of the beast's name. In Greek each letter is given a value. For example, if in my name Brian, B=10, R=100, I=500, A=50, and N=6, therefore, I could be the beast because the number of my name would equal a total of 666. There have been many famous people whose names equaled 666 throughout history, but man always inserts his fallible wisdom into his interpretation making every possible assumption to get the outcome to equal his desire. Kennedy's name equaled 666, but to get that total one had to get the right name. The names John F Kennedy, John Kennedy, J.F.K, J.F. Kennedy, etc., were used until the right number came up.

One significant possibility is that Nero fit the 666 qualifications. The name Nero Caesar in Hebrew totaled 666. Nero's name was written as Neron Kaiser (Nero Caesar, or NRWN QSR. N=50, R=200, W=6, N=50, Q=100, S=60, R=200). Many believe that this would have been easily seen by early Christian believers and that Nero fulfilled the antichrist role in a New Testament millennial period. Though this interpretation does hold a lot of significant value, it doesn't answer our questions regarding the Antichrist's involvement with the two witnesses. To say that our interpretation thus far has been the only way of viewing things would be rather arrogant, so we cannot exclude this as a possibility. Because of the tremendous significance of the Antichrist in end time events and the final battle, it seems best to this author to interpret Nero as a type of antichrist who was a mere shadow of the one to come. We have already discussed how God uses many patterns throughout history to point us to His glorious and final deliverance.

Though these ideas could be possible, I do not believe that we need to worry about it, because when the time comes it will certainly be made obvious. If it isn't obvious, Christians could take the number of the beast unknowingly and negate their free ticket to heaven through Jesus Christ. This will certainly not happen because anyone who receives the mark has a terrible future ahead: "And the smoke of their torment rises for ever and ever. There is no rest day or night for those who worship the beast and his image, or for anyone who receives the mark of his name" (Rev 14:11). Besides, remember that for Christians our focus is on the Seal of God, not the mark of the beast.

CHAPTER 14

Rev 14:1 Then I looked, and there before me was the Lamb, standing on Mount Zion, and with him 144,000 who had his name and his Father's name written on their foreheads. 14:2 And I heard a sound from heaven like the roar of rushing waters and like a loud peal of thunder. The sound I heard was like that of harpists playing their harps. 14:3 And they sang a new song before the throne and before the four living creatures and the elders. No one could learn the song except the 144,000 who had been redeemed from the earth. 14:4 These are those who did not defile themselves with women, for they kept themselves pure. They follow the Lamb wherever he goes. They were purchased from among men and offered as firstfruits to God and the Lamb. 14:5 No lie was found in their mouths; they are blameless.

Chapter 13 focused on the evils and doom of Satan and those on the earth, but chapter 14 now tells us of the deliverance by the Lamb and the joy of heaven.

John saw the Lamb of God (Christ) standing on Mount Zion with the 144,000 who bore the Father's name on their foreheads. This is the opposite of chapter 13 where the mark of the beast was put on the forehead of unbelievers. Now the believers were marked with the Father's name, and made the claim that they belonged to Him. It was the SOLD sign on the souls of men showing that they had been purchased by the blood of the Lamb for the Father.

These verses describe the day we read about in Psalms where Satan is trying to make his stand against the Lord, but the Lord is about to laugh as the Lamb, the Holy King, comes to Mount Zion to rebuke and pass judgment on Satan. We read in Psalms, "The kings of the earth take their stand and the rulers gather together against the LORD and against His Anointed One. 'Let us break their chains,' they say, 'and throw off their fetters.' The One enthroned in heaven laughs; the Lord scoffs at them. Then He rebukes them in His anger and terrifies them in His wrath, saying, '*I have installed My King on Zion, My holy hill*'" (Psa 2:2-6).

Mount Zion is Jerusalem as seen in many Old Testament passages. This Holy Mount will play a very important part, not only in the last days, but for an eternity. As seen above it is the place God comes to claim His possessions and to judge the world. But Zion is also the Mount of God on which He will establish His throne FOREVER. In fact, many Scripture passages suggest we will flee to Jerusalem for our protection. Since the Lamb is coming there, it makes sense that this will be our fortress. Consider the following:

- "Great is the LORD, and most worthy of praise, in the city of our God, His holy mountain. It is beautiful in its loftiness, the joy of the whole earth. Like the utmost heights of Zaphon is Mount Zion, the city of the Great King. God is in her citadels; He has shown Himself to be her fortress" (Psa 48:1-3).

- "For the LORD has chosen Zion, He has desired it for His dwelling: This is My resting place *for ever and ever*; here I *will sit enthroned*, for I have desired it— " (Psa 132:13-14).

- "But you have come to Mount Zion, to the heavenly Jerusalem, the city of the living God. You have come to thousands upon thousands of angels in joyful assembly" (Heb 12:22).

- "This is what Isaiah son of Amoz saw concerning Judah and Jerusalem: *In the last days* the mountain of the Lord's temple will be established as chief among the mountains; it will be raised above the hills, and *all nations will stream to it.* Many peoples will come and say, 'Come, let us go up to the mountain of the LORD, to the house of the God of Jacob. He will teach us His ways, so that we may walk in His paths.' The law will go out from Zion, the Word of the LORD *from Jerusalem*. He will judge between the nations and will settle disputes for many peoples. They will beat their swords into plowshares and their spears into pruning hooks. Nation will not take up sword against nation, nor will they train for war anymore. Come, O house of Jacob, let us walk in the light of the LORD" (Isa 2:1-5).

- "Those who are left in Zion, who remain in Jerusalem, will be called holy, all who are recorded among the living in Jerusalem. The Lord will wash away the filth of the women of Zion; He will cleanse the bloodstains from Jerusalem by a spirit of judgment and a spirit of fire. Then the LORD will create over all of Mount Zion and over those who assemble there a cloud of smoke by day and a glow of flaming fire by night; over all the glory will be a canopy. It will be a shelter and shade from the heat of the day, and a refuge and hiding place from the storm and rain" (Isa 4:3-6).

- "I will *gather all the nations* to Jerusalem to fight against it; the city will be captured, the houses ransacked, and the women raped. Half of the city will go into exile, but the rest of the people will not be taken from the city. Then the LORD will go out and fight against those nations, as He fights in the day of battle. On that day **His feet will stand on the Mount of Olives**, east of Jerusalem, and the Mount of Olives will be split in two from east to west, forming a great valley, with half of the mountain moving north and half moving south" (Zec 14:2-4).

- "*He will raise a banner* for the nations and gather the exiles of Israel; He will assemble the scattered people of Judah from the four quarters of the earth" (Isa 11:12).

- "All you people of the world, you who live on the earth, *when a banner is raised* on the mountains, you will see it, and when a *trumpet sounds*, you will hear it" (Isa 18:3).

- "On this mountain the LORD Almighty will prepare a feast of rich food for all peoples, a banquet of aged wine-- the best of meats and the finest of wines" (Isa 25:6). (The Wedding Banquet of the Lamb coming up in Revelation 19:7).

- "In those days, when your numbers have increased greatly in the land, declares the LORD, men will no longer say, 'The ark of the covenant of the LORD.' It will never enter their minds or be remembered; it will not be missed, nor will another one be made. At that time they will call Jerusalem *The Throne of the LORD,* and all nations will gather in Jerusalem to honor the Name of the LORD. No longer will they follow the stubbornness of their evil hearts" (Jer 3:16-17).

See also, Is 27:13, 65:9, and Jer 30:3.

    Just as we have seen earlier in Revelation, (1:15, 4:5, 6:1, 8:5, 11:19) God's powerful voice is heard like that of thunder and rushing water. However, the sound, though powerful, is comfort to the ears as it is like harps playing. The 144,000, as seen in 7:4, are in heaven singing a new song that only they could learn. We earlier saw the 24 elders around God's throne singing a new song. No doubt, in both cases, their song is of joy and deliverance since they are now in heaven having been taken away from earth (v.3). Just as in 5:9, the song sung was a new one. From the vast number of times we see "new songs" in reference to worship, it is most probable that this song has something to do with salvation and praise. We read in Psalms, "Sing to the LORD a new song, for He has done marvelous things; His right hand and His holy arm have worked salvation for Him" (Psa 98 see also Ps 33:3, 40:3, 96:1, 98:1, 144:9, 149:1, Is 42:10). It is almost as if the singers are worshipping in spirit with a song that only they themselves know. John said, "God is spirit, and His worshipers must worship in spirit and in truth" (John 4:2).

    These 144,000 had not defiled themselves with women. This does not mean that they had never been married or never slept with a woman, but rather in a spiritual sense, they had never prostituted themselves when engaged to God. We read in Corinthians, "I am jealous for you with a godly jealousy. I promised you to one husband, to Christ, so that I might present you as a pure virgin to Him" (2 Cor 11:2). There are many references to the church as the bride of Christ, (John 3:29, 2:9, Rev 19:7, Jer 2:2, Mat 9:15, Mat 25:1-10). The entire book of Hosea compares an adulterous relationship with that of the Israelites and God. Israel had prostituted themselves to other gods, but they were forgiven and invited back. These 144,000 are those who never forsook God, but have waited in spiritual pureness through the blood of the Lamb to be presented to Christ as His bride. In fact, verse four tells us they follow the Lamb wherever He goes because they were purchased by Him (through Christ's blood- Psalm 74:2) and offered as a living sacrifice to Him. Christ is our Shepherd and the sheep will follow Him to safe pastures: "For the Lamb at the center of the throne will be their shepherd; He will lead them to springs of living water" (Rev 7:17).

The fact that these 144,000 were firstfruits simply shows them to be holy as we see from Jeremiah, "Israel was holy to the LORD, the firstfruits of His harvest" (Jer 2:3). James also states, "He chose to give us birth through the Word of truth, that we might be a kind of firstfruits of all He created" (James 1:18).

They are blameless because of Christ and, therefore, walk with Him just as was promised: "Yet you have a few people in Sardis who have not soiled their clothes. They will walk with Me, dressed in white, for they are worthy" (Rev 3:4). We, too, are blameless through Christ:

- "so that you may become blameless and pure, children of God without fault in a crooked and depraved generation, in which you shine like stars in the universe" (Phil 2:15).
- "so that you may be able to discern what is best and may be pure and blameless until the day of Christ" (Phil 1:10).
- "You are witnesses, and so is God, of how holy, righteous and blameless we were among you who believed" (1 Th 2:10).
- "May God Himself, the God of peace, sanctify you through and through. May your whole spirit, soul and body be kept blameless at the coming of our Lord Jesus Christ" (1 Th 5:23).
- "May He strengthen your hearts so that you will be blameless and holy in the presence of our God and Father when our Lord Jesus comes with all His holy ones"(1 Th 3:13).
- "To make her holy, cleansing her by the washing with water through the Word, and to present her to Himself as a radiant church, without stain or wrinkle or any other blemish, but holy and blameless" (Eph 5:26-27).

Part of this state of being "blameless" was that there were no lies found in their mouths. This is again predicted of God's people, "The remnant of Israel will do no wrong; they will speak no lies, nor will deceit be found in their mouths. They will eat and lie down and no one will make them afraid" (Zep 3:13). This blamelessness can only be obtained by becoming one in Christ. As Christians, we are told, "To this you were called, because Christ suffered for you, leaving you an example, that you should follow in His steps. 'He committed no sin, and no deceit was found in His mouth'" (1 Pet 2:21-22).

Rev 14:6 Then I saw another angel flying in midair, and he had the eternal gospel to proclaim to those who live on the earth--to every nation, tribe, language and people. 14:7 He said in a loud voice, "Fear God and give him glory, because the hour of his judgment has come. Worship him who made the heavens, the earth, the sea and the springs of water." 14:8 A second angel followed and said, "Fallen! Fallen is Babylon the Great, which made all the nations drink the maddening wine of her adulteries."

The next thing John saw was another angel flying in the air proclaiming the eternal Gospel. This isn't the first time we see an angel flying in midair (Rev 8:13, 19:7), however, it is the only time in all of the Bible that the Gospel is described as eternal. I find it interesting that we are also told what the message of the ETERNAL Gospel is: "Fear God and give Him glory, because the hour of His judgment has come. Worship Him who made the heavens, the earth, the sea and the springs of water." We know that fearing God is the beginning of wisdom, (Pro 9:10, Psa 111:10), but wisdom is also, for the most part, a synonym for Jesus. That is why you can almost always substitute the word "Christ" in place of "wisdom" and the passage will make sense. Wisdom has always been in existence. It was here even before Creation and, therefore, it must be a quality of Christ. Consider the words of Psalms:

> "For wisdom is more precious than rubies, and nothing you desire can compare with her. 'I, wisdom, dwell together with prudence; I possess knowledge and discretion. To fear the LORD is to hate evil; I hate pride and arrogance, evil behavior and perverse speech. Counsel and sound judgment are mine; I have understanding and power. By me kings reign and rulers make laws that are just; by me princes govern, and all nobles who rule on earth. I love those who love me, and those who seek me find me. With me are riches and honor, enduring wealth and prosperity. My fruit is better than fine gold; what I yield surpasses choice silver. I walk in the way of righteousness, along the paths of justice, bestowing wealth on those who love me and making their treasuries full. The LORD brought me forth as the first of His works, before His deeds of old; *I was appointed from eternity, from the beginning, before the world began. When there were no oceans, I was given birth, when there were no springs abounding with water; before the mountains were settled in place, before the hills, I was given birth*, before He made the earth or its fields or any of the dust of the world. I was there when He set the heavens in place, when He marked out the horizon on the face of the deep, when He established the clouds above and fixed securely the fountains of the deep, when He gave the sea its boundary so the waters would not overstep His command, and when He marked out the foundations of the earth. Then I was the craftsman at His side. I was filled with delight day after day, rejoicing always in His presence, rejoicing in His whole world and delighting in mankind. Now then, my sons, listen to me; blessed are those who keep my ways. Listen to my instruction and be wise; do not ignore it. Blessed is the man who listens to me, watching daily at my doors, waiting at my doorway. *For whoever finds me finds life* and receives favor from the LORD. But whoever fails to find me harms himself; all who hate me love death'" (Prov 8:11-36).

Not only is the Gospel eternal because it bears the existence of wisdom, but also because the message the angel proclaims is one of Creation. Earlier in chapter ten we read, "And he swore by Him who lives for ever and ever, who created the heavens and all that is in them, the earth and all that is in it, and the sea and all that is in it, and said, 'There will be no more delay' (Rev 10:6)! God as Creator is one of the most important doctrines to understand. Without a Creator we have no law giver and, "where there is no law there is no transgression" (Rom 4:15). Without the knowledge that we are sinful, how would we see a need for a Savior? We also see in Romans that God's existence cannot be denied simply by looking at what He has made: "For since the creation of the world God's invisible qualities--His eternal power and divine nature--have been clearly seen, being understood from what has been made, so that men are without excuse" (Rom 1:20). Also in Romans we read that the Israelites had no excuse for not hearing the words of Christ because Creation proclaimed it: "Consequently, faith comes from hearing the message, and the message is heard through the Word of Christ. But I ask: Did they not hear? Of course they did: 'Their voice has gone out into all the earth, their words to the ends of the world'" (Rom 10:17-18). Whose voice went out into all the earth giving the Word of Christ? According to Psalm 19, of which this is a direct quote, it was the voice of the stars: "The heavens declare the glory of God; the skies proclaim the work of His hands. Day after day they pour forth speech; night after night they display knowledge. There is no speech or language where their voice is not heard. Their voice goes out into all the earth, their words to the ends of the world" (Psa 19:1-2). The Gospel is eternal because it bears eternal wisdom. God's creative hand has always been evident.

A second angel follows in verse eight crying out, "Fallen! Fallen is Babylon the Great." Isaiah spoke of this time when he wrote, "Look, here comes a man in a chariot with a team of horses. And he gives back the answer: 'Babylon has fallen, has fallen! All the images of its gods lie shattered on the ground'" (Isa 21:9)! We have already discussed that Babylon is the symbol of moral corruption. Here in Revelation it is the center of Satan's kingdom. We will discuss this further in chapters 17 and 18, but for now it is only important for us to realize that this is the doom of Satan's kingdom. So far in chapter 14 we saw that Jesus came and stood on Zion. What was He doing there? Coming to protect His people and to judge those who have rejected Him. *Here we only get an outline view showing that Christ came and He conquered. The rest of chapter 14 will continue this outline style, however, once we reach chapter seventeen and eighteen, we will rewind to this time period and get a more detailed look at the fall of Babylon.*

Babylon was said to have made all the nations drink of the maddening wine of her adulteries. We read in Jeremiah, "Babylon was a gold cup in the Lord's hand; she made the whole earth drunk. The nations drank her wine; therefore they have now gone mad. Babylon will suddenly fall and be broken. Wail over her! Get balm for her pain; perhaps she can be healed. 'We would have healed Babylon, but she cannot be healed; let us leave her and each go to his own land, for her judgment reaches to the skies, it rises as high as the clouds'" (Jer 51:7-9).

In addition to the above interpretation, Babylon could also fit the description of Jerusalem at the time of John. In verse 8 Babylon was called the great city. In Revelation 11:8 we see that a "great city" is mentioned. This city turns out to be Jerusalem, which was figuratively called Sodom and Egypt, two other ungodly nations. We will look at this in more depth in chapter 17.

Rev 14:9 A third angel followed them and said in a loud voice: "If anyone worships the beast and his image and receives his mark on the forehead or on the hand, 14:10 he, too, will drink of the wine of God's fury, which has been poured full strength into the cup of his wrath. He will be tormented with burning sulfur in the presence of the holy angels and of the Lamb. 14:11 And the smoke of their torment rises for ever and ever. There is no rest day or night for those who worship the beast and his image, or for anyone who receives the mark of his name." 14:12 This calls for patient endurance on the part of the saints who obey God's commandments and remain faithful to Jesus. 14:13 Then I heard a voice from heaven say, "Write: Blessed are the dead who die in the Lord from now on." "Yes," says the Spirit, "they will rest from their labor, for their deeds will follow them."

A third angel followed up the warning to worship and fear our Creator. This time, however, the message was not to warn of the doom of Satan's kingdom, but Satan's followers. Anyone who receives the mark of the beast will have no hope of peace, joy or comfort, only God's wrath in its full strength. Hell will await with eternal burning sulfur.

The imagery of God pouring out His wrath in a cup is common in Old Testament prophecy as we see from the following verses:

- "In the hand of the LORD is a cup full of foaming wine mixed with spices; He pours it out, and all the wicked of the earth drink it down to its very dregs. As for me, I will declare this forever; I will sing praise to the God of Jacob" (Psa 75:8-9).
- "Awake, awake! Rise up, O Jerusalem, you who have drunk from the hand of the LORD the cup of His wrath, you who have drained to its dregs the goblet that makes men stagger" (Isa 51:17).
- "This is what the LORD, the God of Israel, said to me: 'Take from My hand this cup filled with the wine of My wrath and make all the nations to whom I send you drink it. When they drink it, they will stagger and go mad because of the sword I will send among them'" (Jer 25:15-16).

This is exactly what *will happen* in the 15th and 16th chapter of Revelation when we see that seven angels will be given seven bowls of God's wrath to pour out on the ungodly. At that point, however, all believers will be in heaven since the seventh trumpet will have already sounded. That is why Psalm 75:9 said, "As for me. . . I will sing praise."

The burning sulfur is also a trademark judgment from God. Sodom and Gomorrah were destroyed by burning sulfur (Gen 19:24), and so will the wicked in the end times: "On the wicked He will rain fiery coals and burning sulfur; a scorching wind will be their lot" (Psa 11:6). See Revelation 19:20, 20:10, and 21:8.

We are also warned that this will call for patient endurance for believers of Christ and followers of His commands. After all, Christ said, "If you love Me, you will obey what I command" (John 14:15). Patience is an important virtue for a Christian, as we are reminded in Hebrews, "We do not want you to become lazy, but to imitate those who through faith and patience inherit what has been promised" (Heb 6:12). Good things come to those who wait. The events that lead up to the seventh trumpet will be trying and terrible times. Jesus even said, "If those days had not been cut short, no one would survive, but for the sake of the elect those days will be shortened" (Mat 24:22). Praise God for our deliverance that we may never see the cup of God's wrath.

In verse 13 the joy of those who follow God is seen. A voice from heaven tells John to write down that all who die in the Lord from now on will be blessed. One reason they are so blessed is that they will rest from their labor and their deeds will follow them. Yes God does keep track of our good deeds, however, there is no record for the believers' sins. Scripture supports the fact that there are different glories or degrees of heaven. This is a puzzling thing for many Christians, but the Bible makes it clear. As an analogy, if one person is represented by a 16 ounce cup and another person is represented by a 32 ounce cup, both will be filled with as much glory as they can hold when they get to heaven. The sixteen ounce cup would not desire more because he cannot hold any more. He is as full as he knows how to be. Those who love God enough to stand firm in these last days will indeed be blessed because of their perseverance and love for God. One must be careful to realize this is NOT works righteousness. Good works will not get you to a higher glory in heaven, but your faith will. The more you love God the more you see Him. The more faith you have, the more you will produce good fruit in keeping with repentance (Mat 3:8). James warns, "But someone will say, 'You have faith; I have deeds.' Show me your faith without deeds, and I will show you my faith by what I do. You believe that there is one God. Good! *Even the demons believe that*--and shudder. You foolish man, do you want evidence that faith without deeds is useless? Was not our ancestor Abraham considered righteous for what he did when he offered his son Isaac on the altar? You see that his faith and his actions were working together, and his faith was made complete by what he did" (James 2:18-22). Clearly we must be careful about having faith in faith. Believing in Jesus does not get you to heaven, because even Satan believes in Jesus. Allowing Jesus to be your personal Savior whom you love, adore and follow daily because of your faith in Him; that is our free ticket to heaven. Again, James writes, "You see that a person is justified by what he does and *not* by faith alone" (James 2:24). It will take great faith that will be blessed, to do what the saints in chapter 12 did: They, "overcame him by the blood of the Lamb and by the word of their testimony; they did not love their lives so much as to shrink from death" (Rev 12:11).

Let us look at a few Scripture verses showing us degrees of heaven:
- "The man who plants and the man who waters have one purpose, and *each will be rewarded according to his own labor.* For we are God's fellow workers; you are God's field, God's building. By the grace God has given me, I laid a foundation as an expert builder, and someone else is building on

it. But each one should be careful how he builds. For no one can lay any foundation other than the one already laid, which is Jesus Christ. If any man builds on this foundation using gold, silver, costly stones, wood, hay or straw, his work will be shown for what it is, because **the Day** will bring it to light. It will be revealed with fire, and the fire will test the quality of each man's work. If what he has built survives, he will receive his reward. If it is burned up, he will suffer loss; *he himself will be saved,* **but** *only as one escaping through the flames*" (1 Cor 3:8-15).

- "I tell you the truth: Among those born of women there has not risen anyone greater than John the Baptist; yet he who *is* **least in the kingdom of heaven is greater than he**" (Mat 11:11).
- "Anyone who breaks one of the least of these commandments and teaches others to do the same will be called **least in the kingdom of heaven**, but whoever practices and teaches these commands will be called **great in the kingdom of heaven**" (Mat 5:19).
- "The first one came and said, 'Sir, your mina has earned ten more.' 'Well done, my good servant!' his master replied. 'Because you have been trustworthy in a very small matter, *take charge of ten cities.*' The second came and said, 'Sir, your mina has earned five more.' His master answered, '*You take charge of five cities*'" (Luke 19:16-19).
- Speaking symbolically of the wedding banquet of the Lamb: "When someone invites you to a wedding feast, do not take the place of honor, . . . But when you are invited, take the lowest place, so that when your host comes, he will say to you, 'Friend, move up to a better place.' Then you will be honored in the presence of all your fellow guests" (Luke 14:8-10).
- "Those who are wise will shine like the brightness of the heavens, and those who lead many to righteousness, like the stars for ever and ever" (Dan 12:3).

Blessed indeed, will be those who suffer for Christ!

Rev 14:14 I looked, and there before me was a white cloud, and seated on the cloud was one "like a son of man" with a crown of gold on his head and a sharp sickle in his hand. 14:15 Then another angel came out of the temple and called in a loud voice to him who was sitting on the cloud, "Take your sickle and reap, because the time to reap has come, for the harvest of the earth is ripe." 14:16 So he who was seated on the cloud swung his sickle over the earth, and the earth was harvested.

Verse 14 continues to run through a turn of events in a quick outline form. The beginning of this chapter showed God coming out of heaven and standing on His holy mountain of Zion to protect His people from those that hate them. Then Babylon had fallen because of God's Word against those who took the number of the beast. Now it is all over and God is going to harvest the people on earth. First He will gather the wheat, or believers, up to heaven with Him (must take place at the seventh trumpet). Second, He will harvest the chaff, or unbelievers, and set them down in the valley of destruction where He will destroy them with the seven bowl judgments. The judgment will be described in greater detail in chapters 15, 16 and 18. (Chapter 17 shows why the judgment needed to take place). Then chapter 19-22 will show in greater detail what happens to us, the believers in Christ, when we are harvested. In short, just as 1:19 does, chapter 14 gives a good outline for the remainder of the book.

John sees one like a son of man (1:13, Mat 8:20, 9:6, John 13:31); God, coming on the clouds just as prophesied. When the disciples saw Jesus go to heaven in the clouds, an angel stood by and said, "This same Jesus, who has been taken from you into heaven, will come back *in the same way* you have seen Him go into heaven" (Acts 1:11). When Christ comes He will certainly be in the clouds. Clouds have often represented God's *shekinah* glory as He filled the temple (Ex 33:19), covered Mount Sinai (Ex 19:16, 24:15), or led the Israelites through the desert (Ex 13:21, 14:19, 16:10). In fact, the Scriptures have over 97 references to God's presence in the clouds.

Daniel saw the same vision as John saw here in verse 14: "In my vision at night I looked, and there before me was one like a son of man, coming with the clouds of heaven" (Dan 7:13).

He is wearing a gold crown of victory and authority and also holds a sickle, of which to harvest the earth. Once more, a parable of Jesus is seen being fulfilled here in Revelation. We read in Matthew, "He answered, 'The one who sowed the good seed is *the Son of Man*. The field is the world, and the good seed stands for the sons of the kingdom. The weeds are the sons of the evil one, and the enemy who sows them is the devil. *The harvest is the end of the age*, and the *harvesters are angels.*' As the weeds are pulled up and burned in the fire, so it will be at the end of the age. The Son of Man will send out His angels, and they will weed out of His kingdom everything that causes sin and all who do evil. They will throw them into the fiery furnace, where there will be weeping and gnashing of teeth. Then the righteous will shine like the sun in the kingdom of their Father. He who has ears, let him hear" (Mat 13:37-43). What a beautiful scene on which our hope is set; the great deliverance of our LORD! Interestingly, according to the above parable, the ungodly are taken first: "Let both grow together until the harvest. At that time I will tell the harvesters: First collect the weeds and tie them in bundles to be burned; then gather the wheat and bring it into My barn" (Mat 13:30).

With the close of verse 16 the believers are harvested and brought into the barn: "His winnowing fork is in His hand to clear His threshing floor and to gather the wheat into His barn, but He will burn up the chaff with unquenchable fire" (Luke 3:17). Next we will see the chaff being gathered so that it may be burned.

Rev 14:17 Another angel came out of the temple in heaven, and he too had a sharp sickle. 14:18 Still another angel, who had charge of the fire, came from the altar and called in a loud voice to him who had the sharp sickle, "Take your sharp sickle and gather the clusters of grapes from the earth's vine, because its grapes are ripe." 14:19 The angel swung his sickle on the earth, gathered its grapes and threw them into the great winepress of God's wrath. 14:20 They were trampled in the winepress

outside the city, and blood flowed out of the press, rising as high as the horses' bridles for a distance of 1,600 stadia.

A second angel came out of heaven holding a sickle. Then a third angel, who was in charge of the element of punishment (fiery bowls of God's wrath, Rev 15:17, 8:3), told the second angel to harvest the unbelievers into bundles and set them down in a predetermined place where they could be trampled upon with God's wrath.

In the Old Testament times we read of a major event where Babylon had captured Judah and took them captive for 70 years. God had also promised that Babylon would fall and Judah would be delivered. This deliverance took place exactly 70 years after Judah's captivity. Babylon's destruction foreshadowed the great day of our deliverance spoke of in these verses. We read in Jeremiah, "This is what the LORD Almighty, the God of Israel, says: 'The Daughter of Babylon is like a threshing floor at the time it is trampled; the time to harvest her will soon come'" (Jer 51:33). As Jesus said, "As soon as the grain is ripe, he puts the sickle to it, because the harvest has come" (Mark 4:29).

Joel also talked of this day, "Let the nations be roused; let them advance into the *Valley of Jehoshaphat,* for *there I will sit to judge* all the nations on every side. *Swing the sickle, for the harvest is ripe.* Come, trample the grapes, for the winepress is full and the vats overflow-- so great is their wickedness! Multitudes, multitudes in the valley of decision! For the day of the LORD is near in the valley of decision. The sun and moon will be darkened, and the stars no longer shine. The LORD will **roar from Zion and thunder from Jerusalem;** the earth and the sky will tremble. But the LORD will be a refuge for His people, a stronghold for the people of Israel" (Joel 3:12-16).

As to the winepress itself, this imagery of treading upon the blood of grapes for treading upon the blood of men was common (Lam 1:15, Deut 32:14). Christ clearly used this to reserve its true meaning for this day discussed here. In Isaiah we read, "I have trodden the winepress alone; from the nations no one was with Me. I trampled them in My anger and trod them down in My wrath; their blood spattered My garments, and I stained all My clothing. For the day of vengeance was in My heart, and the year of My redemption has come" (Isa 63:3-4). Revelation will show that God will tread on them; not with His feet, but rather His Word, "Out of His mouth comes a sharp sword with which to strike down the nations. 'He will rule them with an iron scepter.' He treads the winepress of the fury of the wrath of God Almighty" (Rev 19:15).

The unbelievers who were just harvested were set down in the valley of decision or the valley of Megiddo. This is where we get the word *armageddon* which means "hill of Megiddo". This valley has also been called the Valley of Jezreel which runs along Mount Carmel past Megiddo. Today it is a very fertile valley. The important thing here, however, is that they are "outside the city." Just as Jesus was killed outside the city, they will also be outside the city. In Hebrews we read, "And so Jesus also suffered outside the city gate to make the people holy through His own blood" (Heb 13:12). Bloodshed was considered to be unholy and would thus defile the city, especially since this will certainly be a true Holy city when Christ comes again. More importantly, based upon upcoming chapters, it seems that these people are also trying to rise up against Jerusalem, where God's people were taken to be protected. Keeping in mind that this chapter is more of an outline form, we do not get many of the details. It seems very possible that the result of the armageddon battle will be "blood rising as high as the horses bridles." In 16:14 we see the kings are "gathered" for battle against God's people. Where are God's people? In the section on 14:1-5 I listed a number of verses showing that God's people would be gathered to Jerusalem or Mount Zion. It is likely that this will be the draw that brings the unbelievers against Jerusalem. Then, God will "gather all nations and bring them down to the Valley of Jehoshaphat. There I will enter into judgment against them" (Joel 3:2).

In regard to the volumes of blood described, Josephus recorded that when Rome took over Jerusalem in 70 AD there was so much blood that it even put out small fires. However, to have blood so deep that it reaches the horses bridles for 1600 stadia (about 200 miles, almost the same distance it is from north to south across Palestine) is hard to imagine. This clearly speaks to the tremendous amount of non-Christian people that are on earth and the great bloodshed there will be.

Once more, before beginning chapter 15, I believe it may be important to run through the main points of each chapter to keep our mind in order.

- In chapter one we saw a basic introduction showing us who wrote this, how and from whom John received it, and what he saw while the message was given. We saw a description of a Judge (God) among His churches and holding the angels of those churches in His hands.
- In chapter two we shifted back to earth to see the churches that God was watching over. They symbolized churches throughout all of time. Each church brought us closer to the present era with their attributes getting worse and worse until finally ending with Laodicea, a lukewarm church that rejected God as Creator. During this time period the seals are to be opened.
- In chapter three we continued through those seven churches.
- In chapter four we shifted back to heaven and returned to the Judge who was taking His seat on the throne. Around Him were the angels, saints and disciples praising Him. The imagery was the seating of a courtroom with the Judge and jury about to pass judgment on the guilty.
- In chapter five we saw Christ with God, having a scroll, or deed to the earth, while the praises continued. He was ready to open the scroll so that the earth and its inhabitants could be judged. In other words, the guilty verdict was being read.
- Chapter six described six seal judgments as the scrolls were opened. With each seal opened, a judgment took place.
- Chapter seven was our commercial break, or interlude, between the sixth and seventh seal. Here the 144,000 were sealed by God in

order to be protected by the judgments affecting the people on earth. We also saw a great multitude of saints from all nations praising God in heaven.

- Chapter eight showed the seventh seal opened which brought forth the blowing of the first four trumpets. As with all of the sevens, the first four follow a certain theme, the next two another theme, and the last of the series (seventh) was one of rest.
- Chapter nine continued the blowing of the remaining three trumpets. We saw terrible creatures that inflicted pain, injury and death upon the unbelievers.
- Chapter ten was our interlude, or commercial break, between the sixth and seventh trumpet. We saw Christ coming not to judge as much as to claim ownership of the earth and His people with the deed to the earth, or open scroll.
- Chapter eleven shows us two witnesses, probably Moses and Elijah, who were instrumental in God's plan to bring about the Antichrist's power and popularity. This part covers the entire seven year tribulation period. The first three and one-half years were marked by the preaching of repentance, and the next three and one-half years were under the rule of the Antichrist. The second part of chapter eleven then told of the blowing of the seventh trumpet. At this point, all believers went to heaven as the seven bowl judgments were about to be poured out on the ungodly.
- Chapter twelve rewound and took a quick preview approach to all of history. It began with Satan's fall, went through the birth of Christ, and led up to the dragon, Satan himself, waiting to call the Antichrist out of the sea. It began the description of the evil trinity.
- Chapter thirteen showed how Satan called out the beast from the sea, or the Antichrist. The Antichrist in turn called up the False Prophet from the earth. Together they go after and persecute Christians. (This takes place before the seventh trumpet). The beast and his number are worshipped.
- Chapter 14 changed focus and showed us the believers in heaven who had overcome this beast and his image. God then blew the trumpet and the earth was harvested. The Christians were very likely gathered to a renewed Jerusalem and the non-believers were gathered together and set down in the valley of decision so that they could be judged in the Great Battle of the Lord. Therefore, chapters 12, 13, and 14 were a type of interlude breaking up the sounding of the seventh trumpet and the pouring out of the bowl judgments. These three chapters gave a quick and more detailed summary of what was going on during the seven seals and six trumpets. Now we are ready to see the seven angels receive and pour out the bowls upon the ungodly in chapters fifteen and sixteen.

CHAPTER 15

Section 5 (Revelation 15:1-18:24)
Seven Bowl Judgments

Rev 15:1 I saw in heaven another great and marvelous sign: seven angels with the seven last plagues--last, because with them God's wrath is completed. 15:2 And I saw what looked like a sea of glass mixed with fire and, standing beside the sea, those who had been victorious over the beast and his image and over the number of his name. They held harps given them by God 15:3 and sang the song of Moses the servant of God and the song of the Lamb:

As we discussed in 11:19, chapter fifteen takes place after the seventh trumpet is blown when the saints are in heaven.

John saw a great and marvelous sign. Seven angels came out of the temple of God in heaven to finalize God's judgment on the earth. These bowls will not be actually poured out until chapter 16, right now we are seeing the preparation and praise made in heaven. These were good angels, and one of them will later show John the church in heaven, the bride of the Lamb (Rev 21:9). Again, seven is appearing to show complete destruction is about to fall on Satan and the earth. Also, we read in Leviticus, "If you remain hostile toward Me and refuse to listen to Me, I will multiply your afflictions seven times over, as your sins deserve" (Lev 26:21). God will leave no sin unpunished for those who have not been made clean by the Blood of Christ.

John also saw God's throne in heaven because he described something like a sea of glass and fire. This is exactly how the throne of God was described earlier in 4:6. Next to this were the saints who had been victorious over the beast, his image and number, all described in chapters 12 and 13. As told in 12:11, they were victorious because of Christ's blood and the word of their testimony about Him.

A better view of what John is seeing may be given to us in Ezekiel's description of God's throne above: "Then there came a voice from above the expanse over their heads as they stood with lowered wings [cherubim]. Above the expanse over their heads was what looked like a throne of sapphire, [sea of glass] and high above on the throne was a figure like that of a man. I saw that from what appeared to be His waist up He looked like glowing metal, as if full of fire, and that from there down He looked like fire [mixed with fire]; and brilliant light [God's glory] surrounded Him. Like the appearance of a rainbow in the clouds on a rainy day, so was the radiance around Him. This was the appearance of the likeness of the glory of the LORD. When I saw it, I fell facedown, and I heard the voice of one speaking" (Ezek 1:25-28). Even in Exodus Moses saw the same picture when he "saw the God of Israel. Under His feet was something like a pavement made of sapphire, clear as the sky itself" (Exo 24:10). The best thing about all of this is that God's throne is among us, the saints. In the description of heaven in chapter 21 we see that the very streets we will walk on will be as the foundation of God's throne: "The twelve gates were twelve pearls, each gate made of a single pearl. The great street of the city was of pure gold, *like transparent glass.* I did not see a temple in the city, because the Lord God Almighty and the Lamb are its temple" (Rev 21:21-22).

Each saint had a harp to sing praises to God. Earlier in 5:8 we saw the 24 elders and the four living creatures fell down before God's throne and sang praises. Upon our deliverance we will be able to do no different, because our hearts and spirits will be overcome by joy. We read in Psalms, "They will celebrate your abundant goodness and joyfully sing of your righteousness" (Psa 145:7).

The song they sing is that of Moses, either in Exodus 15 or Deuteronomy 32. In Exodus we see Moses sang a song of deliverance to praise God for saving them from the Egyptians as they crossed the Red Sea. This song was sung every Sabbath evening in remembrance of this salvation. Here the song must portray that same joy and praise because of their deliverance from the beast.

It is also interesting that Moses is mentioned here in Revelation. Why not Abraham, Noah, Paul, Daniel or any other great faith hero? It is possible that it is because Moses is most likely one of the two witnesses mentioned in chapter 11, and is, therefore, very involved in these end time deliverances. Moses may very well be there singing with the saints because, he too, was delivered from the beast (11:7-12).

Rev 15:3b "Great and marvelous are your deeds, Lord God Almighty. Just and true are your ways, King of the ages. 15:4 Who will not fear you, O Lord, and bring glory to your name? For you alone are holy. All nations will come and worship before you, for your righteous acts have been revealed."

The song sung by the saints can be broken up into three categories: 1) ways, 2) works, 3) worth, and 4) worship.

Great and marvelous are God's deeds (works). This is foundational to the Christian faith, that there is nothing we can do by ourselves, but it is God's grace and work that brings us to be with Him. Therefore, we praise God for His work in bringing us to His throne. The psalmist declares, "How great are Your works, O LORD, how profound Your thoughts" (Psa 92:5)! Jeremiah also wrote, "Who should not revere you, O King of the nations? This is Your due. Among all the wise men of the nations and in all their kingdoms, there is no one like You" (Jer 10:7).

"Just and true are your *ways.*" Throughout all ages Christ has been "just" and fair in His judgments. It was not without warning that these judgments and deliverances had come. God's plan, or "way," is concluding exactly as He wanted. We read in Jeremiah, "the LORD is the true God; He is the living God, the eternal King" (Jer 10:10). Indeed God is the King of the ages and we must conclude as Timothy said, "Now to the King eternal, immortal, invisible, the only God, be honor and glory for ever and ever. Amen" (1 Tim 1:17).

"Who will fear You Lord and bring glory to Your Name?" Only God deserves glory and honor (worth). It is the fear of the Lord that is the beginning of wisdom (Ps 111:10). We also see that the fear of the Lord is eternal: "The fear of the LORD is pure, enduring forever. The ordinances of the LORD are sure and altogether righteous" (Psa 19:9). Therefore, God's worth is now and forever more.

"All nations will *worship* before you." Paul wrote, "As surely as I live, says the Lord, every knee will bow before Me; every tongue will confess to God. So then, each of us will give an account of himself to God" (Rom 14:11–12). In Philippians also, we read of Christ: "Therefore God exalted Him to the highest place and gave Him the Name that is above every name, that at the Name of Jesus every knee should bow, in heaven and on earth and under the earth, and every tongue confess that Jesus Christ is Lord, to the glory of God the Father" (Phil 2:9-11, see also Ps 86:9, 2:9-11, Mal 1:11, Isa 66:23, and 45:22-23).

Even the words sung here echo the truths found in the song of Moses as seen in Exodus, "Who among the gods is like You, O LORD? Who is like You-- majestic in holiness, awesome in glory, working wonders" (Exo 15:11)?

Rev 15:5 After this I looked and in heaven the temple, that is, the tabernacle of the Testimony, was opened. 15:6 Out of the temple came the seven angels with the seven plagues. They were dressed in clean, shining linen and wore golden sashes around their chests. 15:7 Then one of the four living creatures gave to the seven angels seven golden bowls filled with the wrath of God, who lives for ever and ever. 15:8 And the temple was filled with smoke from the glory of God and from his power, and no one could enter the temple until the seven plagues of the seven angels were completed.

In verse five, John saw the temple in heaven opened up. As we explained back in 11:19, this is very important in order to understand the timing and order of these events. The words, "after this" can mean after the seventh trumpet. In chapter 11 we saw God gave us a very brief outline explanation of the seven bowl judgments. He simply showed us that after the seventh trumpet blew, the temple in heaven would be opened and then there would be thunder, lightning and an earthquake. In between the opening of the temple here in verse five, and the great thundering and shaking in 16:8-9, are the bowl judgments.

The temple was called the Tabernacle of Testimony because it was not only the dwelling place of God during the 40 year desert wandering, but it also housed the tablets of the Ten Commandments (Ex 32:15, 38:21, Dt 10:5, Nu 1:50). Therefore, we see an image of the law being brought forth. It is because the inhabitants of the earth are law breakers that they are about to be judged. The tabernacle (God's presence) has testified against them: "All who rely on observing the law are under a curse, for it is written: 'Cursed is everyone who does not continue to do everything written in the Book of the law.' Clearly no one is justified before God by the law, because, 'The righteous will live by faith.' The law is not based on faith; on the contrary, 'The man who does these things will live by them.' Christ redeemed us from the curse of the law by becoming a curse for us" (Gal 3:10 -13). Without the blood of Christ, they were lost. We also read why Christ went to this tabernacle: "For Christ did not enter a man-made sanctuary that was only a copy of the true one; He entered heaven itself, now to appear for us in God's presence. Nor did He enter heaven to offer Himself again and again, the way the high priest enters the Most Holy Place every year with blood that is not his own" (Heb 9:24).

  The temple was opened so that the seven angels who would pour out the wrath of God could come out and prepare to do their job. They were dressed in clean linen and also wore gold sashes around their chests. The clean linen stands for the righteous acts of the saints (19:8) and the gold sashes very likely represent the fact that they are priests since the Old Testament priests were also instructed to wear such a thing (Ex 28:4). This is exactly what God told us earlier we would be, "You purchased men for God from every tribe and language and people and nation. You have made them to be a kingdom and priests to serve our God, and they will reign on the earth" (Rev 5:9-10).

  It is important to note that no one can enter the temple until the seven bowls are completed. Keep in mind that the temple will be God Himself in heaven (Rev 21:22). The fact that we can't enter the temple yet suggests that the wedding banquet of the Lamb has not yet taken place. We must wait until all of God's plan has been fulfilled to *completely* inherit this unity with our new bodies.

CHAPTER 16

Rev 16:1 Then I heard a loud voice from the temple saying to the seven angels, "Go, pour out the seven bowls of God's wrath on the earth." 16:2 The first angel went and poured out his bowl on the land, and ugly and painful sores broke out on the people who had the mark of the beast and worshipped his image.

Now that we see the temple is filled with God's glory, and no one but God Himself can be in the temple, there can be no question that the voice coming from within is God's. He tells the seven angels to go and pour out His wrath on the nations. We read in Psalms, "Pour out Your wrath on the nations that do not acknowledge You, on the kingdoms that do not call on Your name" (Psa 79:6). Zephaniah tells us that the cause of this wrath is jealous anger: "'Therefore wait for Me,' declares the LORD, 'for the day I will stand up to testify. I have decided to assemble the nations, to gather the kingdoms and to pour out My wrath on them-- all My fierce anger. The whole world will be consumed by the fire of My jealous anger'" (Zep 3:8).

When the first bowl is poured out on the land, ugly and painful sores break out on all of the ungodly. If you look at the outline provided with this book you will see that the first four bowl judgments are very similar to the first four trumpets, however, they are NOT the same. This only testifies to the orderliness of God. The trumpets began the destruction and the bowls finish it. Where 1/3 of the land is affected with the trumpets, all of the land is affected with the bowls, etc. That is why we saw earlier that the sign in heaven was, "seven angels with the seven last plagues--last, because with them God's wrath is completed" (Rev 15:1).

The painful sores produced by this first bowl reminds us of God's promise of wrath to the Israelites when they rejected Him. He said, "The LORD will afflict your knees and legs with painful boils that cannot be cured, spreading from the soles of your feet to the top of your head" (Deu 28:35). Even in Revelation these people were given warning to stay away from the beast and his image: "A third angel followed them and said in a loud voice: 'If anyone worships the beast and his image and receives his mark on the forehead or on the hand, he, too, will drink of the wine of God's fury, which has been poured full strength into the cup of His wrath. He will be tormented with burning sulfur in the presence of the holy angels and of the Lamb'" (Rev 14:9-10). It seems that pain inflicted upon the body is an appropriate way to punish one who has tried to satisfy the earthly pleasures and lusts of the body throughout his life. God also used this same type of punishment in Egypt when Pharaoh refused to let the Israelites go (Ex 9:9-11).

Rev 16:3 The second angel poured out his bowl on the sea, and it turned into blood like that of a dead man, and every living thing in the sea

died. 16:4 The third angel poured out his bowl on the rivers and springs of water, and they became blood.

The second bowl was poured out on the sea and it ALL turned to blood, just as the second trumpet affected only 1/3 of it. This time not a single living thing survives. Once more this echoes the plagues of Egypt when the waters were turned to blood (Ex 7:17, Ps 78:44).

The third bowl, just as the third trumpet, was poured out on the fresh water and it ALL turns to blood. Now that the oceans, rivers, and underground springs are blood, there is no more drinking water anywhere for the people left on earth. Just as the boils brought about intense bodily suffering, so, too, will this drought. We read in Jeremiah, "O LORD, the hope of Israel, all who forsake You will be put to shame. Those who turn away from You will be written in the dust because they have forsaken the LORD, the spring of living water" (Jer 17:13). While the ungodly will thirst forever, the Christians will have their thirst quenched forever, "whoever drinks the water I give him will never thirst. Indeed, the water I give him will become in him a spring of water welling up to eternal life" (John 4:14). God even promised earlier in Revelation that "living water" would be part of our reward "For the Lamb at the center of the throne will be their shepherd; He will lead them to springs of living water. And God will wipe away every tear from their eyes" (Rev 7:17). What exactly is this living water? We see Jesus' explanation to the woman at the well: "'Whoever believes in Me, as the Scripture has said, streams of living water will flow from within him.' By this He meant the Spirit, whom those who believed in Him were later to receive" (John 7:38-39). What a precious gift *living* water is! The most abundant *natural* (or eternal) resource was rejected by these ungodly people left on earth.

Rev 16:5 Then I heard the angel in charge of the waters say: "You are just in these judgments, you who are and who were, the Holy One, because you have so judged; 16:6 for they have shed the blood of your saints and prophets, and you have given them blood to drink as they deserve." 16:7 And I heard the altar respond: "Yes, Lord God Almighty, true and just are your judgments."

Verse five tells us that the angel in charge of all the waters acknowledges God's righteous and fair judgment on these people. He also calls God the one who is and was, but appropriately leaves out the "who is to come" that has been used all the time prior to this (1:4, 1:8), because now Christ has come again for the final time. We did see this same acknowledgment of Christ's reign beginning earlier in chapter 11:17 showing that chapter sixteen is giving us more details about what went on in chapter eleven's outline form.

God is also called the "Holy One." We know that God alone can hold this title, for "Who will not fear you, O Lord, and bring glory to Your Name? For You alone are holy" (Rev 15:4).

The reason God's judgment was fair was because those being judged had killed the prophets and saints (Rev 6:9). Now they were getting what they dished out, however, their final outcome will not be rewarded as that of the saints. Isaiah told of God's judgment, "I will make your oppressors eat their own flesh; they will be drunk on their own blood, as with wine. Then all mankind will know that I, the LORD, am your Savior, your Redeemer, the Mighty One of Jacob" (Isa 49:26). Because God is our Redeemer we will join in the hallelujah chorus and sing, "Hallelujah! Salvation and glory and power belong to our God, for true and just are His judgments. He has condemned the great prostitute who corrupted the earth by her adulteries. He has avenged on her the blood of His servants" (Rev 19:1-2).

Rev 16:8 The fourth angel poured out his bowl on the sun, and the sun was given power to scorch people with fire. 16:9 They were seared by the intense heat and they cursed the name of God, who had control over these plagues, but they refused to repent and glorify him.

Now the fourth angel pours his bowl out on the sun and intense heat scorches people with fire. Rather than recognize their sin and confess to God with repentance, their hardened hearts can only curse the Name of God. They clearly recognize that God had control over these plagues, yet they refuse to repent and give God glory. Isn't this so typical of sinful man? As long as things are going well in our lives God is okay, but we still forget about Him because we have all we need. But as soon as trouble comes, we wonder why God is doing this. Instead of repentance, blame and scorn result. These people will complain and blame God for their troubles just as the Israelites did in their 40 years of wandering.

I have a cousin who is an RN at a hospital in Lincoln, Nebraska. She shared an interesting experience with me. There was a man from the nearby prison in the hospital dying of cancer. Part of my cousin's job was to pronounce a person's death, so she would listen for a heartbeat sometimes a full five minutes after seeing a flat line. When this man died, however, he revived after a short time. When he did, all that came out of his mouth was foul and evil cursing of God. He didn't waste his time with simple, vial profanity, he only wanted to curse God. This happened a second time, and he finally died for an eternity. The demons, and those whom they get to follow them, will hate God with all intensity. There is no love in hell, not even the love of hate. This is the hopelessness of those who refuse to repent and worship God.

Through all of this God is still just in these judgments, for He certainly has "given her time to repent of her immorality, but she is unwilling" (Rev 2:21).

Rev 16:10 The fifth angel poured out his bowl on the throne of the beast, and his kingdom was plunged into darkness. Men gnawed their tongues in agony 16:11 and cursed the God of heaven because of their pains and their sores, but they refused to repent of what they had done.

Now that we have seen the first four bowl judgments, we will see a change in theme, keeping with our four/three split, as observed in every other series of seven. So far, all four bowls have affected people indirectly because the bowls were poured out on the land, water, and sun. The people were indeed affected by this, but they haven't seen anything yet.

Now the fifth angel pours his bowl out directly upon the throne of the beast so that his entire kingdom is thrown into darkness where people gnaw their tongues in agony and continue to curse God because of their torment. This is none other than hell, where there is "weeping and gnashing of teeth" (Matt 8:12, 13:42, 13:50, 22:13, 24:51, 25:30).

The kingdom was thrown into darkness. Again, we may see a parallel with the Egyptian plagues, where "Moses stretched out his hand toward the sky, and total darkness covered all Egypt for three days. No one could see anyone else or leave his place for three days. Yet all the Israelites had light in the places where they lived" (Exo 10:22-23). We see that those whom God's hand is against have no light. John wrote, "When Jesus spoke again to the people, He said, 'I am the light of the world. Whoever follows Me will never walk in darkness, but will have the light of life'" (John 8:12). We see that Jesus is the light of the world, and without Him there is no joy, love, peace, comfort, life or salvation. For those who believe in Him, however, there will be all good things given. Isaiah also wrote concerning the doom of these people, "Why consult the dead on behalf of the living? To the law and to the testimony! If they do not speak according to this word, they have no light of dawn. Distressed and hungry, they will roam through the land; when they are famished, they will become enraged and, looking upward, will curse their king and their God. Then they will look toward the earth and see only distress and darkness and fearful gloom, and they will be thrust into utter darkness. Nevertheless, there will be no more gloom for those who were in distress" (Isa 8:19-9:1).

When a dog gnaws his teeth it is usually a sign of great pain, fear and anger. What a visual description of the torment going on in the body, soul and spirit of these now damned unbelievers. This is not something I want anybody I know to experience. I pray that this motivates us to be bold enough to put aside pride and worry of embarrassment so that we will preach and stand on God's Word firmly, to be a good example and witness for Christ.

Rev 16:12 The sixth angel poured out his bowl on the great river Euphrates, and its water was dried up to prepare the way for the kings from the East. 16:13 Then I saw three evil spirits that looked like frogs; they came out of the mouth of the dragon, out of the mouth of the beast and out of the mouth of the false prophet. 16:14 They are spirits of demons performing miraculous signs, and they go out to the kings of the whole world, to gather them for the battle on the great day of God Almighty.

When the sixth angel poured out his bowl, the Euphrates River dried up in order for the eastern kings to cross with their armies. In verse fourteen we see that the kings of the "whole world" will be gathered, but for now only those from the east are mentioned. These kings are clearly evil and will be those whom God will destroy in the great battle of the Lord (19:11ff). Though viewed in a different context, this drying up of the river may be very similar to the event spoke of in Isaiah, "The LORD will dry up the gulf of the Egyptian sea; with a scorching wind He will sweep His hand over the Euphrates River. He will break it up into seven streams so that men can cross over in sandals" (Isa 11:15). In any case, the kings of the east are walking into God's trap and fulfilling His purpose: "I make known the end from the beginning, from ancient times, what is still to come. I say: My purpose will stand, and I will do all that I please. From the east I summon a bird of prey; from a far-off land, a man to fulfill My purpose" (Isa 46:10-11; see 41:2 also).

There are also three evil spirits that come out of the mouth of the evil trinity: Dragon (Satan), beast out of the sea (Anitchrist), and the beast out of the earth (False Prophet). The spirits come out as frogs, which according to Leviticus 11:10, were unclean animals and, therefore, the imagery shows the defilement and negative goal of these spirits. These were not mere men who were persecuting and leading the saints astray. They were demon possessed men controlled by Satan himself whose main goal is to destroy the saints and steal as many followers of Christ as possible. Through deception, miracles (13:13) and spiritual warfare, the spirits go out to deceive and gather the leaders of the world to march out against Jerusalem and the holy people (19:11-21).

Christ warns us in Timothy "The Spirit clearly says that in later times some will abandon the faith and follow deceiving spirits and things taught by demons" (1 Tim 4:1). In Matthew He also said, "For false christs and false prophets will appear and perform great signs and miracles to deceive even the elect--if that were possible" (Mat 24:24). In the next chapter we will see that "They will make war against the Lamb, but the Lamb will overcome them because He is Lord of lords and King of kings--and with Him will be His called, chosen and faithful followers" (Rev 17:14; see also 19:19 and 20:8).

Other Scriptures showing this gathering of kings follow:

- "I will gather all nations and bring them down to the Valley of Jehoshaphat. There I will enter into judgment against them concerning My inheritance, My people Israel, for they scattered My people among the nations and divided up My land.. . . . Come quickly, all you nations from every side, and assemble there. Bring down your warriors, O LORD" (Joel 3:2,11)!

- "'Therefore wait for Me,' declares the LORD, 'for the day I will stand up to testify. I have decided to assemble the nations, to gather the kingdoms and to pour out My wrath on them-- all My fierce anger. The whole world will be consumed by the fire of My jealous anger. Then will I purify the lips of the peoples, that all of them may call on the Name of the LORD and serve Him shoulder to shoulder'" (Zep 3:8-9).

- "I will gather all the nations to Jerusalem to fight against it; . . .Then the LORD will go out and fight against those nations, as He fights in the day of battle. On that day His feet will stand on the Mount of Olives, east of Jerusalem, and the Mount of Olives will be split in two from east to west, forming a great valley, with half of the mountain moving north and half moving south" (Zec 14:2-4).

- "At the time of the end the king of the South will engage him in battle, and the king of the North will storm out against him with chariots and cavalry and a great fleet of ships. He will invade many countries and sweep through them like a flood. He will also invade the Beautiful Land. Many countries will fall, but Edom, Moab and the leaders of Ammon will be delivered from his hand" (Dan 11:40-41).

Rev 16:15 "Behold, I come like a thief! Blessed is he who stays awake and keeps his clothes with him, so that he may not go naked and be shamefully exposed." 16:16 Then they gathered the kings together to the place that in Hebrew is called Armageddon.

Verse 15 begins the third of seven beatitudes in Revelation (1:3, 14:13, 19:9, 20:6, 22:7, and 22:14). The message is that Christ will come like a thief when most people do not expect Him because they are not watching for Him. The blessings will be given to those who stay up, watch, and wait for Jesus to come. By watching, we will not be caught naked nor will we remain naked in heaven. Nakedness is a picture of unholiness as well as unreadiness: "I counsel you to buy from Me gold refined in the fire, so you can become rich; and white clothes to wear, so you can cover your shameful nakedness" (Rev 3:18). In fact, God will give us white robes of righteousness in heaven (Rev 19:8). We are told it is good to watch for the Lord's second coming, "It will be good for those servants whose Master finds them watching when He comes. I tell you the truth, He will dress Himself to serve, will have them recline at the table and will come and wait on them" (Luke 12:37 Note, God serves us, what a humbling experience to have One so great serve you). We don't want to miss this great banquet He has prepared for us. Again, there is a warning for the unbeliever though, "But understand this: If the owner of the house had known at what hour the thief was coming, he would not have let his house be broken into" (Luke 12:39). We must be very careful in thinking that, as Christians, we won't know when the end is coming, for Jesus said, "But you, brothers, are not in darkness so that this day should surprise you like a thief. You are all sons of the light and sons of the day. We do not belong to the night or to the darkness. So then, let us not be like others, who are asleep, but let us be alert and self-controlled" (1 Th 5:4). It is only the unbeliever who will be caught in their nakedness.

The beautitude of verse 15 served as a type of interlude between the sixth and seventh bowl judgment, just as there has been a break of some sort after the sixth one of each series of sevens.

Verse 16 closes off the sixth trumpet by showing that the work of the evil spirits of verse 14 had been accomplished. The kings had been deceived and gathered to a place called Armageddon. The word Armageddon means, "hill of Megiddo." It is no accident that the ancient city of Megiddo lies within the Valley of Jezreel or the Valley of Decision where this last battle is to take place. Some of the verses in reference to this may be seen in the section covering verse 14.

Rev 16:17 The seventh angel poured out his bowl into the air, and out of the temple came a loud voice from the throne, saying, "It is done!" 16:18 Then there came flashes of lightning, rumblings, peals of thunder and a severe earthquake. No earthquake like it has ever occurred since man has been on earth, so tremendous was the quake. 16:19 The great city split into three parts, and the cities of the nations collapsed. God remembered Babylon the Great and gave her the cup filled with the wine of the fury of his wrath. 16:20 Every island fled away and the mountains could not be found. 16:21 From the sky huge hailstones of about a hundred pounds each fell upon men. And they cursed God on account of the plague of hail, because the plague was so terrible.

When the seventh and final bowl is poured out into the air God fills the temple, announcing "It is done." Much like on the cross, once the end of an important part of God's historical plan is completed, He announces it to the world. Once again, for the last time, during the seventh of any of our series, something else begins. For the unbeliever that will be the eternal torment of hell, but for the believers, this marks the beginning of the wedding banquet of the Lamb, which we will read about further in chapter 19.

After God's final announcement, there was thunder, lightning, and a severe earthquake bringing forth the final doom of Satan's kingdom while Christians are safe in heaven: "The LORD will roar from Zion and thunder from Jerusalem; the earth and the sky will tremble. But the LORD will be a refuge for His people, a stronghold for the people of Israel" (Joel 3:16). The earthquake is greater than anything that has ever taken place. It was so great that EVERY mountain and island were no more. Daniel recorded, "At that time Michael, the great prince who protects Your people, will arise. There will be a time of distress such as has not happened from the beginning of nations until then. But at that time Your people--everyone whose name is found written in the book--will be delivered" (Dan 12:1; see also Mat 24:21). Isaiah spoke of this day hundreds of years earlier:

"Terror and pit and snare await you, O people of the earth. Whoever flees at the sound of terror will fall into a pit; whoever climbs out of the pit will be caught in a snare. *The floodgates of the heavens are opened*, the foundations of *the earth shake*. The earth is broken up, *the earth is split asunder, the earth is thoroughly shaken*. The earth reels like a drunkard, it sways like a hut in the wind; *so heavy upon it is the guilt of its rebellion that it falls--never to rise again*. In that day the LORD will punish the *powers in the heavens above and the kings on the earth below*. They will be herded together like prisoners bound in a dungeon; they will be shut up in prison and be punished after many days. The moon will be abashed, the sun ashamed; *for the LORD Almighty will reign on Mount Zion and in Jerusalem,* and before its elders, gloriously" (Isa 24:17-23).

The great city was split into three parts and all other cities destroyed. The great city seems to be Babylon, the throne of the beast. It is mentioned in the second half of verse 19 and we also see it coming up in chapter 17, "The woman you saw is *the great city* that rules over the kings of the earth" (Rev 17:18). In 18:5 we see why this city is being destroyed, "for her sins are piled up to heaven, and God has remembered her crimes" (Rev 18:5). The reason for three parts is not known for sure, but it could imply that it was completely split or destroyed since three symbolizes a number of completeness.

Regarding the islands being removed, Isaiah wrote, "The sky receded like a scroll, rolling up, and every mountain and island was removed from its place" (Rev 6:14). In addition to this great destruction, 100 pound hailstones fell on the people as one last judgment of God's wrath. Once more we are reminded of God's wrath that fell upon the Egyptians (Ex 9:23). Hail is often associated with God's most fierce wrath, "Therefore this is what the Sovereign LORD says: 'In My wrath I will unleash a violent wind, and in My anger hailstones and torrents of rain will fall with destructive fury'" (Ezek 13:13), and, "I will execute judgment upon him with plague and bloodshed; I will pour down torrents of rain, hailstones and burning sulfur on him and on his troops and on the many nations with him" (Ezek 38:22). Woe to those upon whose head this hail shall fall. As usual, a hardened heart can do nothing but continue to curse God, as they may very well do for an eternity. Though this plague will end, the torment, pain and suffering never will.

As mentioned earlier, Babylon could fit the description of Jerusalem at the time of John as well. We see again that this city is called the "great city." In Revelation 11:8 we saw that a "great city" was mentioned, and it turned out to be Jerusalem, which was figuratively called Sodom and Egypt, two other ungodly nations. Taking the text literally, this implies that Babylon, or the great city, is indeed Jerusalem (see Rev 11:8; 16:19; 17:18; 18:10). This being the case, the Fall of Jerusalem in 70 AD does typify the end. Interestingly, we see that the "great city" had hail stones thrown upon her that weighed about 100 pounds (16:21). Josephus records that when the Romans came and took Jerusalem they hurled great "white stones" that weighed about 100 pounds each. Could this description fulfill John's vision in 16:21? This is significant if Revelation is describing the divorce of the harlot Israel because in Old Testament times the punishment of prostitution was stoning. After all, John does open and close the book with the warnings that this would "soon take place" (1:1, 22:6), because the "time is near" (1:3,22:10). For John, 70 AD was very near. The fall of Jerusalem would therefore be a Battle of Armageddon in itself where the woman (Jerusalem) would be destroyed. The old, earthly Jerusalem was to be destroyed and the new Jerusalem coming in chapter 21 would fill the void. In other words, Judaism and the rejection of the Messiah would be left desolate (Mat 23:38) while Christianity would flourish. This also fits with what we have been discussing so far. We saw in 11:1-2 that the siege of Jerusalem by the Gentiles was to last for 42 months, or three and one-half years. The Roman siege began in the spring of AD 67 and ended in September of AD 70, exactly 42 months. Also, in 11:2 the temple was the focus of the trampling. During John's day the temple existed, however, today it does not. Even in Matthew, the focus of the Olivet discourse was the temple, "Jesus left the temple and was walking away when His disciples came up to Him to call His attention to its buildings. 'Do you see all these things?' He asked. 'I tell you the truth, not one stone here will be left on another; every one will be thrown down'" (Mat 24:1-2). Luke also supports Jerusalem being the center of this great destruction: "For this is the time of punishment in fulfillment of all that has been written. How dreadful it will be in those days for pregnant women and nursing mothers! There will be great distress in the land and wrath against this people. They will fall by the sword and will be taken as prisoners to all the nations. Jerusalem will be trampled on by the Gentiles until the times of the Gentiles are fulfilled" (Luke 21:22-24). All of this, and more, was to take place in one generations time. We already discussed this in reference to Matthew 24, however, a new question arises? Could the "one generation" prophecy also be a dual fulfillment? Luke goes on to say the Son of Man would appear in the clouds and the heavenly bodies would be shaken before he makes the "one generation" comment, could this be interpreted two ways with neither one being a lie? IF so, the end time events will take place in one generations time as the people living through it (referred to as THIS generation) are represented. In addition, the Jerusalem siege, which was typifying end time events, would also take place in one generation's time.

In Revelation 18:11 we see the merchants will mourn for Babylon, the great city. When Jerusalem fell, many merchants did mourn because she was indeed a strong economic force due to the selling of Temple sacrifices and offerings.

CHAPTER 17

Rev 17:1 One of the seven angels who had the seven bowls came and said to me, "Come, I will show you the punishment of the great prostitute, who sits on many waters. 17:2 With her the kings of the earth committed adultery and the inhabitants of the earth were intoxicated with the wine of her adulteries."

Technically, Revelation should be over, but God is going to backtrack and explain His actions by showing the great sins of the city and why Babylon must be destroyed. Up to this point we have been calling the throne of Satan Babylon, but it is very possible that this is figurative, as this chapter will also give great detail into what the city really is. Chapter 18 will give greater details as to the actual destruction. But for now, the key is in verse one where the angel says, "Come, I will show you the punishment."

This prostitute is simply a woman representing a so called "church" as we will see. She is called a prostitute because she has not kept herself spiritually pure. We have already shown that this is simply turning away from our groom to be; the Lord Jesus Christ (See notes on 14:4).

She is sitting on many waters. Verse 15 tells us straight out that the waters are "peoples, multitudes, nations and languages." Simply put, the waters are people of all nations, not just one city. The prostitute sits on the waters and perhaps rules or leads them. In any case, the kings of the earth follow her ways and join her in the adulteries she promotes and practices. We read in Romans, "Although they know God's righteous decree that those who do such things deserve death, they not only continue to do these very things but also approve of those who practice them" (Rom 1:32). The nations not only follow these adulteries, but get drunk on them. They don't just drink them, they indulge and take in as much as they can. Isaiah wrote "She will return to her hire as a prostitute and will ply her trade with all the kingdoms on the face of the earth" (Isa 23:17). From this we are beginning to see why God is judging this city. She has lead others astray, as is evident in chapter 19, which states, "for true and just are His judgments. He has condemned the great prostitute who corrupted the earth by her adulteries. He has avenged on her the blood of His servants" (Rev 19:2, see also Rev 14:8).

An alternate, or perhaps double fulfillment of this woman is Jerusalem. We know that the Old Testament uses much imagery of Israel prostituting herself to other Gods. Jeremiah shows God sees Himself as Israel's Husband, "'Return, faithless people,' declares the LORD, 'for I am your Husband' (Jer 3:14; see also 31:32). When Israel "cheated" on God He sent the prophets to testify against them: "When the LORD began to speak through Hosea, the LORD said to him, 'Go, take to yourself an adulterous wife and children of unfaithfulness, because the land is guilty of the vilest adultery in departing from the LORD'" (Hosea 1:2). Therefore, in Revelation God is painting a picture of Jerusalem as a prostitute just like Babylon and the other enemies of God. That is why in 11:8 Jerusalem was called Sodom and Egypt. God sits on His throne to judge them

(Rev 4:2), and the scroll of Revelation chapter 5 is His "divorce certificate" as Jeremiah said, "I gave faithless Israel her certificate of divorce and sent her away because of all her adulteries" (Jer 3:8). This being the case, the seven seals of Revelation 5 could be referenced to in the prophetic judgments of Leviticus 26:18-28 where it mentions God's judgment being given "seven times over."

If the above be true, Jerusalem is the prostitute that sits on Rome. What does this mean? Jerusalem was controlled by Rome until its destruction in 70 AD. In 18:24 we will see that the blood of the saints and prophets were "found within her." This could fit Rome as it certainly shed the blood of many saints, but it could also be Jerusalem where Christian persecution first began (Acts 8:1, 4:3, 5:18). In either case, Revelation 19:2 shows God will avenge her for this innocent bloodshed.

Rev 17:3 Then the angel carried me away in the Spirit into a desert. There I saw a woman sitting on a scarlet beast that was covered with blasphemous names and had seven heads and ten horns. 17:4 The woman was dressed in purple and scarlet, and was glittering with gold, precious stones and pearls. She held a golden cup in her hand, filled with abominable things and the filth of her adulteries. 17:5 This title was written on her forehead: MYSTERY BABYLON THE GREAT THE MOTHER OF PROSTITUTES AND OF THE ABOMINATIONS OF THE EARTH.

The angel then carried John into the desert where he got a bird's eye view of this woman or church. She was sitting on a scarlet beast covered with blasphemous names. She also had seven heads and ten horns. Although this picture seems difficult to understand, God clearly explains it to us in later verses. The seven heads are explained in verse nine where they are said to be seven hills on which the woman, or city, sits. The ten horns are explained in verse 12 as ten kings who must rule on these seven hills within this city. The beast appears to be a city from where the woman rules. Here we have the beginning of a good possibility that this city is actually Rome, where the Vatican sits. We see in Daniel that, in more than one instance, four kingdoms that were to come upon the earth were described in beast form; Babylonian, Medo-Persian, Greek and Roman. Interestingly, they came out of the sea, "Four great beasts, each different from the others, came up out of the sea" (Dan 7:3). This is the same place that the beast, or Antichrist, comes from in Revelation 13:1. In Revelation chapter 12 we saw Satan, or the dragon, waiting by the shore for the beast to come. In Daniel we see that the fourth beast was Rome, the empire which took over the Greeks and which still remains in power today. In one of the descriptions of the fourth beast we see a striking similarity from that which we are reading about here in Revelation. We are told that the fourth beast is a kingdom that will have ten horns (Rev 17:3), will reign 3 ½ years while going after the saints (Rev 11), and will be destroyed by God (Rev 11, 14-16). The same story is told in Daniel in more than one place, but one example follows:

> "He gave me this explanation: 'The fourth beast is a fourth kingdom that will appear on earth. It will be different from all the other kingdoms

and will devour the whole earth, trampling it down and crushing it. The ten horns are ten kings who will come from this kingdom. After them another king will arise, different from the earlier ones; he will subdue three kings. He will speak against the Most High and oppress His saints and try to change the set times and the laws. The saints will be handed over to him for a time, times and half a time. But the court will sit, and his power will be taken away and completely destroyed forever. Then the sovereignty, power and greatness of the kingdoms under the whole heaven will be handed over to the saints, the people of the Most High. His kingdom will be an everlasting kingdom, and all rulers will worship and obey Him'" (Dan 7:23-27).

The very fact that the kingdom Daniel was talking about was Rome indicates that John's Babylon here in Revelation is actually Rome, the city on which the Antichrist will sit. An interesting thought that we will continue to pursue through the next couple of chapters is that the Vatican, or the Roman Catholic seat of power through the papacy, will play a large part in the end times. We see in verse three that the woman was sitting on a scarlet beast and in verse four she wore purple and scarlet clothing. Today the Catholic bishops and cardinals wear scarlet and purple robes. We know that this woman is called the great prostitute in verse one and, therefore, she is considered to be religious or spiritual because she is "cheating" on God. God only calls the spiritual strays "prostitutes." Therefore, the woman must be associated with a church of some kind.

The colors of the woman could also be significant for Jerusalem. In Exodus we read of the same colors used for the priestly clothing, tabernacle and offerings: "Tell the Israelites to bring Me an offering. You are to receive the offering for Me from each man whose heart prompts him to give. These are the offerings you are to receive from them: gold, silver and bronze; blue, purple and scarlet yarn and fine linen; goat hair; ram skins dyed red and hides of sea cows" (Exo 25:2-5). It is interesting that the description of the temple colors were called, "Babylonian colors" by Josephus (Josephus, Wars V.5.4) and, therefore, supports the description of the woman given in verse five. Spiritual prostitution did, in a way, begin with Israel. John seems to be playing the earthly Jerusalem (Judaism) against the heavenly Jerusalem (Christianity), evidenced both at the destruction of the city in 70 AD, and in the future. Perhaps that is why it appears that the same angel shows John the prostitute (17:1) and the Bride of Christ (21:9). Likewise, John was shown both the wilderness (17:3) and the holy mountain (21:10). God wants to make a contrast between the prostitute and the true saints. Furthering this line of thought, we see in Exodus that the priests were to wear a sign on their forehead: "Make a plate of pure gold and engrave on it as on a seal: HOLY TO THE LORD. Fasten a blue cord to it to attach it to the turban; it is to be on the front of the turban. It will be on Aaron's forehead" (Exo 28:36-38). Likewise, the woman in Revelation receives the opposite message as the "Mother of prostitutes and of the abominations of the earth." Because Aaron was a priest in the temple, this makes the mention of priestly colors all the more significant here. It is showing that though Israel was "Holy to the Lord," they cheated and became harlots or prostitutes.

We saw that the seven heads represented seven hills (v. 9) and Rome has always been known as the "city of seven hills." As earlier stated, other cities throughout history have had seven hills, however, Rome is the most famous and it fits with Daniel labeling the fourth beast as Rome. If only the city of seven hills was mentioned perhaps there would not be enough evidence to attach Roman significance to this woman on the beast. However, there are many descriptions of Rome given here. In verse four we see that the woman is rich with gold and precious stones. Anyone who has ever seen the Vatican can attest that it is one of the most magnificent architectural sites today, but at the same time, the least Christ-like icon religion could have. Christ came to serve and didn't find wealth something to be sought after, or even important. Those who saw Christ as a business investment were told by Jesus, "Foxes have holes and birds of the air have nests, but the Son of Man has no place to lay His head" (Mat 8:20). James warns, "Your gold and silver are corroded. Their corrosion will testify against you and eat your flesh like fire. You have hoarded wealth in the last days" (James 5:3). Jesus said in Luke, "sell your possessions and give to the poor. Provide purses for yourselves that will not wear out, a treasure in heaven that will not be exhausted, where no thief comes near and no moth destroys. For where your treasure is, there your heart will be also. Be dressed ready for service" (Luke 12:33-35). Despite this example of Christ, the Vatican is a symbol of wealth and power, both religious and political. Indeed, other churches get caught up in materialism and fancy building projects, however, none that also dress in purple and scarlet, sit on a city of seven hills and that fit Daniel's fourth beast of ten horns, etc..

In any case, the woman has a cup filled with abominable things and of adulteries. Adulteries would be cheating on your spouse, or in a religious sense, worshipping idols and cheating on Christ, our bridegroom. Again, the Catholic church has made saint worship central to their faith, especially the adultery of praying to Mary. This is by no means the only way to cheat on Christ, however, if Rome is the correct interpretation here, it is not difficult to label the adulteries of the Vatican with its saints and supposed infallible popes. The Old Testament gives further insight into the golden cup: "Babylon was a gold cup in the Lord's hand; she made the whole earth drunk. The nations drank her wine; therefore they have now gone mad. Babylon will suddenly fall and be broken" (Jer 51:7-8).

The name on the woman's forehead is MYSTERY, BABYLON THE GREAT THE MOTHER OF PROSTITUTES AND OF THE ABOMINATIONS OF THE EARTH. In ancient times, Babylon was the political, commercial, and religious center of the world. It was well known for its lack of morals and material luxuries that led people astray and, therefore, the "mother" of prostitution in a spiritual sense. It was Babylon that was the center of the tower of Babel. It was from Babylon that the evil Euphrates River flowed. It was Babylon who captured God's people. It was Babylon that God promised to destroy over and over throughout Isaiah, Jeremiah, Daniel and other prophets. We see the sorrow that Babylon brought upon the Israelites, "By the rivers of

Babylon we sat and wept when we remembered Zion. There on the poplars we hung our harps, for there our captors asked us for songs, our tormentors demanded songs of joy; they said, 'Sing us one of the songs of Zion'" (Psa 137:1-3). But the Lord promised to, "carry out His purpose, His decree against the people of Babylon. You who live by many waters and are rich in treasures, your end has come, the time for you to be cut off' (Jer 51:12-13).

Rev 17:6 I saw that the woman was drunk with the blood of the saints, the blood of those who bore testimony to Jesus. When I saw her, I was greatly astonished. 17:7 Then the angel said to me: "Why are you astonished? I will explain to you the mystery of the woman and of the beast she rides, which has the seven heads and ten horns. 17:8 The beast, which you saw, once was, now is not, and will come up out of the Abyss and go to his destruction. The inhabitants of the earth whose names have not been written in the book of life from the creation of the world will be astonished when they see the beast, because he once was, now is not, and yet will come.

This spiritual harlot was drunk from the killing of the true saints who would not shrink from death for the testimony of Jesus Christ.

John was astonished when he saw her, very likely because he was shocked to see the "church" killing the saints. Sometimes it is difficult to separate the woman from the beast since they rule together almost as one mind. We do know that Babylon is considered to have been the place of saint slaughter, "In her was found the blood of prophets and of the saints, and of all who have been killed on the earth" (Rev 18:24). Because of chapter 12 we know that Satan's power is involved where we see the connection of the ten horns and seven heads: "Another sign appeared in heaven: an enormous red dragon with seven heads and ten horns and seven crowns on his heads" (Rev 12:3). Since we have already discussed that the seven heads are hills and the ten horns are kings, we see that the dragon (Satan) will give power to, and control ten kings. As we started this book I made the point that we would only let Scripture speak for itself, and though Rome seems to fit many qualifications for the seven hills etc., we must remember that Scripture doesn't identify the city as Rome unless you count Daniel's visions of the fourth beast. Though Babylon may be Rome, it could also be a world government with its main control center being Rome, hence the need for ten kings. This also may give further insight into the "many waters" (v. 1) upon which the church and beast sit.

The angel seems to say to John that this is a simple vision to understand and, therefore, there is no need for astonishment or mystery because he will show John exactly who this woman and beast are. Further explanation was given telling that the beast once was, now is not, but will come again out of the Abyss. This time, however, only to go to his destruction. This indicates that the beast cannot simply represent a city, but moreso the power behind the city, namely Satan. We know that the Abyss is the dreaded place where demons reside. In Luke, Jesus cast out the legion of demons and they begged Him repeatedly, "not to order them to go into the Abyss" (Luke 8:31). Earlier in chapter 9:1 we saw that Satan was given a key to the Abyss to let his demon followers out. Chapters

12 and 13 showed that Satan gave his power to the Antichrist and the Antichrist gave power to the False prophet. Simply put, Satan gives power to his demons to possess and control human bodies. Some possible explanations are that Satan himself, who once was, but now is bound, will be loosed for a short time. We read in chapter 20 of God's control of Satan: "He threw him into the Abyss, and locked and sealed it over him, to keep him from deceiving the nations anymore until the thousand years were ended. After that, he must be set free for a short time" (Rev 20:3). However, there are inconsistencies with this interpretation. Since the beast comes out of the Abyss, it is therefore more probable that there is a demon who will be loosed and possess certain individuals (ten horns). The main character being the Antichrist himself. How would the Antichrist fit the "once was" description? We know that the Bible says, "Dear children, this is the last hour; and as you have heard that the Antichrist is coming, even now many antichrists **have come**. This is how we know it is the last hour" (1 John 2:18). In Daniel's day, Antiochus Epiphenes fit the description of, and certainly was a type of Antichrist. The interesting thing is that verse 8 here in Revelation says that those whose names are NOT in the book of life are astonished. Christians don't seem to be the ones who will be shocked by the appearance of this beast. We expect it to come.

Even in Daniel, some of the most difficult things to understand about Scripture are the dual prophecies; those that represent more than one fulfillment. For example, Babylon, though a true world power, also represented a future power here in Revelation. It was also representative of generic evil. Therefore, Babylon doesn't necessarily mean an exact geographical location, but rather Babylonian in spirit. Therefore, when we discuss this beast it is most likely that more than one description may be fitting. It may be that it is not only a city, but also the Antichrist, and because of its ten horns, other demonic beings. That is why it is difficult to find any one explanation to fit in all areas of the beast's description. When we view the beast as simply the demonic powers with an emphasis on the Antichrist, who leads the world astray and kills the saints, all descriptions fit.

Rev 17:9 "This calls for a mind with wisdom. The seven heads are seven hills on which the woman sits. 17:10 They are also seven kings. Five have fallen, one is, the other has not yet come; but when he does come, he must remain for a little while. 17:11 The beast who once was, and now is not, is an eighth king. He belongs to the seven and is going to his destruction.

Verse nine explains what we have already been discussing about the seven heads being seven hills where the woman and beast reside. Something we have not discussed, but also supports our interpretation of the beast having more than one meaning, is that the heads are both hills and kings.

We are told this calls for wisdom. We must remember that wisdom is not knowledge. You won't get wisdom from reading the political or academic books. We have plenty of fools with their doctorates at Harvard, Yale and other universities. I say fools because, "The fool says in his heart, 'There is no God'"

(Ps 14:1). Wisdom only comes through searching God's Word and through prayer. James reminds us, "If any of you lacks wisdom, he should ask God, who gives generously to all without finding fault, and it will be given to him. But when he asks, he must believe and not doubt" (James 1:5-6). My prayer for all of us, dear brothers and sisters, is that God gives us this desired and important piece of Himself. Yes, Wisdom is God and God is Wisdom because Wisdom is eternal. We read in Proverbs: "The LORD brought Me forth as the first of His works, before His deeds of old; I was appointed from eternity, from the beginning, *before the world began.* When there were no oceans, I was given birth, when there were no springs abounding with water; before the mountains were settled in place, before the hills, I was given birth, before He made the earth or its fields or any of the dust of the world. I was there when He set the heavens in place, when He marked out the horizon on the face of the deep, when He established the clouds above and fixed securely the fountains of the deep, when He gave the sea its boundary so the waters would not overstep His command, and when He marked out the foundations of the earth. Then I was the *craftsman at His side.* I was filled with delight day after day, rejoicing always in His presence, rejoicing in His whole world and delighting in mankind. Now then, My sons, listen to Me; blessed are those who keep My ways" (Prov 8:22-32). Clearly, Jesus is Wisdom. It is interesting that in almost every passage that the Word "wisdom" is used, one can substitute the word "Jesus" in its place and the sentence still makes sense. Wisdom can only come from God's Word who is Jesus Christ, the Living Word made Flesh (John 1:1-3).

These seven kings are broken into five that have already fallen at the time John was writing this, one that was ruling then, and one that would come for a short time. We know historically that before the days of John, five major kings ruled in Rome: Julius Caesar, Augustus, Tiberias, Claudius, and Coligula. Depending on the accuracy of the dating of Revelation, Nero may have been ruling while John was writing the book and, therefore, could be the sixth king who "now is." The one who had not yet come, but would reign a short period could then be Galba who ruled only seven months. Diocletian came to power about a year later and actively persecuted the saints (Both Nero and Diocletian acted with an attitude or Antichrist spirit - 1 John 2:18). In fact, as you recall from the beginning of Revelation we see John had been exiled to the island of Patmos because of his faith. However, we cannot say for sure that the interpretation of the Roman kings fulfilling these verses in Revelation is an accurate one. Some believe that the seven simply represents the Roman powers all together in the symbolic number of completeness. The one who has not yet come is unidentified, but most likely the Antichrist. We know that the beast is actually an eighth king who belongs to the seven. In chapter 13 the Antichrist (beast out of the sea) gave power to the False Prophet (beast out of the earth). Also, the seventh king will only reign for a "little while" just as the Antichrist is said to do. Also, the eighth king, or perhaps the false prophet, goes down to his destruction in 19:20. Paul warns us about this man of lawlessness and perhaps about saying that he has already come: "Concerning the coming of our Lord Jesus Christ and our being gathered to Him, we ask you, brothers, not to become easily unsettled or alarmed by some prophecy, report or letter supposed to have come from us, saying that the day of the Lord has already come. Don't let anyone deceive you in any way, for that day will not come **until** the rebellion occurs and the man of lawlessness is revealed, the man doomed to destruction. He will oppose and will exalt himself over everything that is called God or is worshipped, so that he sets himself **up in God's temple**, proclaiming himself to be God. Don't you remember that when I was with you I used to tell you these things? And now you know what is holding him back, so that he may be revealed at the **proper time**. For the secret **power of lawlessness** is already at work; **but** the one who now holds it back will continue to do so till he is taken out of the way. **And then the lawless one** will be revealed, whom the Lord Jesus will overthrow with the breath of His mouth and destroy by the **splendor of His coming** [Must be future]. The coming of the lawless one will be in accordance with the work of Satan displayed in all kinds of **counterfeit miracles, signs and wonders** [did Nero do this?], and in every sort of evil that deceives those who are perishing. They perish because they refused to love the truth and so be saved. For this reason God sends them a powerful delusion so that they will believe the lie and so that all will be condemned who have not believed the truth but have delighted in wickedness" (2 Th 2:1-12).

The bottom line seems to be that historically these ten kings make sense. However, futuristically they could make sense as well. The many foreshadowings of Scripture leave it open that the ten historical kings of Rome merely typified the ten kings to come at the end. Repeatedly, Scripture tells us of events that only partially fulfill a prophecy because they are simply pointing to a greater fulfillment.

Rev 17:12 "The ten horns you saw are ten kings who have not yet received a kingdom, but who for one hour will receive authority as kings along with the beast. 17:13 They have one purpose and will give their power and authority to the beast. 17:14 They will make war against the Lamb, but the Lamb will overcome them because he is Lord of lords and King of kings--and with him will be his called, chosen and faithful followers."

If the ten horns and heads are kings there are a total of 17 kings involved in these end times. This could easily be a world power through the United Nations, however, Scripture does not say that for sure so we will assume not for now. We can only leave it in the back of our minds as we watch events progress closer to these days described. One thing is for sure, when the time comes, you won't have to wonder.

These ten kings give the beast their authority and their loyalty to him. Again, it seems that the beast will be a leader whom everyone trusts and looks to for deliverance of some kind. However, they will only rule for one hour, or a very short time, because God will destroy them (see 18:10,17,19).

One act of loyalty to the beast is the battle against Christ. Jesus, however, remains triumphant because He is the Supreme authority. As we will see in chapter 19, He overcomes the beast and his followers by the Sword of His mouth (Word of God - Heb 4:12). Indeed the saints will come with Him because we have been given authority from God Himself, the King of all kings and the Lord of all lords (see Dan 2:487, Deut 10:17, Psa 136:3 and 1 Tim 6:15). After all, "Do you not know that the saints will judge the world" (1 Cor 6:2)? Also, "Enoch, the seventh from Adam, prophesied about these men: 'See, the Lord is coming with thousands upon thousands of His holy ones to judge everyone, and to convict all the ungodly of all the ungodly acts they have done in the ungodly way, and of all the harsh words ungodly sinners have spoken against Him'" (Jude 1:14-15). This is what Daniel spoke of when he prophesied of the Antichrist, "He will cause deceit to prosper, and he will consider himself superior. When they feel secure, he will destroy many and take his stand against the Prince of princes. Yet he will be destroyed, but not by human power" (Dan 8:25).

Another reason to believe that these kings are demon possessed comes from chapter 16 where we saw, "They are spirits of demons performing miraculous signs, and they go out to the kings of the whole world, to gather them for the battle on the great day of God Almighty" (Rev 16:14). In all of this we need to remember the words of Jesus: "I have told you these things, so that in Me you may have peace. In this world you will have trouble. But take heart! I have overcome the world" (John 16:33).

Rev 17:15 Then the angel said to me, "The waters you saw, where the prostitute sits, are peoples, multitudes, nations and languages. 17:16 The beast and the ten horns you saw will hate the prostitute. They will bring her to ruin and leave her naked; they will eat her flesh and burn her with fire. 17:17 For God has put it into their hearts to accomplish his purpose by agreeing to give the beast their power to rule, until God's words are fulfilled. 17:18 The woman you saw is the great city that rules over the kings of the earth."

Because the waters on which the prostitute sits are many people of all nations, this may suggest that this empire controls the world, or at least is the central command for it. Since the woman is the spiritual side of this chapter it could possibly be interpreted as the Vatican, which is extremely powerful worldwide, and also very involved politically. The beast represents the political side of this chapter and will be involved in world government, which is something the Scriptures say is coming. It doesn't take a politician to see how our world is indeed headed for this united force. It has been planned for years and is becoming more of a reality all the time with the United Nations. Whether the UN will continue, fail or grow we do not know, but one thing is for sure, there will be a world government that unites all the kings together.

The beast and the kings under him will hate the woman or prostitute. We discussed how this woman was spiritual in nature, though prostituting herself against God, her groom. The Antichrist is political in nature, and though for a time will appeal to and befriend the woman, he will eventually turn on her and devour her. We see in verse 17 that this is what God had planned. The church organization and city represented by the woman will hand over her power to the beast. Whether out of necessity or desire we are not told, but we just saw that the woman has a lot of power because she sits on "many waters" or many nations. Therefore, when the political force also gains religious control, a one world government will take place. You can be sure that this will not be a republic or a democracy. However, this will only be until God's Word is established by bringing the ultimate and final destruction of the kingdom of Babylon and her king; Satan.

When the beast takes control Scripture says that he will bring the woman to her ruin and leave her naked. Ezekiel prophesied that God promised to do just that to those who prostitute themselves against Him: "Therefore I am going to gather all your lovers, with whom you found pleasure, those you loved as well as those you hated. I will gather them against you from all around and will strip you in front of them, and they will see all your nakedness. I will sentence you to the punishment of women who commit adultery and who shed blood; I will bring upon you the blood vengeance of My wrath and jealous anger" (Ezek 16:37-38).

The chapter closes by telling us that the woman is the "great city" that rules over the earth. Scripture calls this city Babylon (see 18:19) and we will see its destruction in the next chapter. Though it is the beast that turns on her, it is no doubt God's divine judgment. Jeremiah tells us, "This is what the LORD Almighty, the God of Israel, says: I am about to fulfill My words against this city through disaster, not prosperity. At that time they will be fulfilled before your eyes" (Jer 39:16). Just as Jonah symbolically foretold of Jesus's death and resurrection, the Old Testament Babylonian events were all symbolic of the Babylon of the end times.

CHAPTER 18

Rev 18:1 After this I saw another angel coming down from heaven. He had great authority, and the earth was illuminated by his splendor. 18:2 With a mighty voice he shouted: "Fallen! Fallen is Babylon the Great! She has become a home for demons and a haunt for every evil spirit, a haunt for every unclean and detestable bird. 18:3 For all the nations have drunk the maddening wine of her adulteries. The kings of the earth committed adultery with her, and the merchants of the earth grew rich from her excessive luxuries."

Chapter eighteen now shows us a descriptive view of the destruction that God said was coming upon the woman as foretold in chapter 17. The announcement of her fall is made by an angel that has such great splendor, that the whole earth is illuminated. This can only be Christ, the light of the world. As already discussed in earlier chapters, often times the "angel of the Lord" in Old Testament times was Jesus. In Exodus 34:29 we see the face of Moses glowed because he had seen God's glory. Psalms tells us, "He wraps Himself in light as with a garment" (Psa 104:2). Timothy also declared of God, "Who alone is immortal and who lives in unapproachable light, whom no one has seen or can see. To Him be honor and might forever. Amen" (1 Tim 6:16).

Fallen is Babylon! The message that so many prophets had proclaimed has now reached its final fulfillment. It has become desolate and a home for jackals: "So desert creatures and hyenas will live there, and there the owl will dwell. It will never again be inhabited or lived in from generation to generation," (Jer 50:39), and "Babylon will be a heap of ruins, a haunt of jackals, an object of horror and scorn, a place where no one lives" (Jer 51:37, see also Is 13:21, 34:11-15, and Zeph 2:14-15). All of these things seem to point to unclean things, more specifically, demons or evil spirits. Verse two makes reference to detestable birds. Many times in Scripture we see that birds represent Satan or his demons. We see in the parable of the sower that birds tried to eat up the seed that was sown (Mark 4:4). The seed represented God's Word. When God was going to give Abram His covenant, the birds of prey (unclean birds- Lev 11) tried to keep it from happening (Gen 15:11).

The nations were led astray by Babylon and her alluring idolatries. We have already discussed much of this in the section on 14:8 so we will not go into great detail. Suffice it to say that the nations were drunk on moral corruption that was readily available in Babylon (Ezek 27:9-25, Rev 17:2). They lavished themselves in material things and earthly treasures, failing to listen to the warnings of Jesus, "Do not store up for yourselves treasures on earth, where moth and rust destroy, and where thieves break in and steal" (Mat 6:19). Eventually, they became so distracted by things that they no longer had time for Christ. They kept drinking sin in to quench the desires of the flesh. As Luke shows us, when Christ comes many will perish, because while He was away they were too caught up in worldly cares to follow Him: "A certain man was preparing a great banquet and invited many guests. At the time of the banquet He sent His servant to tell those who had been invited, 'Come, for everything is now ready.' But they all alike began to make excuses. The first said, 'I have just bought a field, and I must go and see it. Please excuse me.' Another said, 'I have just bought five yoke of oxen, and I'm on my way to try them out. Please excuse me.' Still another said, 'I just got married, so I can't come'" (Luke 14:16-20). Let us not make our world, our country, our workplace, our home, or our body a desolate home for demons. It is too easy to get to busy with our lives and forget about God.

Rev 18:4 Then I heard another voice from heaven say: "Come out of her, my people, so that you will not share in her sins, so that you will not receive any of her plagues; 18:5 for her sins are piled up to heaven, and God has remembered her crimes. 18:6 Give back to her as she has given; pay her back double for what she has done. Mix her a double portion from her own cup. 18:7 Give her as much torture and grief as the glory and luxury she gave herself. In her heart she boasts, 'I sit as queen; I am not a widow, and I will never mourn.' 18:8 Therefore in one day her plagues will overtake her: death, mourning and famine. She will be consumed by fire, for mighty is the Lord God who judges her.

Verse four echoes Jeremiah who wrote about the inhabitants of Babylon: "Come out of her, My people! Run for your lives! Run from the fierce anger of the LORD" (Jer 51:45). The comforting thing is God has promised to deliver His people and they will praise Him for their deliverance. In Isaiah we read, "Leave Babylon, flee from the Babylonians! Announce this with shouts of joy and proclaim it. Send it out to the ends of the earth; say, 'The LORD has redeemed His servant Jacob'" (Isa 48:20). Even in the New Testament we see warnings about living in the midst of sinners. Paul wrote to the Corinthians, "What agreement is there between the temple of God and idols? For we are the temple of the living God. As God has said: 'I will live with them and walk among them, and I will be their God, and they will be My people. Therefore come out from them and be separate'" (2 Cor 6:16-17). We know that when Lot lived among the Sodomites, his family was affected by the cup of their sins. Out of ten people in his family, only two survived. The rest perished because they refused to "come out of her." We read in Genesis, "With the coming of dawn, the angels urged Lot, saying, 'Hurry! Take your wife and your two daughters who are here, or you will be swept away when the city is punished'" (Gen 19:15). Other verses warning to flee from Babylon follow:

- "Flee from Babylon! Run for your lives! Do not be destroyed because of her sins. It is time for the Lord's vengeance; He will pay her what she deserves" (Jer 51:6).
- "Flee out of Babylon; leave the land of the Babylonians, and be like the goats that lead the flock. For I will stir up and bring against Babylon an alliance of great nations from the land of the north. They will take up their positions against her, and from the north she will be captured.

Their arrows will be like skilled warriors who do not return empty-handed. So Babylonia will be plundered" (Jer 50:8-10).

- "The LORD will lay bare His holy arm in the sight of all the nations, and all the ends of the earth will see the salvation of our God. Depart, depart, go out from there! Touch no unclean thing! Come out from it and be pure, you who carry the vessels of the LORD. But you will not leave in haste or go in flight; for the LORD will go before you" (Isa 52:10-12).

Verse five tells us why we are to flee from the seat of the woman. Jeremiah also said the same: "We would have healed Babylon, but she cannot be healed; let us leave her and each go to his own land, for her judgment reaches to the skies, it rises as high as the clouds" (Jer 51:9).

If we continue to read on in Jeremiah 50 and 51 we see that Revelation 18 is almost the same text. Verse six sounds much the same: "Shout against her on every side! She surrenders, her towers fall, her walls are torn down. Since this is the vengeance of the LORD, take vengeance on her; do to her as she has done to others" (Jer 50:15). Similarly, the Psalmist writes, "O Daughter of Babylon, doomed to destruction, happy is He who repays you for what you have done to us—" (Psa 137:8). Verse six says that Babylon would receive a double portion from her "own cup." Simply put, she will have double trouble as we saw what was in her cup earlier, "The woman was dressed in purple and scarlet, and was glittering with gold, precious stones and pearls. She held a golden cup in her hand, filled with abominable things and the filth of her adulteries" (Rev 17:4).

Babylon will have the heart of Satan (Eze 28:2-8) and will be boastfully proud as the ungodly are, "He says to himself, 'Nothing will shake me; I'll always be happy and never have trouble'" (Psa 10:6). This is a sobering thought for us here in America who have much the same attitude. Zephaniah could be speaking to the U.S. when we writes, "This is the carefree city that lived in safety. She said to herself, 'I am, and there is none besides me.' What a ruin she has become, a lair for wild beasts! All who pass by her scoff and shake their fists. Woe to the city of oppressors, rebellious and defiled" (Zep 2:15 –16)! She boasts about sitting as Queen and never being a widow. If there are any doubts that the Old Testament prophecies foretold of these events, Isaiah puts them to rest, "You said, 'I will continue forever-- the eternal queen!' But you did not consider these things or reflect on what might happen. Now then, listen, you wanton creature, lounging in your security and saying to yourself, 'I am, and there is none besides me. I will never be a widow or suffer the loss of children'" (Isa 47:7-8).

All of this will take place in a single day just as Isaiah had also said, "Both of these will overtake you in a moment, on a single day: loss of children and widowhood. They will come upon you in full measure, in spite of your many sorceries and all your potent spells" (Isa 47:9; see also Jer 50:31-32). History tells us that this is true. Over and over in God's judgments upon sinful nations, prosperity was one of their last calls to repentance. Instead of giving God thanks for His gifts, they became accustomed to luxury and were distracted away from God. When everyone was on top of the world financially and politically, God brought them to their destruction quickly. Even Luke tells us this will happen in the last days, "While people are saying, 'Peace and safety,' destruction will come on them suddenly, as labor pains on a pregnant woman, and they will not escape. But you, brothers, are not in darkness so that this day should surprise you like a thief" (1 Th 5:3-4). We would do well to listen to this passage. YOU brothers should not be surprised if you are in God's Word. He will show you the times are near and His Holy Spirit will keep you from being distracted by the cares of this world that keep us from seeing the handwriting on the wall. May God's Wisdom be on you all!

Rev 18:9 "When the kings of the earth who committed adultery with her and shared her luxury see the smoke of her burning, they will weep and mourn over her. 18:10 Terrified at her torment, they will stand far off and cry: "'Woe! Woe, O great city, O Babylon, city of power! In one hour your doom has come!'

When those who had participated with the adulteries of the woman see her destruction, they will mourn over her. Note, they will not mourn for her, but over her. The weeping will be for themselves because they selfishly turn inward to see what opportunities, entertainment and perhaps financial possibilities they have lost.

At the same time they will be terrified because of her torment. They will be shocked that such a great power could be destroyed, let alone in one hour, and they will now stand leaderless. The torment itself will send chills up the spine of all who witness this great event. The smoke of her burning will never end, showing that this was her eternal judgment (see 19:3).

Rev 18:11 "The merchants of the earth will weep and mourn over her because no one buys their cargoes any more-- 18:12 cargoes of gold, silver, precious stones and pearls; fine linen, purple, silk and scarlet cloth; every sort of citron wood, and articles of every kind made of ivory, costly wood, bronze, iron and marble; 18:13 cargoes of cinnamon and spice, of incense, myrrh and frankincense, of wine and olive oil, of fine flour and wheat; cattle and sheep; horses and carriages; and bodies and souls of men.

Verse eleven shows the true reason for the mourning over Babylon. Greed and selfishness, the very thing that caused this judgment will continue on.

A long list of merchandise is listed in verses 12 and 13, but the item that stands out is the last object of trade – the souls of men. The very life of man was being sold to the devil as people traded material wealth and worldly pleasures for true riches and an eternal life of love, joy and peace.

The list of things mentioned is not as important as the general theme they all possess, that being wealth. All these items are "costly" and show man's true god in Babylon was money and self. Ezekiel 27 also shows the great wealth of Babylon, foreshadowing this event here.

Rev 18:14 "They will say, 'The fruit you longed for is gone from you. All your riches and splendor have vanished, never to be recovered.' **Rev 18:15** The merchants who sold these things and gained their wealth from her will stand far off, terrified at her torment. They will weep and mourn 18:16 and cry out: "'Woe! Woe, O great city, dressed in fine linen, purple and scarlet, and glittering with gold, precious stones and pearls! 18:17 In one hour such great wealth has been brought to ruin!' "Every sea captain, and all who travel by ship, the sailors, and all who earn their living from the sea, will stand far off. 18:18 When they see the smoke of her burning, they will exclaim, 'Was there ever a city like this great city?' 18:19 They will throw dust on their heads, and with weeping and mourning cry out: "'Woe! Woe, O great city, where all who had ships on the sea became rich through her wealth! In one hour she has been brought to ruin!**

Verses 14–19 simply repeat what was already said showing the complete destruction and utter sorrow of this judgment.

The seamen, as well as those on the land, will be terrified as their source of food literally falls. They will throw dust on their heads in mourning for themselves. They do not realize that food does not come from their work, but God's blessings. Ezekiel again seems to add flavor to this with his description: "The shorelands will quake when your seamen cry out. All who handle the oars will abandon their ships; the mariners and all the seamen will stand on the shore. They will raise their voice and cry bitterly over you; they will sprinkle dust on their heads and roll in ashes. They will shave their heads because of you and will put on sackcloth. They will weep over you with anguish of soul and with bitter mourning. As they wail and mourn over you, they will take up a lament concerning you: 'Who was ever silenced like Tyre, *surrounded by the sea?*' When your merchandise went out on the seas, you satisfied many nations; with your great wealth and your wares you enriched the kings of the earth. Now you are shattered by the sea in the depths of the waters; your wares and all your company have gone down with you. All who live in the coastlands are appalled at you; their kings shudder with horror and their faces are distorted with fear. The merchants among the nations hiss at you; you have come to a horrible end and will be no more" (Ezek 27:28-36). It is interesting that in Ezekiel it mentions that this city was "surrounded by the seas." We have been talking about the woman here in Revelation fitting the description of Rome in many ways. One more to add to the list is that Rome, as well, is surrounded by seas.

Rev 18:20 Rejoice over her, O heaven! Rejoice, saints and apostles and prophets! God has judged her for the way she treated you.'" 18:21 Then a mighty angel picked up a boulder the size of a large millstone and threw it into the sea, and said: "With such violence the great city of Babylon will be thrown down, never to be found again.

In contrast, the saints, prophets and apostles rejoice because of the woman's destruction. The prayer of the saints from chapter six has now been answered: "They called out in a loud voice, 'How long, Sovereign Lord, holy and true, until You judge the inhabitants of the earth and avenge our blood'" (Rev 6:10)? This praise of deliverance will continue with greater detail in chapter 19.

Jeremiah wrote, "'Then heaven and earth and all that is in them will shout for joy over Babylon, for out of the north destroyers will attack her,' declares the LORD" (Jer 51:48). Earlier in 17:13 we saw that the woman was going to give her power to the beast because she would trust him, however, the beast would turn on her and bring her to destruction. This is one more example of how God uses other people, (sometimes not Christian) to bring His judgments upon the world. The Jeremiah passage quoted above shows us that the beast comes out of the north. Daniel, Isaiah and Ezekiel all confirm this to be true as well (Dan 11, Ezek 26:7, Is 41:25). Therefore we can see that the beast has been identified as the Antichrist who will come out of the north.

Verse 21 shows that a mighty angel threw a large boulder into the sea as a sign or symbol of Babylon's destruction. In case there is still doubt that the Old Testament prophets were only talking about the Babylon of their day, Jeremiah wrote, "When you finish reading this scroll, tie a stone to it and throw it into the Euphrates. Then say, 'So will Babylon sink to rise no more because of the disaster I will bring upon her. And her people will fall.' The words of Jeremiah end here" (Jer 51:63-64).

Rev 18:22 The music of harpists and musicians, flute players and trumpeters, will never be heard in you again. No workman of any trade will ever be found in you again. The sound of a millstone will never be heard in you again. 18:23 The light of a lamp will never shine in you again. The voice of bridegroom and bride will never be heard in you again. Your merchants were the world's great men. By your magic spell all the nations were led astray. 18:24 In her was found the blood of prophets and of the saints, and of all who have been killed on the earth."

Verse 22 shows the joy of Babylon is gone even though the saints have now received their joy. Isaiah talks about this joy of the saints and the utter sorrow of the unbelievers at the destruction of Babylon:

> "The gaiety of the tambourines is stilled, the noise of the revelers has stopped, the joyful harp is silent. No longer do they drink wine with a song; the beer is bitter to its drinkers. The ruined city lies desolate; the entrance to every house is barred. In the streets they cry out for wine; all joy turns to gloom, all gaiety is banished from the earth. The city is left in ruins, its gate is battered to pieces. So will it be on the earth and among the nations, as *when an olive tree is beaten, or as when gleanings are left after the grape harvest* [remember the harvest of Revelation 14:14ff] They raise their voices, they shout for joy; *from the west* they acclaim the Lord's majesty. Therefore in the east give glory to the LORD; exalt the name of the LORD, the God of Israel, in the

islands of the sea. From the ends of the earth we hear singing: 'Glory to the Righteous One'" (Isa 24:8-16).

We also read in Ezekiel:

"I will put an end to your noisy songs, and the music of your harps will be heard no more. I will make you a bare rock, and you will become a place to spread fishnets. You will never be rebuilt, for I the LORD have spoken, declares the Sovereign LORD. This is what the Sovereign LORD says to Tyre: Will not the coastlands tremble at the sound of your fall, when the wounded groan and the slaughter takes place in you? Then all the princes of the coast will step down from their thrones and lay aside their robes and take off their embroidered garments. Clothed with terror, they will sit on the ground, trembling every moment, appalled at you. Then they will take up a lament concerning you and say to you: 'How you are destroyed, O city of renown, peopled by men of the sea! You were a power on the seas, you and your citizens; you put your terror on all who lived there. Now the coastlands tremble on the day of your fall; the islands in the sea are terrified at your collapse.' This is what the Sovereign LORD says: 'When I make you a desolate city, like cities no longer inhabited, and when I bring the ocean depths over you and its vast waters cover you, then I will bring you down with those who go down to the pit, to the people of long ago. I will make you dwell in the earth below, as in ancient ruins, with those who go down to the pit, and you will not return or take your place in the land of the living. I will bring you to a horrible end and you will be no more. You will be sought, but you will never again be found, declares the Sovereign LORD'" (Ezek 26:13-21).

Regarding the light of the lamp and the joy of marriage in verse 23 Jeremiah wrote, "I will banish from them the sounds of joy and gladness, the voices of bride and bridegroom, the sound of millstones and the light of the lamp" (Jer 25:10). Also, "I will bring an end to the sounds of joy and gladness and to the voices of bride and bridegroom in the towns of Judah and the streets of Jerusalem, for the land will become desolate" (Jer 7:34). And, "For this is what the LORD Almighty, the God of Israel, says: Before your eyes and in your days I will bring an end to the sounds of joy and gladness and to the voices of bride and bridegroom in this place" (Jer 16:9). I believe that the lack of the voice of the bridegroom has deeper meaning. Understanding that God is talking about the final doom of Babylon we see that God will never be their voice or help again. The Scriptures make it very clear that the church is the bride and Christ is the Bridegroom. Nahum wrote, "all because of the wanton lust of a harlot, alluring, the mistress of sorceries, who enslaved nations by her prostitution and peoples by her witchcraft. 'I am against you,' declares the LORD Almighty" (Nahum 3:4-5).

Once more God gives reason for His judgment on this city in verse 24. Because she shed the blood of the saints, she, too, will have her blood shed.

Jeremiah said, "Babylon must fall because of Israel's slain, just as the slain in all the earth have fallen because of Babylon" (Jer 51:49). Note that God is not judging the blood shed only in the last days, but the blood of all the righteous men that ever walked the earth. As it states in Matthew, "And so upon you will come all the righteous blood that has been shed on earth, from the blood of righteous Abel to the blood of Zechariah son of Berekiah, whom you murdered between the temple and the altar" (Mat 23:35). The Hebrew Bible begins with Genesis (where Abel was killed) and ends in 2 Chronicles (where Zechariah was killed). All others books of the Bible are placed between Genesis and 2 Chronicles. Therefore, God is saying that from A to Z or from the beginning of time (Genesis) to the end (2 Chronicles), ALL the righteous blood is being avenged.

CHAPTER 19

Section 6 (Revelation 19:1-22:21)
The Believer's Hope

Rev 19:1 After this I heard what sounded like the roar of a great multitude in heaven shouting: "Hallelujah! Salvation and glory and power belong to our God, 19:2 for true and just are his judgments. He has condemned the great prostitute who corrupted the earth by her adulteries. He has avenged on her the blood of his servants." 19:3 And again they shouted: "Hallelujah! The smoke from her goes up for ever and ever."

Whereas chapter 18 focused on judgment, chapter 19 now focuses on salvation. Chapters 12-18 can get somewhat gloomy, so chapters 19-22 are quite refreshing.

"After this," implies after the fall of Babylon. There was heard a great roar of a multitude of voices in heaven shouting and praising God for their deliverance. It was by the blood of Christ that the blood of the saints had been avenged. Not only did salvation belong to God, but also glory and power. It is interesting the word *hallelujah* does not appear anywhere else in the New Testament outside of Revelation. Here, we will see it used four times in the first six verses of chapter 19. This praise is certainly not without merit as we saw from chapter four, "You are worthy, our Lord and God, to receive glory and honor and power, for You created all things, and by Your will they were created and have their being" (Rev 4:11).

God's judgments are true and just, as we saw this proclamation come from the altar in 16:7. Christ condemned the great prostitute (17:1) and we saw a description of her destruction in chapter 18. Therefore, it is easy to see how these chapters form one simple theme of God's judgment and salvation.

We see that the prostitute will never be restored, her judgment was final in this, the last hour. Isaiah wrote of this eternal torment when he recorded, "It will not be quenched night and day; its smoke will rise forever" (Isa 34:10, see also Rev 14:11).

Rev 19:4 The twenty-four elders and the four living creatures fell down and worshipped God, who was seated on the throne. And they cried: "Amen, Hallelujah!" 19:5 Then a voice came from the throne, saying: "Praise our God, all you his servants, you who fear him, both small and great!"

At the sound of these praises, the 24 elders and the living creatures (4:4-6) fell down and worshipped God; the Judge sitting on His throne. This will be the last time we see the elders in Revelation. They cry out "AMEN," that is to agree with the praises given by the voice of the multitude in the first three verses. Amen means, "it shall be so," or "it is true."

From the throne came a voice, probably from one of the four living creatures, telling all those in heaven to praise God because a long awaited and joyous celebration is about to take place; a celebration that only God could give through the death and resurrection of the Lamb. It made no difference what their status was, small or great, they all praised Him for their salvation as promised, "He will bless those who fear the LORD-- small and great alike" (Psa 115:13, see also Rev 20:12).

Rev 19:6 Then I heard what sounded like a great multitude, like the roar of rushing waters and like loud peals of thunder, shouting: "Hallelujah! For our Lord God Almighty reigns. 19:7 Let us rejoice and be glad and give him glory! For the wedding of the Lamb has come, and his bride has made herself ready. 19:8 Fine linen, bright and clean, was given her to wear." (Fine linen stands for the righteous acts of the saints.)

Again, the voice like a multitude, full of power, shouted, Hallelujah! Once more the living creatures are probably the source of this praise. The reason for this praise was that God was reigning. No longer was He only *coming*, He *had come* and was ruling in His kingdom. There is much rejoicing going on because the long awaited wedding ceremony has come. The wedding banquet of the Lamb when the Bride (Church) becomes one in a very literal sense with the Bride-groom (Christ).

When will this take place? It seems right at the blowing of the seventh trumpet as we saw back in chapter 11, where we read, "The kingdom of the world has become the kingdom of our Lord and of His Christ, and He will reign for ever and ever" (Rev 11:15).

We are being presented with white linen, which represents our righteous acts. Note it is not just righteousness, but righteous acts that come in response to our righteousness. Just as a bride was to wear a white wedding dress only if she were a virgin, so, too, we are being presented to Christ as virgins. It is as Paul said, "I am jealous for you with a godly jealousy. I promised you to one Husband, to Christ, so that I might present you as a pure virgin to Him" (2 Cor 11:2). Also, it is neat to see that even the angels have this white linen to wear (Rev 15:6).

Once more Revelation makes the parable promises of the New Testament so much more vivid and tangible. We see many times this wedding banquet is foretold. In Matthew we read about the ten virgins:

> "At that time the kingdom of heaven will be like ten virgins who took their lamps and went out to meet the bridegroom. Five of them were foolish and five were wise. The foolish ones took their lamps but did not take any oil with them. The wise, however, took oil in jars along with their lamps. The Bridegroom was a long time in coming, and they all became drowsy and fell asleep. At midnight the cry rang out: 'Here's

the Bridegroom! Come out to meet him!' Then all the virgins woke up and trimmed their lamps. The foolish ones said to the wise, 'Give us some of your oil; our lamps are going out.' 'No,' they replied, 'there may not be enough for both us and you. Instead, go to those who sell oil and buy some for yourselves.' But while they were on their way to buy the oil, the Bridegroom arrived. The virgins who were ready went in with him to the wedding banquet. And the door was shut. Later the others also came. 'Sir! Sir!' they said. 'Open the door for us!' But He replied, 'I tell you the truth, I don't know you'" (Mat 25:1-12).

In this parable we see that the bride waits anxiously for the Groom to come. Those that do not keep ready will not be allowed into the kingdom of heaven. You see, there is a real wedding coming and it is easy for us to think of it as a nice story so that we forget about its truth and become impatient or tired. This aspect is given in detail as well as the significance and importance of the white linen in the parable of the wedding banquet:

"The kingdom of heaven is like a king who prepared a wedding banquet for his son. He sent his servants to those who had been invited to the banquet to tell them to come, but they refused to come. Then he sent some more servants and said, 'Tell those who have been invited that I have prepared my dinner: My oxen and fattened cattle have been butchered, and everything is ready. Come to the wedding banquet.' But they paid no attention and went off--one to his field, another to his business. The rest seized his servants, mistreated them and killed them. The king was enraged. He sent his army and destroyed those murderers and burned their city. Then he said to his servants, 'The wedding banquet is ready, but those I invited did not deserve to come. Go to the street corners and invite to the banquet anyone you find.' So the servants went out into the streets and gathered all the people they could find, both good and bad, and the wedding hall was filled with guests. But when the king came in to see the guests, he noticed a man there who was not wearing wedding clothes. 'Friend,' he asked, 'how did you get in here without wedding clothes?' The man was speechless. Then the king told the attendants, 'Tie him hand and foot, and throw him outside, into the darkness, where there will be weeping and gnashing of teeth.' For many are invited, but few are chosen" (Mat 22:2-14).

Without the righteous acts that come from being righteous through the blood of Christ, hell is our destination. No unclean thing can enter heaven or else it wouldn't be heaven. We must be cleansed and made pure before we can get married. Therefore, white linen was given, clearly robes of salvation for us, as Isaiah tells us: "I delight greatly in the LORD; my soul rejoices in my God. For He has clothed me with garments of salvation and arrayed me in a robe of righteousness, as a bridegroom adorns His head like a priest, and as a bride adorns herself with her jewels" (Isa 61:10). We talked earlier about the Old Testament tabernacle foreshadowing heaven. Even the priests could not enter into the tabernacle without these white linen robes of righteousness: "When they enter the gates of the inner court, they are to wear linen clothes; they must not wear any woolen garment while ministering at the gates of the inner court or inside the temple" (Ezek 44:17). Nothing is without meaning in the Scriptures. God uses literal items with symbolic meaning. Even in Zecheriah we see this picture of clothing being cleansed, "The angel said to those who were standing before Him, 'Take off his filthy clothes.' Then He said to Joshua, 'See, I have taken away your sin, and I will put rich garments on you'" (Zec 3:4). What a beautiful gift for a wedding.

Earlier in 3:12 we saw that those who overcame the world were to be made permanent pillars in the new Temple God was going to make. We will see that God is the Temple in the new Jerusalem that comes down out of heaven (Rev 21:22). This is what the wedding banquet of the Lamb does, it makes us permanent pillars in Christ. We will see in chapter 21, "I saw the Holy City, the new Jerusalem, coming down out of heaven from God, prepared as a bride beautifully dressed for her husband" (Rev 21:2). See the section on 3:12 for other New Testament verses dealing with this glorious union. If you think about it, in an earthly marriage the bride also gets a new name just as we will in heaven (2:11). Marriage on earth is a beautiful foreshadowing of a greater marriage to come. It is sad that the world does not view a marriage like that today, but even the Scriptures say of marriage, "For this reason a man will leave his father and mother and be united to his wife, and the two will become one flesh. This is a profound mystery--but I am talking about Christ and the church" (Eph 5:31-32). Though a mystery, it is plain to see we will be united with Christ as one in the Spirit, and one in the Lord.

Rev 19:9 Then the angel said to me, "Write: 'Blessed are those who are invited to the wedding supper of the Lamb!'" And he added, "These are the true words of God." 19:10 At this I fell at his feet to worship him. But he said to me, "Do not do it! I am a fellow servant with you and with your brothers who hold to the testimony of Jesus. Worship God! For the testimony of Jesus is the spirit of prophecy."

After John saw the heavenly wedding banquet, he was instructed to write down a message to the seven churches, including us. The message was a word of encouragement showing that all who are invited to the wedding supper are blessed. As we saw from the parable of the wedding banquet, many were invited, but not all came. Therefore, since John had just observed the wedding taking place, he must only be referring to all those that were invited AND came. Before Jesus began telling this parable, others recognized what a blessing this day would be: "When one of those at the table with Him heard this, he said to Jesus, 'Blessed is the man who will eat at the feast in the kingdom of God'" (Luke 14:15).

These words are not John's, but God's and, therefore, true. Upon hearing this John fell down at the feet of the angel to worship, but the angel quickly warned not to do it because, as an angel, he was a servant just like John himself. Only God was to be worshipped. It seems strange that John would do this. Some suggest that John maybe didn't know it was an angel and thought it was God. This is possible since in 7:4 John didn't know who the saints were. However, it still seems strange that he wouldn't recognize the angel because he is in the spirit and in tune with pretty much everything else that is going on. Though in the spirit, he is still flesh and could have been caught up in it all. Not only did John begin bowing before an angel here, but also in chapter 22:8. Therefore, I tend to think God did have John confused as to who was who and allowed this to happen so that he could send us a message today. In a world of saint worship and "spiritual" awareness through which the dead are contacted (viewed as either spirits, aliens, or highly evolved beings), it serves as a great verse to show GOD ONLY is to be worshipped and prayed to. If angels do not deserve prayer and worship, no man, dead or alive, should receive them either.

The verse closes by saying that preaching about Christ is the spirit of prophecy. Indeed Christ is the Beginning and the End, the Alpha and the Omega, the First and the Last and, therefore, preaching about Jesus is what prophecy is all about. Prophecy is the telling of future events and understanding present situations and needs as they affect our eternity. Jesus is the center of all our needs in every situation for an eternal future. The spirit of prophecy is 100% truth. Yet Jesus said, "I am the way and the truth and the life. No one comes to the Father except through Me" (John 14:6). Therefore, do not get caught up in end time prophecies centered on which country will do what, and who the Antichrist is going to be, etc.. Instead, look deeply into the blessing of the great invitation that has been given for the wedding of the Lamb. He is the center of this prophecy. Even the beginning of Revelation stated that this was the "Revelation of Jesus Christ" (Rev 1:1). This book is not about angels, horses, seals, or trumpets, but about God's salvation through His Son, Jesus Christ. Praise be to GOD!!!!!!

Rev 19:11 I saw heaven standing open and there before me was a white horse, whose rider is called Faithful and True. With justice he judges and makes war.

With the reminder of verse ten that Jesus is the center of prophecy, we now see Him coming on a white horse. Earlier we saw a white horse coming with the first seal. That was the Antichrist wearing a different type of crown (see note on first seal). We are told very clearly that this is the true Christ because He is the Faithful and True, who was earlier identified as Christ (Rev 3:14). In addition, the description of verse 16 can be none other than Jesus, our Lord. Christ is being faithful in that He is keeping His promise to come back, to judge and to redeem. Jesus is true because He is the only real or true God, not like the Antichrist will claim to be.

It is also noted that Christ judges and makes war. This is not the type of Christ-like figure that most think of when they picture Jesus, but that is exactly who He is – a loving Savior and a harsh Judge, the Lion and the Lamb. Many believe that the wars in the Old Testament are evidence that the Bible is not inspired because any loving God would not kill like that. A loving Judge would. It says here in verse 11 that with justice He makes war. His judgments are not without cause or unjust. In Genesis, Abraham was not allowed to enter the promised land right away because, "the sin of the Amorites has not yet reached its full measure" (Gen 15:16). God would not judge them at that time because there were still some Amorites that believed in God, and He loved them. However, once the time had come when all had rejected Him, Christ had to justly judge them. He could have just rained down fire and brimstone, but instead He used the Israelites as His instrument of judgment. I personally believe that this is to foreshadow end times as well. God will do the same thing once more. He is coming not to just judge a few nations, but to judge the world. However, He will not do so until the Gospel is "preached to all nations" (Mark 13:10). Once the sin of this world reaches its full measure He will come to destroy it and all the unbelievers, just as He did before in the Old Testament. Once again, He will use us, His saints, as instruments in this judgment, as we will see in verse 14. Therefore as Moses said of God, "The LORD is a warrior; the LORD is His name" (Exo 15:3).

The only way to be just is to be true. That is why He is called the Faithful and True. We read in Psalms, "They will sing before the LORD, for He comes, He comes to judge the earth. He will judge the world in righteousness and the peoples in His truth" (Psa 96:13). In other words, it is the Word of God that will judge the nations. We know that "In the beginning was the Word, and the Word was with God, and the Word was God. . . .that Word became flesh" (John 1:1,14). Not only is Christ the "Word of God," but also Truth itself: "I am the Way and the Truth and the Life" (John 14:6). Therefore, the Word is truth, which is why Isaiah writes, "with righteousness He will judge the needy, with justice He will give decisions for the poor of the earth. He will strike the earth with the rod of His mouth; with the breath of His lips He will slay the wicked" (Isa 11:4). In verse 15 we see that it is the sharp sword (God's truthful Word – Heb 4:12) that strikes men down. We have that Word with us today in the Holy Scriptures and, therefore, have a measuring rod for truth, for right and wrong. There will be no excuse for those who deliberately go against, or do not follow the Bible.

Rev 19:12 His eyes are like blazing fire, and on his head are many crowns. He has a name written on him that no one knows but he himself. 19:13 He is dressed in a robe dipped in blood, and his name is the Word of God.

Now we have a greater description of Christ on this white horse. Similar to what John saw when Christ was coming to take His seat on the judgment throne, His eyes are like blazing fire. This shows His intent is to judge and make war. He has many crowns on His head showing Him to be King of kings. As we mentioned in the section on 6:2, the Antichrist imitates this, however, the crowns are different.

Christ, as well, has a new name written on Himself that only He knows. This is the same proclamation that was promised to all the saints: "He who has an ear, let him hear what the Spirit says to the churches. To him who overcomes,

I will give some of the hidden manna. I will also give him a white stone with a new name written on it, known only to him who receives it" (Rev 2:17).

In verse 13 we see that the robe of Christ had been dipped in blood, an obvious reference to His sacrifice on the cross. Some believe that the blood is not His own, but rather that of His enemies because of Isaiah: "Why are Your garments red, like those of one treading the winepress? I have trodden the winepress alone; from the nations no one was with Me. I trampled them in My anger and trod them down in My wrath; their blood spattered My garments, and I stained all My clothing" (Isa 63:2-3). Because of the fact that no one is with Him, it seems more likely that the blood is in reference to His own, which gives Him the right to judge justly (see verse 14). His name being the Word of God once again leaves no room for doubt as to who this person is (John 1:1-3).

Rev 19:14 The armies of heaven were following him, riding on white horses and dressed in fine linen, white and clean. 19:15 Out of his mouth comes a sharp sword with which to strike down the nations. "He will rule them with an iron scepter." He treads the winepress of the fury of the wrath of God Almighty. Rev 19:16 On his robe and on his thigh he has this name written: KING OF KINGS AND LORD OF LORDS.'

Coming right behind Christ on His white horse were the armies of heaven. They, too, were dressed in white linen, which as already discussed, represents their righteous acts. Earlier in chapter three we saw that those who follow Christ, "will walk with Me, dressed in white, for they are worthy" (Rev 3:4).

Out of Christ's mouth comes a sword, which is the instrument of judgment that strikes down the nations. In 1:16 we saw this image of Christ as well. Hebrews clearly tells us that God speaks and His Word is like a sword, "For the Word of God is living and active. Sharper than any double-edged sword, it penetrates even to dividing soul and spirit, joints and marrow; it judges the thoughts and attitudes of the heart. Nothing in all creation is hidden from God's sight. Everything is uncovered and laid bare before the eyes of Him to whom we must give account" (Heb 4:12-13). Even Isaiah said, "with righteousness He will judge the needy, with justice He will give decisions for the poor of the earth. He will strike the earth with the rod of His mouth; with the breath of His lips He will slay the wicked. Righteousness will be His belt and faithfulness the sash around His waist. The wolf will live with the lamb, the leopard will lie down with the goat, the calf and the lion and the yearling together; and a little child will lead them" (Isa 11:4-6). As we see from Thessalonians, one of the main people being destroyed by this sword is the Antichrist, "And then the lawless one will be revealed, whom the Lord Jesus will overthrow with the breath of His mouth and destroy by the splendor of His coming" (2 Th 2:8). In Old Testament times this sword was also active, "Assyria will fall by a sword that is not of man; a sword, not of mortals, will devour them" (Isa 31:8).

This destruction is described as God treading the winepress, an image already discussed in 14:14.

Christ will rule with an iron scepter just as prophesied, "She gave birth to a son, a male child, who will rule all the nations with an iron scepter. And her child was snatched up to God and to His throne" (Rev 12:5). Even the Psalmist recorded such a vision, "You will rule them with an iron scepter; You will dash them to pieces like pottery" (Psa 2:9). There can be no question that this is the ultimate destruction and judgment of the wicked.

As for the white armies following, we know that the saints will judge the world. Many Scripture passages show this to be true. Consider the following and glean other details about this glorious day:

- "Enoch, the seventh from Adam, prophesied about these men: 'See, the Lord is coming **with** thousands upon thousands of His holy ones to judge everyone, and to convict all the ungodly of all the ungodly acts they have done in the ungodly way, and of all the harsh words ungodly sinners have spoken against Him" (Jude 14,15).
- "Then the LORD will go out and fight against those nations, as He fights in the day of battle. On that day His feet will stand on the Mount of Olives, east of Jerusalem, and the Mount of Olives will be split in two from east to west, forming a great valley, with half of the mountain moving north and half moving south. You will flee by My mountain valley, for it will extend to Azel. You will flee as you fled from the earthquake in the days of Uzziah king of Judah. Then the LORD My God will come, and **all the holy ones with Him.** On that day there will be no light, no cold or frost. It will be a unique day, without daytime or nighttime--a day known to the LORD. When evening comes, there will be light. On that day living water will flow out from Jerusalem, half to the eastern sea and half to the western sea, in summer and in winter. The LORD will be King over the whole earth. On that day there will be one LORD, and His name the only name" (Zec 14:3-9).
- "May He strengthen your hearts so that you will be blameless and holy in the presence of our God and Father when our Lord Jesus comes **with all His holy ones**" (1 Th 3:13).
- "They will make war against the Lamb, but the Lamb will overcome them because He *is Lord of lords and King of kings--* **and with Him will be His called**, chosen and faithful followers" (Rev 17:14).

However, it may not just be the saints that are coming with Christ here, but also His angels. We see from Deuteronomy, "The LORD came from Sinai and dawned over them from Seir; He shone forth from Mount Paran. He came with *myriads of holy ones* from the south, from His mountain slopes" (Deu 33:2). Also from Psalms, "The chariots of God are tens of thousands and thousands of thousands; the Lord has come from Sinai into His sanctuary" (Psa 68:17).

Christ's robe and thigh bore the name "King of kings" and "Lord of lords." Again, this is not a prophetic or symbolic name, but a true one. Even Timothy said, "I charge you to keep this command without spot or blame until the appearing of our Lord Jesus Christ, which God will bring about in His own time--God, the blessed and only Ruler, the King of kings and Lord of lords, who alone is immortal and who lives in unapproachable light, whom no one has seen or can see. To Him be honor and might forever. Amen" (1 Tim 6:13-16).

Rev 19:17 And I saw an angel standing in the sun, who cried in a loud voice to all the birds flying in midair, "Come, gather together for the great supper of God, Rev 19:18 so that you may eat the flesh of kings, generals, and mighty men, of horses and their riders, and the flesh of all people, free and slave, small and great."

Next, an angel standing in the sun called out for the birds to come and eat the flesh of the unbelievers that the Rider on the white horse was about to destroy. There are many Scripture passages alluding to this event. Matthew wrote, "Wherever there is a carcass, there the vultures will gather" (Mat 24:28). Even more clearly, Ezekiel said, "Son of man, this is what the Sovereign LORD says: 'Call out to every kind of bird and all the wild animals: Assemble and come together from all around to the sacrifice I am preparing for you, the great sacrifice on the mountains of Israel. There you will eat flesh and drink blood. You will eat the flesh of mighty men and drink the blood of the princes of the earth as if they were rams and lambs, goats and bulls--all of them fattened animals from Bashan. At the sacrifice I am preparing for you, you will eat fat till you are glutted and drink blood till you are drunk. At My table you will eat your fill of horses and riders, mighty men and soldiers of every kind,' declares the Sovereign LORD" (Ezek 39:17-20). Jeremiah also said, "Has not my inheritance become to me like a speckled bird of prey that other birds of prey surround and attack? Go and gather all the wild beasts; bring them to devour" (Jer 12:9).

We just saw that there was a sword coming out of Christ's mouth. In Isaiah we clearly see that that sword shed blood, which is why the birds are being called, "The sword of the LORD is bathed in blood, it is covered with fat-- the blood of lambs and goats, fat from the kidneys of rams. For the LORD has a sacrifice in Bozrah and a great slaughter in Edom" (Isa 34:6). Jeremiah wrote, "But that day belongs to the Lord, the LORD Almighty-- a day of vengeance, for vengeance on His foes. The sword will devour till it is satisfied, till it has quenched its thirst with blood. For the Lord, the LORD Almighty, will offer sacrifice in the land of the north by the River Euphrates" (Jer 46:10).

It will make no difference how small or great these men are, they will all have judgment passed on them in the Valley of Decision. Though the saints will celebrate a wedding banquet, the ungodly will not feed, but be fed upon, at this "great supper." It is important to realize once more that demons have often been represented by birds in Scripture and thus this great supper could be the beginning of a never ending feeding frenzy upon the souls of men who do not believe.

Rev 19:19 Then I saw the beast and the kings of the earth and their armies gathered together to make war against the rider on the horse and his army. 19:20 But the beast was captured, and with him the false prophet who had performed the miraculous signs on his behalf. With these signs he had deluded those who had received the mark of the beast and worshipped his image. The two of them were thrown alive into the fiery lake of burning sulfur. 19:21 The rest of them were killed with the sword that came out of the mouth of the rider on the horse, and all the birds gorged themselves on their flesh.

Now that the birds have had their call to come, John sees the people who follow their leaders, who follow the beast (least to greatest), going up against Christ and His followers. However, the beast, the leader of all the evil people on earth, is captured along with his main support, the false prophet. This is sometimes referred to as the battle of Armageddon, however, it really is no battle at all, only a slaughter.

The false prophet had performed many miracles on behalf of the beast (Ch 13) and had led many astray. Jesus warned us about this, "For false christs and false prophets will appear and perform great signs and miracles to deceive even the elect--if that were possible" (Mat 24:24).

Both the beast and his false prophet were thrown into the lake of fire, which is hell. In 20:14 we see that this lake of fire is the second death, an eternal one. That is not to say non-existent, but eternal death from Christ. No hope, no joy, no salvation, no peace, nothing but torment forever and ever. Daniel also saw the Antichrist being destroyed: "Then I continued to watch because of the boastful words the horn was speaking. I kept looking until the beast was slain and its body destroyed and thrown into the blazing fire" (Dan 7:11).

One VERY IMPORTANT thing to notice is that the "two of them" were thrown into hell. We will see that is vital to our chronological understanding of the next chapter. In the next chapter we will see that the thousand year millenium is about to take place. AFTER that is over, the dragon, or Satan, is cast into the lake of fire where the beast and false prophet HAD BEEN thrown. We will discuss this further in chapter 20.

CHAPTER 20 INTRODUCTION

Next to the rapture, the thousand year reign of Christ is one of the most argued over events in religious circles today. Some believe we are living through the millenium right now. They say that verse one must be a figurative chain, a figurative key, so why not a figurative thousand years? However, there are problems with this interpretation, just as there are with others out there. This author's opinion is that this will be an event that has thus far been unimaginable and inexperienced and, therefore, unexplainable. In an attempt to view only what Scripture says and what past history has shown, the basic meaning of Revelation should be revealed. However, no commentary on this chapter, let alone the entire book will be 100% accurate. As we look ahead, one simply cannot tell the future. It is much easier to look back and see how history fits a prophecy once it is fulfilled. On the other hand, sometimes God uses dual prophecies, whereas the prophecy may fit, yet a greater fulfillment is yet to come. For example, in the Old Testament we know that David was a type of Christ, as was Isaac (Gal 4). Clearly, neither one was the ultimate fulfillment of the promise of the Savior in Genesis. As we saw in chapter 11, Elijah was prophesied to come, and he did come in the spirit of John the Baptist, however, a greater fulfillment seems to be coming. For now all that we can say is, "pray for us, too, that God may open a door for our message, so that we may proclaim the mystery of Christ, for which I am in chains. Pray that I may proclaim it clearly, as I should" (Col 4:3 –4). How does one explain the color blue to one that has been blind from birth? Without an experience to have some association with, there can be no understanding or frame of reference. Much like heaven, the millenium must be understood simply by faith and what little Scripture says about it. Who are we to say that it is, or is not, a thousand years? Because Christ said it was, I believe it, but how to understand it, I do not know. Different aspects have fascinated me. For example, we know that God created the universe in six days, Jonah was in the belly of a fish for three days, the Israelites wandered in the desert for 40 years and there were 12 tribes of Israel. Does that mean God only *symbolically* created the earth in six days or the Israelites only *symbolically* wandered in the desert. Yes and No! All of the above events truly happened in the time specified, however, they did symbolize something else as well. We know that 40 was used in times of testing and, therefore, the 40 year desert wandering really lasted 40 years and it was also a time of testing. Jonah was really in the fish for three days, and this symbolically represented Christ's death and resurrection (Mat 12:39ff). The argument is also made that Revelation is prophetic and that it is different than the historical books of Genesis, Exodus etc.. To gain support for a symbolic 1,000 years, verses like these below are used to show the number 1,000 as being used symbolically:

- Psa 50:10 "for every animal of the forest is mine, and the cattle on a thousand hills."

- Deu 1:11 "May the LORD, the God of your fathers, increase you a thousand times and bless you as He has promised!"
- Deu 7:9 "Know therefore that the LORD your God is God; He is the faithful God, keeping His covenant of love to a thousand generations of those who love Him and keep His commands."
- Psa 68:17 "The chariots of God are tens of thousands and thousands of thousands; the Lord has come from Sinai into His sanctuary."
- Psa 84:10 "Better is one day in Your courts than a thousand elsewhere; I would rather be a doorkeeper in the house of my God than dwell in the tents of the wicked."

The above verses use the number 1,000 as exaggerations, or over emphasized points. The questions become: Does Revelation use this number in the same way? Are numbers typically figurative? Daniel was able to glean from Scripture that the Jews were going to be in Babylon for 70 years (Dan 9:2). He knew this because of his study of prophetic Scripture in Jeremiah 25:11-12 and Isaiah 23:15-17. Again, we see a number that symbolizes completeness, yet it was still a literal 70 years. What if Daniel thought this was a symbolic number? Did he ever think that? Scripture never gives any indication of numbers ever being symbolic without, at the same time, making a literal point. In fact, even in Daniel and Ezekiel we see many examples of numbers that were not figurative in their fulfillment. In Daniel the beasts were representative of empires, but the numbers of horns and numbers of animals etc., were very literal. The key is Daniel used Scripture to understand events in his lifetime. We, too, must do the same. One more point on symbolism before leaving, if Revelation is symbolic and figurative, why does John point out when things are figurative (11:8)? Why is the throne of God in Revelation 4:6, 21:11, and 22:1 described the same way in Exodus 24:10, a HISTORICAL book. In Revelation 12:14 we see God helps deliver His people by the wings of an eagle, yet the same thing is described in Exodus 19:4. In Revelation 11 the two witnesses use the same miracles that Moses and Elijah did in Exodus and Kings (Both stopped it from raining for 3 ½ years, turned water to blood, etc.). In Revelation 15 the saints sing the song of Moses that was recorded in Deuteronomy 32 and Exodus 15. These are just a few of many examples of how the Old Testament historical books explain what we see in Revelation. This alone should make one doubt that Revelation may *only* be understood as all being symbolic without literal aspects. On the other hand, remember the prophecy about John the Baptist: "As is written in the book of the words of Isaiah the prophet: 'A voice of one calling in the desert, prepare the way for the Lord, make straight paths for Him'" (Luke 3:4). Taking this too literally, one may have said John was going to build highways throughout the desert. Having been told that John the Baptist fulfilled this prophecy, we now know that Isaiah was referring to the hearts of people being prepared for the Gospel through repentance. Taking things too literal can also become dangerous.

We will examine a number of views dealing with this literal/symbolic issue and let the reader decide for himself which way to lean. The only thing I encourage is that one enter without any presuppositions. We must stop believing things because our church says so, or our pastor, or our mom and dad, or even our emotions, rather let the Spirit of God lead and direct you through His Word alone. Doctrine is a very good thing and we are encouraged to, "hold firmly to the trustworthy message as it has been taught, so that he can encourage others *by sound doctrine* and refute those who oppose it" (Titus 1:9). We are also to, "teach what is in accord with sound doctrine" (Titus 2:1). The problem, however, is that every church has a doctrine they see as sound. How do we know which doctrine is the right doctrine. One way NOT to find out is to be close minded. If we believe things because the church or pastor says so, that is no measure of truth because the church down the street may have a different opinion. God's Word is the ONLY measuring rod for truth for everyone. When churches get too caught up with doctrine they can hinder the Gospel because doctrine is elevated above the Word. True, the doctrines come from the Word, but sometimes we study our doctrines and then apply Scripture into them rather than studying the Bible and applying our doctrines into it. If we do not allow ourselves to explore the Bible unrestrained by doctrines, we hinder the Spirit's work because we have already made up our mind on interpretation before we begin reading. Many churches will not allow their members to visit other churches or read the material published by other denominations. To do this is no better than the Pope telling the church that they do not need to read their Bibles because he will interpret it for them. He will fill them in on what it says. What are they afraid of? That God's Word will not be powerful enough to overcome false doctrines. God's Word is the only measure of truth, not me and my interpretation here, not your church, not your pastor, not any person. That does not mean we are not to share and examine others opinions, but be careful about the bias within us all (myself included). It is better to ere on the side of God's Word than on one's opinion or upbringing. As Timothy said, "For the time will come when men will not put up with sound doctrine. Instead, to suit their *own desires*, they will gather around them a great number of teachers *to say what their itching ears want to hear*" (2 Tim 4:3).

CHAPTER 20

Rev 20:1 And I saw an angel coming down out of heaven, having the key to the Abyss and holding in his hand a great chain. 20:2 He seized the dragon, that ancient serpent, who is the devil, or Satan, and bound him for a thousand years. 20:3 He threw him into the Abyss, and locked and sealed it over him, to keep him from deceiving the nations anymore until the thousand years were ended. After that, he must be set free for a short time.

After seeing the beast and false prophet thrown into the lake of fiery hell, John saw an angel holding the key to the Abyss and a great chain. This Abyss is a dreaded holding place for demons. The same word is used in Luke, a very literal book, where the demons begged Jesus not to cast them into the Abyss (Luke 8:31). We also see the same word translated as "deep" in Romans where we read, "But the righteousness that is by faith says: 'Do not say in your heart, Who will ascend into heaven?' (that is, to bring Christ down), or 'who will descend into the deep,' (that is, to bring Christ up from the dead)" (Rom 10:7). We also saw this Abyss earlier in 9:1-3, 11:7, and 17:8. It is a very real place and one must be careful to suggest that the Abyss is figurative because Hell is going to be some people's reality. With this said, we need to also be aware that the Abyss is not the "lake of fire," or the Hell we normally think of. The Abyss is only a temporary holding place for demons. Though temporary, it still is an undesirable place for demons (Matt 8:31) and they do get a chance to come up out of it for a time (Rev 9:11, 11:7). The lake of fire is the final doom where there will be "weeping and gnashing of teeth."

Earlier in 9:2 we saw that an angel was given the key to the Abyss at the fifth trumpet. He opened the Abyss and smoke like a gigantic furnace arose bringing forth strange and dreadful locusts that tortured the unbelievers. Whether or not this Abyss is compartmentalized we do not know, but Peter seems to suggest it is when he says, "God did not spare angels when they sinned, but sent them to hell, putting them into gloomy dungeons *to be held* for judgment" (2 Pet 2:4). In any case, they are being held in a dungeon UNTIL Judgment Day. We will see *when* this is in upcoming verses. We know that Jesus went to these prisons to proclaim His victory after the cross, "For Christ died for sins once for all, the righteous for the unrighteous, to bring you to God. He was put to death in the body but made alive by the Spirit, through whom also He went and preached to the spirits in prison who disobeyed long ago when God waited patiently in the days of Noah while the ark was being built. In it only a few people, eight in all, were saved through water" (1 Pet 3:18-20). The point being is, the Abyss was opened to let demons out. Nothing is said of the dragon being there directly, however, in 11:7 we see a beast will come up out of the Abyss. This beast doesn't seem to be Satan, but one of his main men, specifically, the Antichrist. Satan, according to chapter 12, was cast out of heaven down to earth. Also, Satan is later to be cast into the Abyss 1,000 years

AFTER the false prophet and beast are cast into hell (19:20, 20:10). Isaiah recorded that, "In that day the LORD will punish the powers in the heavens above and the kings on the earth below. They will be herded together like prisoners bound in a dungeon; they will be shut up in prison and be punished *after many days*" (Isa 24:21-22). It seems that Satan and many of his followers will be punished AFTER many days, and thus perhaps, after the millenium, whatever that may be.

This binding of Satan has been likened to a chained dog. If one gets too close he will be harmed, but the dog's owner will not allow the dog to go roaming about looking for someone to devour. This chain was used to tie up Satan, the dragon we saw in chapter 12. Once bound, he was thrown and locked up in the Abyss for 1,000 years. During this time, Satan cannot deceive the nations at all. **After** the 1,000 years, however, he will be released for a short period of time. It has also been suggested that because Satan is introduced in chapter 12 as the dragon, and is then never mentioned again until now, suggests that at the beginning of the New Testament era Satan was bound for the 1,000 years (which represents the entire time from Christ to the present). Therefore, all the deceiving that has gone on since then is not from the dragon directly, but rather indirectly, through the beast and false prophet of chapter 13. This interpretation is certainly possible, but there are a few glitches that don't make sense, which we will discuss (As there is with all interpretations). The beast and false prophet are to do miraculous signs, and even call fire down from heaven. Not to mention the fact that there is a 42 month period mentioned in 13:5. The same word used for deceive is used in Matthew where Jesus said, "Jesus answered: 'Watch out that no one deceives you. For many will come in My name, claiming, 'I am the Christ,' and will deceive many'" (Mat 24:4-5). Jesus said that many antichrists would come and deceive. In order to fit the 1,000 year period into the whole New Testament era one must then concede that Satan can only deceive through his beast and false prophet because he is bound. However, there is a MAJOR problem with this idea. The beast and the false prophet are thrown into hell BEFORE the thousand years begin and BEFORE the dragon is bound in the Abyss. How, then, can Satan use the false prophet and the beast if they are already in hell? The only way to get around this is to view Satan's being bound as only a restriction. Otherwise, this could suggest that the 1,000 years are not the New Testament era, but rather a literal 1,000 years to come. On the other hand, there could be things we are not told or not understanding yet.

In other areas, the New Testament period representing the millenium really shines. One such example that seems to fit the New Testament era being the 1,000 years comes from the description of the ten kings of Rome as discussed in Chapter 17:9. It may be good to go back and review this again.

Other support for a figurative 1,000 years comes from 1 John where we see that Satan was bound by Christ's resurrection: "He who does what is sinful is of the devil, because the devil has been sinning from the beginning. The reason the Son of God appeared was to destroy the devil's work" (1 John 3:8). *When* his destruction comes is not mentioned in this verse, however. Also, when we read on we see people can get too close to the chained dog, "No one who is born of God will continue to sin, because God's seed remains in him; he cannot go on sinning, because he has been born of God. This is how we know who the children of God are and who the children of the devil are: Anyone who does not do what is right is not a child of God; nor is anyone who does not love his brother" (1 John 3:9-10). This passage does not say that the devil is bound, rather he is limited to whom he can touch. If we have the power of the Spirit protecting us, we are safe: "Put on the full armor of God so that you can take your stand against the devil's schemes. For our struggle is not against flesh and blood, but against the rulers, against the authorities, against the powers of this dark world and against the spiritual forces of evil in the heavenly realms. Therefore put on the full armor of God, so that *when* the day of evil comes, you may be able to stand your ground" (Eph 6:11-13).

Other verses that show Satan to be bound today follow:

- John 12:31 "Now is the time for judgment on this world; **now** the prince of this world will be driven out."
- Col 2:15 "And having **disarmed** [technically not bound] the powers and authorities, he made a public spectacle of them, **triumphing** over them by the cross."
- Heb 2:14 "Since the children have flesh and blood, he too shared in their humanity so that by his death he might **destroy** him who holds the power of death--that is, the devil—" [present destruction or future?]
- Mat 12:28-29 "But if I drive out demons by the Spirit of God, then the **kingdom of God has come** upon you. Or again, how can anyone enter a strong man's house and carry off his possessions unless he first **ties up the strong man**? Then he can rob his house."

Another interesting word to point out is "nations." Satan is not going to deceive the nations anymore. This word for nations is *ethnos* and means of non-Jewish origin. In other words, Gentiles, and this word is translated as such throughout the New Testament. If one does not focus on the word "bound" as much as the words "deceive the nations" another explanation can be given. The purpose of the binding was so that Satan could not longer deceive the nations. Prior to Christ's coming, the Jewish people had the monopoly on God. However, after Christ's death and resurrection, the Gospel message flourished and Satan could do nothing to stop it. The nations could not be deceived anymore about this truth so ALL NATIONS were now receiving the Gospel. Therefore, Satan was bound at the cross and kept from deceiving the nations any longer.

One last point to make regarding the possibility of the 1,000 years being a literal period. God is a God of patterns and order. We have been tracing the pattern of sevens throughout the book of Revelation, where the first four in a series follow one theme, then two others follow another theme, and the seventh is restful, or is completely different because it introduces the next series of seven. The seven days of creation can be divided up with the first four days being non-living creations, the next two were living creations and the last one was a day of rest. All of time can be divided up into the same pattern so far. Using the genealogical record, we see that there were exactly 4,000 years from Creation to Christ. Now in the year 2000, we have had 2,000 years of New Testament, New Covenant era, and then a seventh 1,000 year reign would be a time of rest when Satan was bound. The book of Hebrews also supports this interpretation:

> "Therefore, since the promise of entering His rest **still stands**, let us be careful that none of you be found to have fallen short of it. For we also have had the gospel preached to us, just as they did; but the message they heard was of no value to them, because those who heard did not combine it with faith. Now we who have believed enter that rest, just as God has said, 'So I declared on oath in My anger, they shall never enter My rest.' **And yet His work has been finished since the creation of the world**. For somewhere He has spoken about the **seventh day in these words**: 'And on the seventh day God rested from all His work.' And again in the passage above He says, 'They shall never enter My rest.' It still remains *that some will enter that rest*, and those who formerly had the gospel preached to them did not go in, because of their disobedience. Therefore God again set a certain day, calling it Today, when a long time later He spoke through David, as was said before: 'Today, if you hear His voice, do not harden your hearts.' For if Joshua had given them rest, God would not have spoken later about another day. **There remains, then, a Sabbath-rest** for the people of God; for anyone who enters God's rest also rests from his own work, just as God did from His. Let us, therefore, make every effort to enter that rest, so that no one will fall by following their example of disobedience" (Heb 4:1-11).

Here we see that the Sabbath day (7th day) is still to come and that it will be a Day of rest. Perhaps that is also why we read in Peter, "By the same word the present heavens and earth are reserved for fire, being kept for the day of judgment and destruction of ungodly men. But do not forget this one thing, dear friends: With the Lord *a day is like a thousand years*, and a thousand years are like a day. The Lord is not slow in keeping His promise" (2 Pet 3:7-9). We must be careful not to extend this thought into theorizing the six days of creation occurred over long periods of time. They were literal, 24 hour days! However, even Martin Luther noted that each day of creation seemed to roughly correspond to a thousand years of history. For example, the first day of creation was separating light from dark. The first thousand years were dominated by Adam and Eve, who were known for causing the separation of good and evil. The second day of creation was separating water from water and creating the firmament above. The second thousand years of time after creation were dominated by Noah who is well known for living through the Flood and the first rainfall (Gen 2:5). The third day of creation was making dry ground and vegetation. The third thousand years was dominated by Abraham who became a great nation to fill the earth. The fourth day of creation consisted of the sun, moon and stars while the fourth thousand years was dominated by Jacob and the twelve tribes of Israel. We have seen in chapter 12, and in Joseph's dream in Genesis, how the stars, sun and moon have represented the twelve tribes. Then, day five of creation created fish and birds and the fifth thousand years was dominated by the New Testament Church and Christ who fed the five thousand with a few fish and the Spirit of God landed on Him in the form of a dove. Both the fish and the bird have been New Testament symbols of faith. The sixth day of creation involved the creation of man, while the sixth thousand years of time have been dominated by man growing in knowledge and spreading the Gospel message throughout the world. The seventh day of creation was rest, as the seventh thousand years may be our "Sabbath rest for all of God's people" as we saw in Hebrews. I realize that there is a fair amount of allegorizing with this, but not too much of a stretch for Luther to identify with. Scripture is filled with this type of allegory, much of which is even explained (see Galatians 4).

Let's take this thought one step further. If each of the six, 24 hour days of creation foreshadowed each of the six thousand years of time on earth before the millenium, there should be other references to this. Consider the following: Hosea states, "For I will be like a lion to Ephraim, like a great lion to Judah. I will tear them to pieces and go away; I will carry them off, with no one to rescue them. Then *I will go back to My place* __until__ they admit their guilt. And they will seek My face; in their misery they will earnestly seek Me. Come, let us return to the LORD. He has torn us to pieces but He will heal us; He has injured us but He will bind up our wounds. **After two days** He will revive us; __**on the third day**__ He will restore us, that we **may live in His presence**" (Hosea 5:14-6:2). First of all, note that the Jews had been abandoned by Christ when He went back to His place. Christ's place can only be understood as heaven here. He would remain there only UNTIL they admit their guilt and recognize Him as the Messiah. Just as Jesus said in Matthew, "For I tell you, you will not see me again *until* you say, 'Blessed is He who comes in the name of the Lord'" (Mat 23:39). Once they do so, they will repent and return to the LORD. When will this take place? According to the Hosea text, AFTER two days! We are nearing two thousand years since Christ *ascended* into heaven. Therefore, we could perhaps expect a massive turning to Christ from the Jewish people. Then, ON the third day, or the seventh thousandth year after creation (millenium), God would restore them so that they can live with Him in His presence. How can we live in Christ's presence unless this is the "Sabbath rest" for God's people that Hebrews spoke of?

The Hosea passage fits nothing that happened in Old Testament history and, therefore, must be a future prophecy, upon which we are about to see fulfilled. There is much evidence showing the Jewish people will turn back to Christ: "I do not want you to be ignorant of this **mystery**, brothers, so that you may not be conceited: Israel has experienced a hardening in part __until__ the full number of the **Gentiles** has come in. And so all Israel will be saved, as it is written: 'The Deliverer will come from Zion; He will turn godlessness away from **Jacob**. And this is My covenant with them when I take away their sins.' As far as the gospel is concerned, they are enemies on your account; but as far as election is concerned, they are loved on account of the patriarchs, for God's gifts and **His call are irrevocable**. Just as you who were **at one time** disobedient to God have now received mercy as a result of their disobedience, so they too have now become disobedient in order that **they too may now receive mercy** as a result of God's mercy to you. For God has bound all men over to disobedience so that He may have mercy on them all" (Rom 11:25-32). Note that the Jews have only experienced a temporary hardening until the Gentiles have had their fill. Jacob is a term used for Jews and, therefore, cannot include Gentiles under spiritual Israel or ingrafted branches (Rom 11:11). Besides, the Jews and Gentiles are intentionally split up in these verses. When we read Romans 11 and 12 carefully, there is no question that the Jews will turn to Christ during the end times. Hosea must be talking about the end times. . . two thousand years after Christ "went to His place" in heaven. I pray that God will open our eyes to see this Gospel opportunity.

Rev 20:4 I saw thrones on which were seated those who had been given authority to judge. And I saw the souls of those who had been beheaded because of their testimony for Jesus and because of the word of God. They had not worshipped the beast or his image and had not received his mark on their foreheads or their hands. They came to life and reigned with Christ a thousand years. 20:5 (The rest of the dead did not come to life until the thousand years were ended.) This is the first resurrection. 20:6 Blessed and holy are those who have part in the first resurrection. The second death has no power over them, but they will be priests of God and of Christ and will reign with him for a thousand years.

During the thousand year millenium, John saw thrones, on which were seated those who were given authority to judge. Paul wrote, "Do you not know that the saints will judge the world" (1 Cor 6:2)? In Matthew we see that "when the Son of Man comes in His glory, and all the angels with Him, He will sit on His throne in heavenly glory. All the nations will be gathered before Him, and He will separate the people one from another as a shepherd separates the sheep from the goats" (Mat 25:31-32). The saints are included in this glorious judgment because Jesus also said, "I tell you the truth, at the renewal of all things, when the Son of Man sits on His glorious throne, you who have followed Me will also sit on twelve thrones, judging the twelve tribes of Israel" (Mat 19:28). When speaking of the Antichrist, Daniel wrote, "As I watched, this horn was waging war against the saints and defeating them, *until* the Ancient of Days came and pronounced judgment in favor of the saints of the Most High, and the time came when they possessed the kingdom" (Dan 7:21-22). According to verse four here in Revelation, we see that the time for us to possess the kingdom has come! This is AFTER the Antichrist came, because these people did not take his image or receive his mark. They are to reign WITH Christ for 1,000 years.

Another thing to point out is that the soul's of those who had been killed on account of their testimony were seen. Whether these soul's had bodies or not we do not know. Some say that since the saints were wearing white linen they must have had bodies to put their clothes on. Others say that the bodies do not come until the second resurrection, after Judgment Day. It does not seem that the seventh trumpet has yet blown during this time and, therefore, would indicate that we do not have our renewed bodies yet (1 Cor 15:52, 1 Thes 4:16). When a person dies they do not receive a new body right away, but their soul does go to be with Christ immediately. It won't be until the seventh trumpet blows that the "perishable will become imperishable." From a literal 1,000 year approach, this fact would suggest that the millenium happens sometime after the two witnesses because the mark of the beast has already been introduced, but before the seventh trumpet.

Verse five tells us that the rest of the dead are not resurrected until the thousand years are over. Who are the rest of the dead? Although we cannot be absolutely sure, it seems that they are all who do not go through the tribulation period. In other words, everyone who dies before the Antichrist begins his persecution of the saints will not come to life until after the 1,000 years are over. We must also be careful not to believe that we are in a state of nonexistence if we die prior to this point. Our souls do go to heaven, however, we are not reunited with our bodies yet. That is why this is called the first resurrection. If you note in verse four it mentioned that the souls of these people were seen and then in verse five it is said they came to life. This could suggest that they were truly united with their bodies early.

The symbolic view of the 1000 years is that this first resurrection takes place whenever you die, and after the New Testament era ends, the second resurrection will take place with the uniting and renewing of the body, spirit and soul. We are already reigning with Christ at our "first resurrection" because Jesus said, "But because of His great love for us, God, who is rich in mercy, made us alive with Christ even when we were dead in transgressions--it is by grace you have been saved. And God rais**ed** (past tense) us up with Christ and seated us with Him in the heavenly realms in Christ Jesus, in order that in the coming ages He might show the incomparable riches of His grace, expressed in His kindness to us in Christ Jesus" (Eph 2:4-7). Therefore, this first resurrection is a spiritual one. Just as in Adam all died a spiritual death, now in Christ we are raised up with Christ. As for the "rest of the dead," they must be interpreted as unbelievers and, therefore, the people who deny Christ will not come to life until the New Testament era is over.

Verse six tells us that all those who take part in this resurrection are blessed. This could show that there is a special blessing for those who take part in this millennial reign. As we will discuss in verses 11-13, there are different glories of heaven. Could there be different glories of resurrections? Luke spoke of the great wedding banquet of the Lamb: "But when you give a banquet, invite the poor, the crippled, the lame, the blind, and *you will be blessed*. Although they cannot repay you, you will be repaid at the resurrection of the righteous" (Luke 14:13-14). A large part of these extra blessings seem to come from the willingness to suffer for Christ. Paul said, "I want to know Christ and the power of His resurrection and the *fellowship of sharing in His sufferings,* becoming like Him in His death, and so, somehow, to attain to the resurrection from the dead" (Phil 3:10-11). Perhaps that is why it is said, "Therefore, since Christ suffered in His body, arm yourselves also with the same attitude, because *he who has suffered in his body is done with sin*" (1 Pet 4:1).

Another verse giving possible insight into this first resurrection states, "For the Lord Himself will come down from heaven, with a loud command, with the voice of the archangel and with the trumpet call of God, and *the dead in Christ will rise first.* **After that**, *we who are still alive and are left will be caught up together with them in the clouds* to meet the Lord in the air. And so we will be with the Lord *forever*" 1 Th 4:16-17). This could suggest that all who die because of Christ rise first and are especially blessed, regardless of the timing of the millenium. However, this is by no means essential in interpreting these verses.

The second death has no power over the resurrected. The second death is the spiritual death in the lake of fire. We are told this plainly in verse 14.

Some believe that David will be raised up at this time because of the words of Jeremiah: "Instead, they will serve the LORD their God and David their king, whom I will raise up for them" (Jer 30:9). When this was written, David had been dead for many years. It is more likely, however, that David here simply represents Jesus, the son of David. Jeremiah said they would serve the Lord AND David their king. Here in Revelation we see verse six tells us these saints will live with God AND Christ. Ezekiel also mentions this, "I will save My flock, and they will no longer be plundered. I will judge between one sheep and another. I will place over them *one shepherd*, My servant David, and He will tend them; He will tend them and be their *shepherd.* I the LORD will be their God, and My servant David will be prince among them. I the LORD have spoken. I will make a covenant of peace with them and rid the land of wild beasts so that they may live in the desert and sleep in the forests in safety. I will bless them and the places surrounding *My hill.* I will send down showers in season; there will be showers of blessing" (Ezek 34:22-26). Not only do we gain insight into the location of this reign surrounding "My hill" (which should be obvious anyway), but again, a passage which refers to Christ as our Shepherd. In Hebrews we read, "May the God of peace, who through the blood of the eternal covenant brought back from the dead our Lord Jesus, that great Shepherd of the sheep . . ." (Heb 13:20). Finally Hosea also records, "Afterward the Israelites will return and seek the LORD their God and David their king. They will come trembling to the LORD and to His blessings in the *last days*" (Hosea 3:5).

All who rise with Christ ARE holy priests. We see in Peter, "You also, like living stones, are being built into a spiritual house to be a holy priesthood, offering spiritual sacrifices acceptable to God through Jesus Christ" (1 Pet 2:5). As we discussed in 3:12 this is a reference to our becoming one with Christ in a way that is unimaginable, yet true for us even today. We will be priests in a temple, that is Christ's body, not an ordinary building, however, we are priests already as well. (See 3:12 for a discussion on being made into the pillar of Christ. Also the section on saints or sinners). Going back to Revelation 1:6 we read, "To Him who loves us and has freed us from our sins by His blood, and **has made** us to be a kingdom and **priests** to serve His God and Father--to Him be glory and power for ever and ever! Amen" (Rev 1:5-6).

SAINTS OR SINNERS?

This brings us to one of the most important and most misunderstood points in God's Holy Word. Are you a saint, a sinner, or perhaps both? Scripture makes is very clear that you are a saint, NOT a sinner. Before you let your mind run free, this does not mean you do not sin, rather, you are a saint that sometimes sins, or a sheep that sometimes acts like a goat. The difference is that you are not a sinner as a noun, rather a sinner when used as a verb. You cannot be both. To use another illustration, if you have a sliver in you, are you a block of wood? NO! Likewise, just because we have sin in us, it doesn't mean we are sinners. Paul even says, "And if I do what I do not want to do, I agree that the law is good. As it is, it is no longer **I myself** who do it, but it is **sin** living **in** me" (Rom 7:16-17). Note Paul is not the sinner, he is the saint that has sin in him. Note also that his identity is not bound up in the sin, but that he "himself" is different than his "body." We are a trinity of body, soul and spirit. It is our body that we often look to as our identity, but the fact is that our body is merely a tent or house for who we really are. It just so happens that we live in a dirty house with sin in it. Paul again states, "Now we know that if the earthly **tent we live in** is destroyed, we have a building from God, an eternal house in heaven, not built by human hands. Meanwhile we groan, longing to be clothed with our heavenly dwelling, because when we are clothed, we will not be found naked" (2 Cor 5:1-3). If our tent blew down, our heavenly body would remain standing, therefore, I am not what you can see physically, my identity is what you can't see, my soul and spirit. You can only see my house, not what is inside. Now let's look at what is inside these tents of ours. Jesus states, "I am the vine; you are the branches. If a man remains **in** Me and I **in** him, he will bear much fruit; **apart** from Me you can do nothing. If anyone does not remain **in** Me, he is like a branch that is thrown away and withers" (John 15:5-6). Note that we are IN Christ. For every verse that states that Christ is in us there are ten that say we are in Him. I know it doesn't FEEL like you are in Christ, but what does the Bible say? It doesn't matter how you feel, it matters what you ARE. If we are in Christ and He is in heaven, we are in heaven! That is also what Scripture says, "Since, then, **you have been raised with Christ**, set your hearts on things above, **where Christ is seated** at the right hand of God. Set your minds on things above, not on earthly things. For **you died**, and **your life is now hidden with** Christ in God. When **Christ, who is your life**, appears, then you also will appear **with** Him in glory. Put **to death**, therefore, whatever belongs to your earthly nature" (Col 3:1-5). Christ IS YOUR LIFE. Christ cannot have in Himself any sin. Your body is not in Christ, but YOU are. Note also that you died! Romans tells us, "For we know that our old self was **crucified** with Him so that the body of sin might be **done away with**, that we should no longer be slaves to sin—" (Rom 6:6). Your old self was killed and, therefore, cannot be resurrected. One might say God didn't change you, He exchanged you. You died with Christ so that you could be made new; "to be made new in the attitude of your minds; and to put on the **new** self, **created** to be like God in true *righteousness and holiness*" (Eph 4:23-24). You are not a sinner, but a righteous and holy being in Christ. Some people are uncomfortable saying that they are a saint because they know their sins. The difference is that Christ has forgiven those sins, nailing them to the cross: "He forgave us all our sins, having canceled the written code, with its regulations, that *was against* [past tense] us and that stood opposed to us; He took it away, nailing it to the cross" (Col 2:13-14). True, we were born sinful. Being born was our ticket to hell. However, through Christ we can be born again and made new in Him. God does not operate or judge on a performance based system, even though we unrightfully do so ourselves. God looks at us and He sees a saint, even when we sin. We look at ourselves and see the sin and not the saint because that's what the devil wants. He wants you to go by what you feel, not what God says. God's definition of a hypocrite is someone who pretends to be what they are not. Satan's definition is someone who acts contrary to the way they *feel*. Satan wants us to act on feelings in order to be blinded by truth. We want to keep pretending we are sinners (noun) because we feel like sinners, even though God tells us we are saints. Paul always writes his letters to the "saints" not the "sinners" of Ephesus or Corinth, etc.. (Rom 15:31, 2 Cor 8:4, 9:1; Eph 1:1; Col 1:26; Jude 1:3). Even in the Old Testament before the law was given (Rom 5:13), Job saw himself as blameless, upright and righteous: "let God weigh me in honest scales and He will know that I am blameless—(Job 31:6; see also 9:21). His friends kept telling him, "no, you are a sinner. Repent and be healed." Who did God say was right? "After the LORD had said these things to Job, He said to Eliphaz the Temanite, 'I am angry with you and your two friends, because you have not spoken of Me what is right, as My servant Job has" (Job 42:7). Job knew he was a blameless saint even though he sinned, because those sins were not counted against him and they certainly didn't change his identity if they were forgiven. God fixed it so that your old self died. If when you were born again the old self was still there, you would be like Siamese twins with one good and one bad. As the Bible puts it, "a house divided against itself cannot stand." But as Jesus said, "If a house is divided against itself, that house cannot stand [remember our bodies are our house]" (Mark 3:25). Ephesians tells us Christ, "chose us **in** Him before the creation of the world to be holy and blameless in His sight" (Eph 1:4). Just as this single page would be pierced if I nailed this book to a wall, we were IN Christ before Creation, we were IN Him as we walked the road to Calvary, we were IN Him as he hung and died on the cross, and we were IN Him when He rose from the dead. We don't resurrect our old self, we leave it on the cross. As Romans so beautifully puts it, "We *were* therefore buried **with** Him through baptism into death in order that, just as Christ *was* raised from the dead through the glory of the Father, **we, too,** may live a **new** life. If we *have been* united with Him like this in His death, we will certainly also be united with Him in His resurrection. For we know that our old self *was* crucified with Him so that the body of sin might be done away with, that we should no longer be slaves to sin—" (Rom 6:4-6). Note the italicized verb tenses in the above Romans passage. They are past tense. We are not called to crucify our old self because Christ already did it. We are His workmanship, "created" in Christ Jesus (Eph 2:10). I once read an analogy of an electric tool. We are like these tools. Without being plugged into the energy source (God) we become nothing but paperweights. Our identity is tied up in the energy source. Without the juice the tool loses its individuality. It is Christ's life in us that gives us our identity.

Some people think that we are to emulate the life of Christ. You can't! God doesn't even want you to try. God doesn't want to simply "help" YOU lead a better life, He wants to do it ALL for you. Likewise, God didn't "help" you get saved, He did it ALL for you. As Habakkuk said, we would be: "guilty men, whose own strength is their god" (Hab 1:11). Most everyone knows the poem "Footprints" which illustrates this "independent" attitude. As you recall, the poem goes through life showing how there were two sets of footprints in the sand until the times were tough and then there were only one. When asked why God left him alone, God said, "Oh, that was when I carried you." Though a beautiful poem, it isn't quite theologically accurate. It implies that I can be independent and only need Christ to carry me when things get too tough for ME to handle. NO! Christ carries us through our entire life.

Romans states, "For if, when we were God's enemies, we were *reconciled to Him through the death of His Son*, **how much more**, having been reconciled, shall we be saved through His life" (Rom 5:10)? So often we focus too much on the death of Christ in this verse, but that is a mistake. Don't get me wrong, that is important, but let us look closer. We are already saved, or reconciled from HELL by His death, but there is "much more." We are also saved by His LIFE. Saved from what? His life through you saves you from bearing the burdens here on earth. Christ's death saved you from hell and His life saves you from hell on earth. Sometimes we make Jesus the focal point of our life, failing to make Him our LIFE. As the Bible clearly tells us, "When Christ, who is your life, appears, then you also will appear with Him in glory" (Col 3:4). If God removed His life from this earth, we would all vanish. Somehow we think our flesh is our identity and we try to work independent from Jesus at times. We can't. No matter how hard WE try, WE can't stop sinning and become a "better" Christian. I used to look at my life and think, "when I stop saying bad words, then I will be a good Christian." Then it was, "when I stop losing my temper, then I will be a good Christian." I kept trying to work my way up the ladder. It wasn't until I realized I was a saint and let God work through me that the Gospel of salvation began to change my heart, which in turn changed my actions. Before, I was trying to change my actions so that my heart would be changed. It didn't work that way. "You, however, are *controlled not by the sinful nature* but **by the Spirit,** if the Spirit of God lives in you" (Rom 8:9). Again, we are not sinners saved by grace, but saints who have the capability to sin, but long to overcome it.

Bill Gillham, in his book *Lifetime Guarantee*, talks about the minds "green highway" in which our thoughts become entrenched into our brain. Once you think about something a line is formed in the brain. The more the same thought pattern is used the more the line becomes a trench. Eventually it turns into a path, a road, and finally a green (color of garbage) highway. If the road is not traveled the grass and weeds will begin to cover it up again. For example, the more one practices a foreign language the easier it becomes to recall information. However, if the road isn't traveled on, the information gets harder and harder to pull up. Eventually, if you don't use your foreign language for many years, those thought patterns almost disappear. The point of all this is that, as a saint that sins, one cannot expect to be good all the time, because the power of sin still resides in our flesh, but that doesn't change who you are. Just because our flesh is there does not mean one isn't capable of sinning less and less as we become closer to God and refuse to use those old green highways. James says, "Submit yourselves, then, to God. Resist the devil, and he will flee from you" (James 4:7). We do have the capability to resist the evil thoughts Satan puts in our mind because Christ is in us and we are in Him. Once a thought enters the brain we have a choice to respond or ignore it. Using Christ's strength we can ignore that thought. The more and more we resist these temptations, the more they dissipate. On the flip side, when things of God are put in our thoughts, those good highways become well traveled and lead to a joy filled life. This is why Paul wrote, "We demolish arguments and every pretension that sets itself up against the knowledge of God, and we take captive every thought to make it obedient to Christ" (2 Cor 10:5). Every thought should be taken captive and analyzed to be sure it is in line with Christ-like obedience. If not, resist and ignore it. Again, we can't do this perfectly, however, as Scripture states, " Physical **training** is of some value, but godliness has value for all things, **holding promise** for both the **present life** and the life to come. This is a trustworthy saying that deserves full acceptance (and for this **we labor and strive**), that we have put our hope in the living God, who is the Savior of all men" (1 Tim 4:8-10). This type of training gives joy for this present life, but it is something we work at and can only obtain by using Christ's strength in us. However, to use it, one needs to recognize it is there. God wants more than our salvation, He wants us to reap the benefits of all the blessings He has to offer us on this side of heaven. Eternal life is yours already. You are already seated with Christ in heaven, so act like it! We are what we think we are. You believe you are a sinner, you will act like it. Believe you are a saint and you will act like a saint. Think about it, does the law ever motivate you to do good? NO! I don't steal because I am afraid of getting caught. I don't steal because I love Jesus and I don't want to do anything that would displease Him: *"For Christ's love compels us*, because we are convinced that one died for all, and therefore all died" (2 Cor 5:14). Likewise, thinking you are a sinner and that you NEED to change won't motivate or give you the strength to become better. Paul shows us that the law KILLS, it doesn't build you up and give LIFE: "He has made us competent as *ministers of a* **New Covenant**--*not of the letter* but of the *Spirit*; for the *letter kills*, but the *Spirit gives life*" (2 Cor 3:6). Realizing you are a saint under the New Covenant, and your response to that tremendous gift will be your Gospel motivation and power to change. Jesus said, "I am the vine; you are the branches. If a man **remains in** Me and **I in him**, he **will** bear much fruit; **apart from Me** you can do nothing" (John 15:5). Branches can never PRODUCE fruit, they can only BEAR fruit that is produced by the life of the VINE through them. That is also why we, as saints, are not under the law. Consider the following:

- 1 Tim 1:9 "We also know that the law is made not for the righteous but for lawbreakers and rebels, the ungodly and sinful, the unholy and irreligious."

- 1 Cor 9:20 "To the Jews I became like a Jew, to win the Jews. To those under the law I became like one under the law (though **I myself am not under the law**), so as to win those under the law."

- Rom 7:6 "But now, by **dying** to what **once bound us, we have been released from the law** so that we serve in the **new way of the Spirit**, and not in the old way of the written code."

- Rom 6:14 "For sin shall not be your master, because **you are not under law**, but under grace."

- Gal 5:18 "But if you are led by the Spirit, **you are not under law**."

- Gal 3:12 "The **law is not based on faith**; on the contrary, The man who does these things will live by them."

- Rom 8:2-3 "Because through Christ Jesus the law of the Spirit of life set me free from the law of sin and death. For what the law was powerless to do in that it was weakened by the sinful nature, God did by sending His own Son in the likeness of sinful man to be a sin offering."

This is the heart of the Gospel message. Not until we stray from Christ does the law need to be in the life of a saint. But thinking as sinners, we love to beat ourselves with the law saying, "This is the third time I have done this," or "This sin is too big to be forgiven," and "I must change before the forgiveness becomes effective." How many times do we ask Christ to forgive us and then go away feeling guilty because we still FEEL that we are bad. That is like saying to Christ, "Thanks for the forgiveness, but I must do more in order to be forgiven. What You did wasn't good enough." Can you see the performance based grade report we give ourselves under the law? Can you see how we lessen the joy available to us in forgiveness? If I am good I FEEL like a saint and if I am bad I FEEL like a sinner, no matter what the Bible says. Again, feelings lie, the Bible does not. One of Satan's biggest tools is our feelings. If we operated all of our lives using feelings as our guide, where would we be? In contrast, think how joy filled we would be using Truth as our guide. The truth is – your a saint! Think about Lot. No matter how hard I try to find "saint-like" qualities in him, I can't, but 2 Peter 2:7 says he was righteous. I try to make him a saint based upon his performance and how I feel about him, but God declared him righteous based on truth (note this was before the law was given, which is the same as after the law was taken away in the New Covenant). We want to live under Moses, but if we do we will die: "For the law was given through Moses; grace and *truth* came through Jesus Christ" (John 1:17). Only God's grace can change a person to be obedient to God's law. You see we are under the "law of love, written in our hearts" (Hebrews 10:16). Law, motivated by love, is Gospel.

Have you ever wondered why we have both the body and blood of Christ in communion? It was in Christ's body that we were crucified and then reborn according to Romans: "So, my brothers, you also died to the law **through the body** of Christ, that you might belong to another, to Him who was raised from the dead, in order that we might bear fruit to God" (Rom 7:4). Through the body of Christ we died to the law and became saints. Hebrews states, "And by that will, we have been made holy through the sacrifice of the body of Jesus Christ once for all" (Heb 10:10). We have been made holy in our Spirt-body (our true identity) through the body of Jesus. What was His blood for? Forgiveness! It is through the necessary shedding of the blood of Christ that we were forgiven, but it was His body that exchanged our identity from sinner to saint: "I have been crucified with Christ and I no longer live, but Christ lives in me" (Gal 2:20).

Remember the testimony of Jesus's words about the Temple, "We heard Him say, 'I will destroy this man-made temple and in three days will build another, not made by man'" (Mark 14:58). What was Jesus talking about? His body! After three days God raised up the Temple of God, Jesus Christ. Understanding that we are IN Christ, that third day resurrection also made us new as well. We are the new Holy of Holies of which Jesus spoke. In the Old Testament the Jews were forgiven when the high priest went behind the veil into the Holy of Holies. If the sinners themselves would have gone behind that veil they would have perished. However, when Christ died that veil was torn in half, allowing free passage into the Holy of Holies. Because of our new identity we are holy and can enter into God's presence. We read in the words of Paul, "What agreement is there between the temple of God and idols? **For we are the temple of the living God**. As God has said: 'I will live with them and walk among them, and I will be their God, and they will be My people'" (2 Cor 6:16). How can this be? Because we are not only forgiven through Christ's blood, we are also made new through Christ's body.

This is also why at Christ's return it is our bodies that are changed, not our spirit or soul (I Cor 15:51-53). Again, our identity is not the body, but the soul and spirit. When we eject from our body, Satan can no longer give us a hard time because our sin is in our body (our building WE live in).

How does repentance fit into all of this? Repentance is mandatory for regeneration. One must *want* to be changed into a new creation before God will do it. If you love your life, chances are you will not repent because there will be no motivation for change. "The man who loves his life will lose it, while the man who hates his life in this world will keep it for eternal life" (John 12:25). As Scofield once said, "Repentance is not an act separate from faith, but saving faith implies that change of mind which is called repentance." There are many Scripture passages which show that repentance was a forerunner to faith. John the Baptist was preaching, "Repent, for the kingdom of heaven *is near*" (Mat 3:2). John knew Jesus was coming and, therefore, he was sent to be a "voice calling in the wilderness" to "prepare the way" for Christ (Mark 1:3). As Jesus began His earthly ministry Matthew states, "From that time on Jesus began to preach, 'Repent, for the kingdom of heaven is near'" (Mat 4:17). Jesus knew that, "Godly sorrow brings repentance that leads to salvation and leaves no regret, but worldly sorrow brings death" (2 Cor 7:10). Peter, as well, preached to the Jews saying, "Repent, then, and turn to God, so that your sins may be wiped out, that times of refreshing may come from the Lord" (Acts 3:19; see also Acts 17:30). Repentance is a big step because often times it means swallowing pride, and worse yet, admitting you are not lord of your ring. The first step in a joy filled life with Christ is to abandon YOUR life and cling to Jesus as LIFE. We read in Colossians, "Since, then, you have been raised with Christ, set your hearts on things above, where Christ is seated at the right hand of God. Set your minds on things above, not on earthly things. For you died, and your life is now hidden with Christ in God. When Christ, *who is your life*, appears, then you also will appear with Him in glory" (Col 3:1-4). The key is to surrender your life for His: "For whoever wants to save his life will lose it, but whoever loses his life for Me will save it" (Luke 9:24).

Maybe some of you are still thinking, "if we don't have the law what is to keep people from going crazy with sin under the Gospel?" Scripture answers that one as well: "What then? *Shall we sin because we are not under law but under grace*? **May it never be!** [Why?] But thanks be to God that though you were slaves of sin, *you became obedient* from *the heart* to that form of teaching to which you were committed, and having *been freed from sin*, you became *slaves of righteousness*" [note, slaves are controlled by their master] (Rom 6:15,17-18 NAS). Paul also asks an important question in the book of Galatians, "I would like to learn just one thing from you: Did you receive the Spirit by observing the law, or by believing what you heard" (Gal 3:2)? What is your answer? By believing right? You received the Spirit by faith alone. Verse three then goes on, "Are you so foolish? After beginning with the Spirit, are you now trying to attain your goal by human effort" (Gal 3:3)? Do we now then try to add to our faith, good works through the law? Never. We are not under the law. You cannot try to live out your sainthood by yourself, you must just believe what Christ says and act like it.

This would not be complete without looking at what sin is. We so often think of sin as being a verb, however, Scripture most frequently calls it a "power" and uses it as a NOUN. In light of what we discussed about the law, it is interesting to take note of Paul's words, "The sting of death is sin, and the *power of sin is the law*" (1 Cor 15:56). For many, this may sound like I am going off the deep end, but please hang in there, and most importantly, take a moment to pray right now that God would give you an open mind to openly and honestly examine what He says, not what we feel.

To find the meaning of anything we go to its origin. For example, if I wanted to know what "gay" meant, I could look it up in a dictionary and find out that that word originally meant happy. Today, because of sin, it now means homosexual. So lets look at the true meaning of sin by going to its origin. Sin first appears in Genesis when God warns Cain about sin: "If you do what is right, will you not be accepted? But if you do not do what is right, sin is crouching at your door; *it* desires to have you, *but you must master it*" (Gen 4:7). The literal translation of the Hebrew says, "you must master HIM." Did you catch that? God has shown us Satan's secret. Sin is a noun with personality and thought. Sin is a power that can give Cain thoughts and suggestions, even making Cain think that these thoughts originated with himself (Satan's biggest trick). You see, God dwells within your spirit (1 Cor 6:17), but sin dwells within your body (Rom 7:23). When we talk about sin, it is important to differentiate between sin as a noun (*hamartia*), and sin as a verb (*hamartano*). I am not supporting the false idea that one can say "the devil made me do it," however, I am saying that we have the power to say "NO" to sin with consistency, though never perfection. To blame sin on the "old man" within me promotes denial and flies in the face of what Romans 6 clearly tells us. To say the "sinful nature" in me causes me to sin suggests that it is normal for a Christian to sin several times a day, sometimes even overtly. This lie comes from the devil, the father of lies, and his secret is exposed when we examine the Scriptures further. We will see that sin is a power as Genesis showed us.

As I have been pointing out, our "old self" was crucified, killed, done away with, and never to be raised up again (Rom 6:6). Satan can't raise him up and God won't. What I am about to say is going to shock some of you, but please read on and I will show you that Scripture says it, not me. *Christians* have only one nature, a divine one, not a sinful one. "Through these He has given us His very great and precious promises, so that through them you may *participate in the divine nature* and **escape** the corruption in the world caused by evil desires" (2 Pet 1:4). I know we feel like we have a sinful nature, but that is Satan's successful secret. Through the power of the Spirit I pray that secret will be exposed in the following paragraphs. Many of you may be thinking of Romans 7:18 which reads, "I know that nothing good lives in me, that is, in my sinful nature. For I have the desire to do what is good, but I cannot carry it out." The Hebrew word used for "sinful nature" is *sarx*. The NIV translation of the Bible took the liberty of translating that word as "sinful nature," 23 of the 151 times it is used. Only the NIV did this. Other Bibles translate it as *flesh* or *body*. The point is, "sinful nature" just isn't there. People often use Romans 7 to show that man has two natures, however, look closely and you will see man only has one nature, a good one. Is Paul happy about failing on his good intentions? Does part of him find delight in his screw up? NO! Paul longs to do good and hates the sin (noun) within him. There are two characters represented in Romans; Paul, and sin. That is why he says, "As it is, it is no longer **I myself** who do it, but it is **sin** living in me" (Rom 7:17). He goes on in the next verse to tell us that the power of sin lives in his flesh, though sin is not Paul's identity. Satan loves to get you to think YOU are the one who comes up with these *sinful* ideas and YOU are responsible for the memory traces within your brain. The fact is, however, SIN is crouching at the door and desires to have you FEEL that YOU screwed up and, if possible, FEEL guilty and unforgiven. In Romans chapters 5-8 the word "sin" appears 41 times and only in one case is it translated as a verb (*hamartano*) in 6:14: "For *sin* (noun) *shall not be your master*, because you are not under law, but under grace. What then? Shall we *sin* (verb) because we are not under law but under grace? By no means" (Rom 6:14-15)! To understand our victory in Christ, one needs to understand sin as a power, as a noun. Therefore, SIN offers thoughts to your flesh for you to consider. SIN then deceives you by making you think these are YOUR thoughts. Only when you *act* upon those thoughts do you become accountable. That is Satan's greatest tool against the saints. Go back and read through Romans 5-8 (in any translation other than NIV) and try and find a place that shows that the old man is still alive. It isn't there.

If the sinful nature is non-existent in a Christian's life, who is our battle with? Paul writes, "I see another law at work in the members of my **body**, waging war against the law of my **mind** and making me a prisoner of the law of sin at work within my members" (Rom 7:23). Here we see our enemy is identified as the "law" or the power of sin. Also, this enemy is not living in my **mind** where thoughts are generated, but in my **body**. Therefore, our mind is at war *against* this evil power that God identified back in Genesis 4. Why is your mind against this power? Because God has written His law in our mind: "I will put My laws in their hearts, and I will write them on their minds" (Heb 10:16). You see, your **mind** *wants* to obey God and, therefore, the evil power in your **body** battles *against the law of God* in your **mind** (Rom 7:23). "For who has known the mind of the Lord that He may instruct him? But we have the mind of Christ" (1 Cor 2:16). Our mind is the good guy, and there is not a battle of a good you and a bad you going on, rather a battle of the good you and the evil power of sin (noun) within your body. One might say you have a bad roommate that you can't get rid of. Does this mean the roommate can MAKE you do things you do not *want* to do? NO!

How can we apply this knowledge to our lives? When the power of sin presents a thought to your mind, the trick is to take that thought captive and reject those that are not in line with Godly things: "We take captive every thought to make it obedient to Christ" (2 Cor 10:5). You see, you are not dead to sinning, you are only dead to the power of sin over you. That is why Paul said, "sin (noun) shall not be your master" (Rom 6:14). Sin can't control you because you have the mind of Christ.

Thinking like a saint does not come naturally, one must train themselves to think that way. This is the first step to godly living. Hebrews states, "But solid food is for the mature, who *by constant use* **have trained themselves** to distinguish good from evil" (Heb 5:14). Solid food is for the mature, who because of practice, have trained themselves to discern good and evil. You simply need to understand and begin acting and practice living like a saint. Christ will overcome the power of sin through you, for you. Simply put, we cannot make promises ourselves because we do not have the strength to do so. We need to promise by saying, "Lord, by Your grace alone, I know You can keep my promise through me." But by being trained to think and act like HE is working through us, the power of sin is subdued. Satan is the accuser. He gives you thoughts and then accuses you of originating them. Those thoughts are not yours unless you take them. The more we practice and train ourselves to see Christ in us as saints, the easier it becomes and the more joy-filled our life will be: "Whatever you have learned or received or heard from me, or seen in me-- *put it into practice.* And the God of peace will be with you" (Phil 4:9).

CAUTION! If you think that now you will keep an eye out for these lies of Satan, "take heed, lest ye fall." Satan wants you to do that. This is putting the cart before the horse. The Bible clearly tells us "The mind of sinful man is death, but the mind controlled by the Spirit is life and peace" (Rom 8:6).

If we set our mind to be tuned into sin-filled ideas of sin, Satan has you already defeated. Instead, if you set you mind on things above, sin (noun) is faced with the challenge of getting through those Godly thoughts to deliver his thoughts. The more we are trained to think in godly ways and put Christ into every part of our life, music, entertainment, work, family, etc., the more Satan's thoughts will stick out like a sore thumb. Then you can take that thought captive, reject it, and stay on track with Christ.

Again, to say we have a sinful nature gives us an excuse to sin, but the Bible does not support that. Paul put it beautifully when he said, "In the same way, count yourselves **dead to sin** but alive to God in Christ Jesus. Therefore *do not let sin reign in your mortal* body so that you obey its evil desires. Do not offer the parts of your body to sin, as instruments of wickedness, but rather offer yourselves to God, as those who have been brought from death **to life**; and offer the parts of your body to Him as instruments of righteousness. For sin shall not be your master, because you are not under law, but under grace" (Rom 6:11-14). Now put this Scripture to practice. All true knowledge is the outgrowth of obedience. Everything else is just information, if not acted upon.

As long as we are on a role of challenging your normal thought process, why don't we ask you the question of where the New Testament begins? Do you realize that Jesus' ministry took place under the LAW, not grace? Jesus came to bring a New Covenant of grace, but His ministry only led up to it, it wasn't under it. Therefore, the four gospels are technically under law, or Old Covenant times. Pentecost will usher in the New Testament era in Acts 2. This is vital in properly understanding many portions of Scripture as recorded in the gospels.

I do believe the Bible is inspired in its entirety. However, we must also remember that things like chapter breaks and verse numberings are not inspired. Likewise, the Old/New Testament break is also man made. Luke records Jesus' words, "In the same way, after the supper He took the cup, saying, 'This cup is the New Covenant in My blood, which is *poured out* for you'" (Luke 22:20). The word "covenant" and "testament" are the same Hebrew word, and therefore, Jesus tells us when the New Covenant would begin -- with the pouring out of His blood. The New Covenant could not have stood under the law any more than Moses's basket could have stayed afloat under the law. When Jesus began His ministry He said, "Repent, for the kingdom of heaven is near" (Mat 4:17). Note that He said it was "near" not "here." God's Holy Spirit, which gives faith, had not yet been poured out upon the earth. Many people would give almost anything to have the chance to go back and walk with Christ as the disciples did. Let me tell you, this is nothing to wish for, because you would have been just as blind as they were without the outpouring of the Spirit. We now live in an era much greater than the disciples, and I believe that Scripture will also show this.

To illustrate that Jesus' ministry was under the law, I would like to point out only a small portion of many examples. You can read the gospels and find the rest yourself, however, do not take me as saying that the gospels are not important. They are just as important as the rest of the law and prophets that testify of Christ. They also have grace mixed with their law. However, once the gospels are over, the New Covenant is ushered in and grace abounds. Let us compare Matthew, who recorded Jesus' words, "For **if** you forgive men when they sin against you, your heavenly Father will also forgive you. But **if you do not** forgive men their sins, your Father will *not* forgive your sins" (Mat 6:14-15). Do you see how Christ's ministry was under law? Does this sound like the Gospel you learned about: *If* you forgive, Christ's death is effective, if not, it isn't either? Now look what happens after the New Covenant is ushered in, "**When** you were *dead in your sins* and in the uncircumcision of your sinful [flesh, *sarx*], God *made you alive with Christ*. He *forgave us all our sins*, having canceled the written code, with its regulations, that **was** *against us* and that stood opposed to us; He took it away, nailing it to the cross" (Col 2:13-14). Now we are forgiven by faith, not by our performance. The Bible isn't contradicting itself here, it simply is recording history under two types of covenants. Jesus' entire ministry was trying to bring people to repentance and leave them no place to look but the cross. He was showing them over and over that the law was death for them, and there was no way out except the cross. Look at Matthew 15 when Jesus talked to the Gentile woman and refused to give her gospel (at first): "He replied, 'It is not right to take the children's bread and toss it to their dogs'" (Mat 15:26). Would any of us say that to someone who was willing to receive Christ today? During Old Covenant times, the gospel was for the Jews only. That is why Christ came, to open the doors for all believers, but that time had not yet come here in Matthew. In Matthew 5 we read, "Blessed are those who hunger and thirst for righteousness, for they will be filled" (Mat 5:6). To be righteous means to be perfect. Once we go past Pentecost we then read, "God made Him who had no sin to be sin for us, so that in Him we might become the righteousness of God" (2 Cor 5:21). In the very next verse of Matthew we read, "Blessed are the merciful, for they will be shown mercy" (Mat 5:7). Again, if I don't show mercy to someone, I, myself, will not be given mercy. I sure hope that I have shown enough to receive enough! But what happens after Pentecost: "Praise be to the God and Father of our Lord Jesus Christ! In His great *mercy* He has given us new birth into a living hope through the resurrection of Jesus Christ from the dead" (1 Pet 1:3). Praise God that He gave us mercy without any merit of our own. Matthew continues, "Blessed are the peacemakers, for they will be called sons of God" (Mat 5:9). But Galatians shows we are already sons of God, "You are all sons of God through faith in Christ Jesus" (Gal 3:26). Finally, Matthew culminates the point of his message by saying, "For I tell you that unless your righteousness *surpasses* that of the Pharisees and the teachers of the law, you will certainly not enter the kingdom of heaven. You have heard that it was said to the people long ago, 'Do not murder, and anyone who murders will be subject to judgment.' But I tell you that anyone who is angry with his brother will be subject to judgment. Again, anyone who says to his brother, 'Raca,' is answerable to the Sanhedrin. But anyone who says, 'You fool!' will be in danger of the fire of hell" (Mat 5:20-22). Note the present tense form of those verbs. Now who could stand under that? Jesus was simply leading them up to the point where He could show the people their utter despair, and their need for Him. Later Jesus would throw them a life-raft in the words, "It is because of Him that you are in Christ Jesus, who has become for us wisdom from God--that is, our righteousness, holiness and redemption" (1 Cor 1:30). This sermon was not for us today, it was for those people under the Old Covenant. That is why Jesus said, "Settle matters quickly with your adversary who is taking you to court. Do it while you are still with him on the way, or he may hand you over to the judge, and the judge may hand you over to the officer, and you may be thrown into prison. I tell you the truth, you will not get out until you have paid the last penny" (Mat 5:25-26). People, Jesus wasn't talking about civil court matters here, that Judge was Christ. Jesus clearly showed them that the only way to heaven under their current system was to, "Be perfect, therefore, as your heavenly Father is perfect" (Mat 5:48). They must have walked away from that sermon wondering if there was any hope. To be perfect meant to be blameless. God provided that hope on the cross and then stated, "We proclaim *Him*, admonishing and teaching everyone with all wisdom, so that we may *present everyone perfect in Christ*" (Col 1:28).

This does not mean that the law is bad, and, that it has no purpose today for unbelievers and those that stray. As Timothy states, "We know that the law is good if one uses it properly. We also know that the law is made not for the righteous but for lawbreakers and rebels" (1 Tim 1:8-9). Hebrews tells us the law is written in our minds (Heb 10:16). But what is that for us as Christians? Romans tell us, "Let no debt remain outstanding, except the continuing debt to love one another, for he who loves his fellowman *has fulfilled the law*. The commandments, 'Do not commit adultery,' 'Do not murder,' 'Do not steal,' 'Do not covet,' and whatever other commandment there may be, are summed up in this one rule: 'Love your neighbor as yourself'. Love does no harm to its neighbor. *Therefore love is the fulfillment of the law*" (Rom 13:8-10). Jesus said there were two main laws: 1) Love the Lord your God with all your heart, and 2) Love your neighbor as yourself. Then He said, "All the law and the Prophets hang on these two commandments" (Mat 22:40). Today, we are under the law of love.

I believe this whole topic is more clear when we also look at the twelve apostles. Which twelve? THE twelve! When Judas hung himself (before Pentecost), Peter decided to replace him, so, they cast lots and the lot fell on Matthias. Isn't it interesting that this is the only time we ever hear the name Matthias. We know nothing about him, his family or his ministry. Not another word was said, and he is never mentioned by anyone again. Why? Well, one thing we know about Peter is that he was always running ahead of the game and doing things his way. I tend to believe it was Peter's idea to replace Judas then, not God's. Matthias was man's choice. They narrowed the choices down and then cast lots even before the Holy Spirit had been given. But I think God's choice was Paul. Look what God said of Paul, "But the Lord said to Ananias, 'Go! This man is **My** *chosen instrument* to carry My name before the Gentiles and their kings and before the people of Israel" (Acts 9:15). After all, Paul is afterward called an apostle over 17 times, yet we never hear of Matthias again. And what a choice God made. Isn't it interesting that we know for certain that Paul wrote at least 13 of the 23 New Testament books (after John). When we examine the life of Paul, I believe there is a good reason for this.

In 2 Corinthians 12 Paul wrote, "I know a man in Christ who fourteen years ago was caught up to the third heaven. Whether it was in the body or out of the body I do not know--God knows. And I know that this man--whether in the body or apart from the body I do not know, but God knows--was caught up to *paradise*. He heard *inexpressible things, things that man is not permitted to tell"* (2 Cor 12:2-4). Later we see that this man is Paul and he, perhaps out of humility, used third person language to describe himself. Have you ever wondered what Lazarus experienced after being brought back from the dead? I have! Well, perhaps Paul could tell you. It is interesting that if we go back 14 years to when Paul said this happened, guess where Paul is? Lystra! It is very possible that Paul was dead and brought back to life and during that period experienced what he mentioned in Corinthians. In Lystra this happened to Paul: "Then some Jews came from Antioch and Iconium and won the crowd over. They stoned Paul and dragged him outside the city, *thinking he was dead*. But after the disciples had gathered around him, he got up and went back into the city. The *next day* he and Barnabas left for Derbe" (Acts 14:19-20). Let me tell you, these Jews were not throwing pebbles at Paul, but baseball size and larger stones. These Jews weren't just a little upset either, they were indignant. They even drug him out of the city after he was supposed to be dead. The disciples gathered or "stood" around him and, according to the text, did nothing. I don't know if you have ever been hurt or banged up before, but one thing I can tell you, you aren't going anywhere fast (if at all) the next day. Paul then "got up" or "rose," before going back to his killers. Can you imagine what the stoners must have thought? Paul then went 30 miles to Derbe the very next day. Again, I can't say for sure, but I think Paul was raised from the dead like Eutychus was (Acts 20:9). After all, Paul was God's chosen servant.

    We also see that Paul was the only disciple personally tutored by Christ after the cross, and even this was "one on one" out in the Arabian desert. Fourteen years later Paul was called to preach the "true faith" (1 Tim 2:7) to the Gentiles. Paul even admits that his knowledge (that he received from the ASCENDED Lord) did not come from the other apostles. In fact, Paul even says, "those men added nothing to my message" (Gal 2:6). Paul had a unique experience that none of the other apostles had: he had been taught openly (not in parables) by the ascended Christ. Add to this as well, that Paul was listening and seeing with open eyes and ears. When the disciples were with Jesus they were continually asking Him to repeat and explain, and even then, they still did not understand. After the Holy Spirit came, however, their eyes were opened and they were, for the most part (not completely), left to recall what Christ had said. Paul had the Holy Spirit and was taught not by the disciples, but by Christ. In fact, three years go by before he even meets the disciples in Jerusalem, and even then he did not see them all. When Paul had his revelation where he was "caught up" to paradise he heard words that were not allowed to be shared yet. Bill Gillham has written a fantastic book called, *What God Wishes Christians knew about Christianity*. Much of what we have been talking about in this "saint or sinner" section has come from his book. He writes, "Could it be that God commanded Paul to share the secret revelation to the churches before his martyrdom? I'm speculating that this may be the case because Ephesians, Colossians, and Philippians have much to say about the glorious truths of our identity in Christ. The first four chapters of Ephesians, as well as many verses in Galatians, Philippians, and Colossians, address this. On the other hand, this topic is treated much more lightly, if at all, in Paul's earlier writings (1 and 2 Thessalonians, 1 and 2 Corinthians, and Romans). The fact that no other New Testament scribes record the truths of our new identity in Christ this extensively makes me suspect that they were revealed more completely to Paul. . . .Sometimes it can get lonely at the top. This is especially true when you feel like you're the only one who is saying or doing something a particular way and you are encountering opposition from those who are ostensibly reading from the same page as you. Did Paul begin to have some doubts about whether his message needed some tweaking? Perhaps so. Human reinforcement is encouraging. God designed the body of Christ this way. The Scriptures say, 'Then after an interval of fourteen years I [Paul] went up again to Jerusalem. . .And it was because of a revelation that I went up; and I submitted to them the gospel which I preach among the Gentiles, but I did so in private to those who were of reputation, for fear that I might be running, or had run, in vain (Gal 2:1-2)'" (pp. 166-167). Paul wrote, "But their minds were made dull, for to this day the same veil remains when the Old Covenant is read. It has not been removed, because only in Christ is it taken away" (2 Cor 3:14). Perhaps Paul was "better versed" in the deeper truths of Scripture, because he was trained when that veil was completely removed. The other 11 disciples had been trained by Christ during His ministry under the law. So when we review Paul's life, we see he was converted, spent three years with Jesus in the desert, went and saw Peter and James, then 14 years later went to the Gentiles. But during these times, Paul was able to say that the apostles contributed nothing to his message (Gal 2:6). This, plus his "revelation," may have meant that God had given Paul a message that unveiled the Gospel, not only to the Gentiles, but to the whole world.

Even the other disciples took note of Paul's message saying, "He writes the same way in all his letters, speaking in them of these matters. His letters contain *some things that are hard to understand*, which ignorant and unstable people distort, as they do the other Scriptures, to their own destruction" (2 Pet 3:16). Peter shows us that Paul's teachings were hard to understand, but more importantly, if one does not take note of them or distorts them, it is to their own demise. We become unstable and ignorant in all of scripture because Paul's truth is foundational for your Christian identity as a saint.

Rev 20:7 When the thousand years are over, Satan will be released from his prison 20:8 and will go out to deceive the nations in the four corners of the earth--Gog and Magog--to gather them for battle. In number they are like the sand on the seashore.

When the thousand years are over, Satan will be released from the Abyss for a short time in order that he may go out and deceive all nations in the four corners of the earth. The millennial reign could be seen as being limited to Jerusalem, not the whole earth and, therefore, the people reigning with Christ would not turn away from Him. We read in Isaiah, "He will raise a banner for the nations and gather the exiles of Israel; He will assemble the scattered people of Judah *from* the four quarters of the earth" (Isa 11:12). If this is true, that explains the many verses that we have seen prior to chapter 20 where God gathers His people to Zion, Jerusalem, or His holy hill. The people of the earth will hate God's people who are protected from them. Once Satan is released, they will see their hope and, therefore, gain courage to march against the city of God and His people. This great battle is called the Battle of Armageddon. Little do they know, but this is all part of God's plan for His divine judgment upon them.

A problem with the literal interpretation for the 1000 years deals with the final battle. In chapter 16 we saw the bowl judgments taking place. There the sixth angel poured out his bowl on the great river Euphrates, which then dried up to prepare the way for the kings of the earth to march against God's people during the battle on the Great Day of the Lord. The problem was that evil spirits came out of the mouth of the dragon (Satan), the beast (Antichrist), and the false prophet, to perform miraculous signs to convince the people to march against God and His people. The question then becomes, why are the beast and the false prophet missing in chapter 20? The answer is because they were cast into hell in chapter 19. But the above verses tell us that only Satan went out to deceive the nations to gather them for battle. Either things are not as cut and dry as one thinks, or there could be two great battles.

The places Satan gathers his followers to, are called Gog and Magog. The number of people gathered will be in the millions upon millions. The best explanation of these events are given by God Himself in the book of Ezekiel:

> "Son of man, set your face against Gog, of the land of Magog, the chief prince of Meshech and Tubal; prophesy against him and say: 'This is what the Sovereign LORD says: I am against you, O Gog, chief prince of Meshech and Tubal. I will turn you around, *put hooks in your jaws* [note they are being led] and bring you out with your whole army--your horses, your horsemen fully armed, and a great horde with large and small shields, all of them brandishing their swords. Persia, Cush and Put will be with them, all with shields and helmets, also Gomer with all its troops, and Beth Togarmah from the far north with all its troops--the many nations with you. Get ready; be prepared, you and all the hordes gathered about you, and take command of them. *After many days* you will be called to arms. *In future years* you will invade a land that has recovered from war, *whose people were gathered from many nations to the mountains of Israel, which had long been desolate.* They had been brought out from the nations, and *now all of them live in safety.* You and all your troops and the many nations with you will go up, advancing like a storm; *you will be like a cloud covering the land* [like sand on the seashore].' This is what the Sovereign LORD says: 'On that day thoughts will come into your mind and you will devise an evil scheme. You will say, "I will invade a land of unwalled villages; I will attack a peaceful and unsuspecting people--all of them living without walls and without gates and bars. I will plunder and loot and turn my hand against the resettled ruins and the people gathered from the nations, rich in livestock and goods, living at the center of the land...." This is what the Sovereign LORD says: In that day, *when My people Israel are living in*

safety, [This has not happened yet] will you not take notice of it? You will come from your place in the *far north*, you and *many nations with you*, all of them riding on horses, a great horde, a mighty army. You will advance against My people Israel like a cloud that covers the land. In days to come, O Gog, I will bring you *against My land*, [note it is not the whole world, only the Holy land] so that the nations may know Me when I show Myself holy *through you before their eyes*.' This is what the Sovereign LORD says: 'Are you not the one I spoke of in former days by My servants the prophets of Israel? At that time they prophesied for years that I would bring you against them. This is what will happen in that day: When Gog *attacks the land of Israel*, My hot anger will be aroused, declares the Sovereign LORD. In My zeal and fiery wrath I declare that at that time *there shall be a great earthquake* [as in the last vial judgments] in the land of Israel. The fish of the sea, the birds of the air, the beasts of the field, every creature that moves along the ground, and all the people on the face of the earth will tremble at My presence [as we see in Matthew 24 and Revelation]. The mountains will be overturned, the cliffs will crumble and every wall will fall to the ground. I will summon a sword against Gog on all My mountains, declares the Sovereign LORD. Every man's sword will be against his brother. I will execute judgment upon him with plague and bloodshed; I will pour down torrents of rain, hailstones and burning sulfur on him and on his troops and on the many nations with him. And so I will show My greatness and My holiness, and I will make Myself known in the sight of many nations. Then they will know that I am the LORD'" (Ezek 38:1-23). Wow! Isn't that an amazing description of these last days?

Interestingly, Ezekiel 39 continues on talking about this great battle:

"Son of man, prophesy against Gog and say: 'This is what the Sovereign LORD says: I am against you, O Gog, chief prince of Meshech and Tubal. I will turn you around and drag you along. I will bring you *from the far north* and send you *against the mountains of Israel*. Then I will strike your bow from your left hand and make your arrows drop from your right hand. On the mountains of Israel you will fall, you and all your troops and the nations with you. *I will give you as food to all kinds of carrion birds and to the wild animals.* You will fall in the open field, for I have spoken, declares the Sovereign LORD. I will send fire on Magog and on those who live in safety in the coastlands, and they will know that I am the LORD. I will make known My holy Name among My people Israel. I will no longer let My holy Name be profaned, and the nations will know that I the LORD am the Holy One in Israel. It is coming! It will surely take place, declares the Sovereign LORD. *This is the day I have spoken of.* Then those who live in the towns of Israel will go out and use the weapons for fuel and burn them up--the small and large shields, the bows and arrows, the war clubs and spears. For seven years they will use them for fuel. They will not need to gather wood from the fields or cut it from the forests, because they will use the weapons for fuel. And they will plunder those who plundered them and loot those who looted them,' declares the Sovereign LORD. 'On that day I will give Gog a burial place in Israel, in the valley of those who travel east toward the Sea. It will block the way of travelers, because Gog and all his hordes will be buried there. So it will be called the *Valley of Hamon Gog*. For seven months the house of Israel will be burying them in order to cleanse the land. All the people of the land will bury them, and the day I am glorified will be a memorable day for them,' declares the Sovereign LORD. 'Men will be regularly employed to cleanse the land. Some will go throughout the land and, in addition to them, others will bury those that remain on the ground. At the end of the seven months they will begin their search. As they go through the land and one of them sees a human bone, he will set up a marker beside it until the gravediggers have buried it in the Valley of Hamon Gog. (Also a town called Hamonah will be there.) And so they will cleanse the land.' Son of man, this is what the Sovereign LORD says: 'Call out to every kind of bird and all the wild animals: assemble and come together from all around to the sacrifice I am preparing for you, the great sacrifice on the mountains of Israel. There you will eat flesh and drink blood. You will eat the flesh of mighty men and drink the blood of the princes of the earth as if they were rams and lambs, goats and bulls--all of them fattened animals from Bashan. At the sacrifice I am preparing for you, you will eat fat till you are glutted and drink blood till you are drunk. At My table you will eat your fill of horses and riders, mighty men and soldiers of every kind,' declares the Sovereign LORD" (Ezek 39:1-20).

Obviously, there is much we do not understand about this day. I believe we will not know until the time comes, but in the meantime, we wait patiently for Christ's second coming.

Ezekiel seems to be a mini-book of Revelation (or extended book, depending on how you look at it). As you have just seen, Ezekiel 38 and 39 go through the final battle as we see here in Chapter 19 and 20 of Revelation. Ezekiel 40-48 will then begin describing the new Jerusalem just as we will see Revelation 21-22 do.

Rev 20:9 They marched across the breadth of the earth and surrounded the camp of God's people, the city he loves. But fire came down from heaven and devoured them. 20:10 And the devil, who deceived them, was thrown into the lake of burning sulfur, where the beast and the false prophet had been thrown. They will be tormented day and night for ever and ever.

Verse nine tells us that the evil army marches up to the city of God or Jerusalem. It is interesting that it is called the "camp" of God's people, showing it to be a single, temporary location. Indeed, God has a special plan for Jerusalem as the Psalmist says, "The LORD loves the gates of Zion more than all the dwellings of Jacob. Glorious things are said of you, O city of God" (Psa 87:2-3).

God brings fire down from heaven and destroys the army of Satan as Ezekiel had described in chapter 38 and 39. There is no battle, the evil kings only think there will be. Then Satan was cast into hell, the same place the beast and false prophet had been throne earlier in chapter 19. Here they will be tormented for an eternity.

Rev 20:11 Then I saw a great white throne and him who was seated on it. Earth and sky fled from his presence, and there was no place for them. 20:12 And I saw the dead, great and small, standing before the throne, and books were opened. Another book was opened, which is the book of life. The dead were judged according to what they had done as recorded in the books. 20:13 The sea gave up the dead that were in it, and death and Hades gave up the dead that were in them, and each person was judged according to what he had done. 20:14 Then death and Hades were thrown into the lake of fire. The lake of fire is the second death. 20:15 If anyone's name was not found written in the book of life, he was thrown into the lake of fire.

The completion of time has come, and John sees a great white throne with the Judge seated on it. The earth and sky fled from His presence, showing that the old way of things is passing away just as Peter had said, "But in keeping with His promise we are looking forward to a new heaven and a new earth, the home of righteousness" (2 Pet 3:13). Jesus also stated, "Heaven and earth will pass away, but My words will never pass away" (Mat 24:35). This is why there was no place for the earth or sky.

All of the dead were standing before the throne waiting for their judgment. Books were opened to determine the extent of the judgment as well. Note that it is not one book, but plural books. Typically, we only think of the Book of Life, which is mentioned after these books. The book of life is mentioned many times throughout Scripture:

- "But now, please forgive their sin--but if not, then blot me out of the book you have written" (Exo 32:32).

- "May they be blotted out of the book of life and not be listed with the righteous" (Psa 69:28).

- "At that time Michael, the great prince who protects your people, will arise. There will be a time of distress such as has not happened from the beginning of nations until then. But at that time your people--everyone whose name is found written in the book--will be delivered" (Dan 12:1).

- "Yes, and I ask you, loyal yokefellow, help these women who have contended at my side in the cause of the gospel, along with Clement and the rest of my fellow workers, whose names are in the book of life" (Phil 4:3).

- "Then those who feared the LORD talked with each other, and the LORD listened and heard. A scroll of remembrance was written in His presence concerning those who feared the LORD and honored His name"(Mal 3:16).

- "However, do not rejoice that the spirits submit to you, but rejoice that your names are written in heaven" (Luke 10:20).

- "He who overcomes will, like them, be dressed in white. I will never blot out his name from the book of life, but will acknowledge his name before My Father and His angels" (Rev 3:5 see also Rev 13:8, 22:19, 21:27, and 17:8).

That is the book of life, but what are the other books? Though we can't be certain, there seem to be books that record your works, not your righteousness.

- In Romans we see that perhaps there is a book of conscience: "since they show that the requirements of the law *are written* on their hearts, their consciences also bearing witness, and their thoughts now accusing, now even defending them" (Rom 2:15).

- Matthew suggests a book for words: "But I tell you that men will have to give account on the day of judgment for every careless word they have spoken. For by your words you will be acquitted, and by your words you will be condemned" (Mat 12:36).

- We also see a record of public works: "For the Son of Man is going to come in His Father's glory with His angels, and then He will reward each person according to what he has done" (Mat 16:27). And, "It is not surprising, then, if His servants masquerade as servants of righteousness. Their end will be what their actions deserve" (2 Cor 11:15).

- Perhaps also a book of secret words: "This will take place on the day when God will judge men's secrets through Jesus Christ, as my gospel declares" (Rom 2:16).

- "The LORD will never be willing to forgive him; His wrath and zeal will burn against that man. All the curses written in this book will fall upon Him, and the LORD will blot out his name from under heaven" (Deu 29:20).

Verse 12 tells us that the dead were judged according to what they had done as recorded in these books. It seems that their bodies will rise for this judgment, "But your dead will live; their bodies will rise. You who dwell in the dust, wake up and shout for joy. Your dew is like the dew of the morning; the earth will give birth to her dead" (Isa 26:19). However, verse 13 suggests that those being judged here are all evil, because they come from the sea and hell. The end result is that they are cast into hell again. This judgment simply makes it official and more complete.

Verse 14 tells us that even death and hades are cast into the lake of fire. Paul wrote, "The last enemy to be destroyed is death" (1 Cor 15:26).

If anyone's name was not found in the Book of Life, they were thrown into the lake of fire, their second and final death. A very important thing to realize is that when a Christian sins and repents, his sins are forgiven and remembered no more. We read in Psalms, "as far as the east is from the west, so far has He removed our transgressions from us" (Psa 103:12). That is why Paul wrote, "Blessed are they whose transgressions are forgiven, whose sins are covered. Blessed is the man whose sin the Lord will never count against him" (Rom 4:7).

Therefore, these books may be primarily for the ungodly, to see which part of hell they are to be thrown into. God will not judge our *salvation* by our works. On the other hand, our works show the measure of our faith, which is why, "as the body without the spirit is dead, so faith without deeds is dead" (James 2:26). While God does record the evil deeds of the ungodly, only the good deeds of the Christian are remembered. It is possible that the plural books are used to judge the dead in Christ, while the book of life was used to determine those who had salvation. That may be why they are separated in their descriptions. If your name is not found in the book of life, you are blotted out, and will be remembered no more. To say it is blotted out suggests that everyone has their name in the Book of Life until they reject God's grace and forgiveness. Family members who are not Christians will no longer be remembered, because that would make for a sad heavenly existence knowing your loved ones are suffering in hell. That is why Isaiah says, "Behold, I will create new heavens and a new earth. *The former things will not be remembered, nor will they come to mind*" (Isa 65:17). Note that this is at the time that the new heavens and earth are being created, just as we saw the earth going away here in Revelation.

Note also that there are degrees of glory in heaven and degrees of punishment in hell. There are many passages supporting this. Consider the following verses:

- "That servant who knows his master's will and does not get ready or does not do what his master wants will be beaten with many blows. But the one who does not know and does things deserving punishment will be beaten with few blows. From everyone who has been given much, much will be demanded; and from the one who has been entrusted with much, much more will be asked" (Luke 12:47-48).
- "The man who plants and the man who waters have one purpose, and each will be rewarded according to his own labor" (1 Cor 3:8).
- "Your mina has earned ten more. 'Well done, My good servant!' his master replied. 'Because you have been trustworthy in a very

small matter, take charge of ten cities.' The second came and said, 'Sir, your mina has earned five more.' His master answered, 'You take charge of five cities.' Then another servant came and said, 'Sir, here is your mina; I have kept it laid away in a piece of cloth. I was afraid of you, because you are a hard man. You take out what You did not put in and reap what You did not sow.' His master replied, 'I will judge you by your own words, you wicked servant! You knew, did you, that I am a hard man, taking out what I did not put in, and reaping what I did not sow? Why then didn't you put my money on deposit, so that when I came back, I could have collected it with interest?' Then he said to those standing by, 'Take his mina away from him and give it to the one who has ten minas.' 'Sir,' they said, 'he already has ten!' He replied, 'I tell you that to everyone who has, *more will be given*, but as for the one who has nothing, even what he has will be taken away'"(Luke 19:17-26).

- "Those who are wise will shine like the brightness of the heavens, and those who lead many to righteousness, like the stars for ever and ever" (Dan 12:3).
- "For no one can lay any foundation other than the one already laid, *which is Jesus Christ*. If any man builds on this foundation using gold, silver, costly stones, wood, hay or straw, his work will be shown for what it is, because the *Day* [note capital "D" means final day] will bring it to light. It will be revealed with fire, and the fire will test the quality of each man's work. If what he has built survives, he will receive his reward. If it is burned up, he will **suffer loss**; he *himself will be saved*, **but** *only as one escaping through the flames*" (1 Cor 3:11-15).
- "I the LORD search the heart and examine the mind, to reward a man according to his conduct, according to what his deeds deserve" (Jer 17:10).
- "For the Son of Man is going to come in His Father's glory with His angels, and then He will reward each person according to what he has done" (Mat 16:27).

For some these glories of heaven are confusing, however, they do not realize that God has much more to offer than just salvation. He wants His children to have the best, and to grow up being the best they can be. He has many blessings that go along with salvation if we will only do what it takes to get them. We can go through life believing in and accepting Jesus as our personal Savior, but doing nothing about it and still be saved. However, if we daily read our Bible and go to the source of these blessings, the Holy Spirit will fill you with joy and peace on this earth, despite trials and temptations. Likewise, those who use their faith and do many good works will be rewarded for showing others the righteousness that comes from Christ. If we hide this information and only keep it a personal and private faith, there may not be as much of a reward.

I like to look at it as a 16 oz. glass versus a 32 oz. glass. In heaven, those who build upon the foundation of Jesus with hay and straw, or nothing of value, will be saved. However, in heaven they will only be a 16 oz. cup plum full to the brim. Those who build upon the foundation of Christ with gold and silver, the precious things of good works and faith sharing etc., will be rewarded with the 32 oz. cup plum full to the brim. Whether you are a 16 oz. or 32 oz. Cup, you will be as happy as you can be. You are plum full and can hold no more. Though one gets more than the other, there is no jealousy because you don't know any better. For example, imagine you just ate all the cake you could eat and you are plum full. Now you see someone else eating cake across the room. Will you covet that cake? Not at all, because you are as full as you can be. If your 16 oz. cup wasn't full you may desire more, but as long as your full, you are satisfied and long for nothing else. God disciplines those He loves, because He not only wants all of His children to be saved, but to be the 32 and 64 oz. cups in heaven. He wants you to be as successful as you can be when you grow up, not into adulthood, but into spiritual maturity.

Therefore, though the dead are judged by the bad they do, the Christians will only be judged by their good and how much of it there was. Their faith (not works) gets their names in the Book of Life, and if your name is there, salvation is yours.

CHAPTER 21

Rev 21:1 Then I saw a new heaven and a new earth, for the first heaven and the first earth had passed away, and there was no longer any sea. 21:2 I saw the Holy City, the new Jerusalem, coming down out of heaven from God, prepared as a bride beautifully dressed for her husband. 21:3 And I heard a loud voice from the throne saying, "Now the dwelling of God is with men, and he will live with them. They will be his people, and God himself will be with them and be their God. 21:4 He will wipe every tear from their eyes. There will be no more death or mourning or crying or pain, for the old order of things has passed away." 21:5 He who was seated on the throne said, "I am making everything new!" Then he said, "Write this down, for these words are trustworthy and true."

After death and all evil had been cast into hell, John saw a new heaven and a new earth being created, just as we ourselves were told: "But in keeping with His promise we are looking forward to a new heaven and a new earth, the home of righteousness" (2 Pet 3:13). This home will be eternal and never changing: "'As the new heavens and the new earth that I make will endure before Me,' declares the LORD, 'so will your name and descendants endure'" (Isa 66:22). And as mentioned earlier, we will no longer remember the things that took place here on this earth: "Behold, I will create new heavens and a new earth. The former things will not be remembered, nor will they come to mind. But be glad and rejoice forever in what I will create, for I will create Jerusalem to be a delight and its people a joy. I will rejoice over Jerusalem and take delight in My people; the sound of weeping and of crying will be heard in it no more" (Isa 65:17-19).

There will be no sea on the new earth, perhaps because there is no need for it. Today the sea is vital to keep the temperature on earth down. Without it, we would burn up. Also, throughout Scripture we see that the depths have been a type of holding place for evil. The dragon comes out of the Abyss, as did one beast in chapter 13. All the evil people in the days of Noah were buried by water. In Matthew the evil spirits called Legion were cast into the water. Scripture does not make this possibility certain, but the depths also hold a lot of uncertainties, and there will not be anything unknown in heaven.

On this new earth will be a new Jerusalem, as spoke of many times in the Bible:

- "For here we do not have an enduring city, but we are looking for the city that is to come" (Heb 13:14).
- "Instead, they were longing for a better country--a heavenly one. Therefore God is not ashamed to be called their God, for He has prepared a city for them" (Heb 11:16).

- "But you have come to Mount Zion, to the heavenly Jerusalem, the city of the living God. You have come to thousands upon thousands of angels in joyful assembly" (Heb 12:22).
- "In My Father's house are many rooms; if it were not so, I would have told you. I am going there to prepare a place for you. And if I go and prepare a place for you, I will come back and take you to be with Me that you also may be where I am" (John 14:2-3).
- "Awake, awake, O Zion, clothe yourself with strength. Put on your garments of splendor, O Jerusalem, the holy city. The uncircumcised and defiled will not enter you again" (Isa 52:1).

Perhaps the most fascinating of all passages regarding this new city is that we will become one with Christ in it. As we saw in the section on 3:12, we will become pillars in the temple, yet the Temple is Christ according to 21:22. We read, "Him who overcomes I will make a pillar in the temple of My God. Never again will he leave it. I will write on him the name of My God and the name of the city of my God, the new Jerusalem, which is coming down out of heaven from my God; and I will also write on him My new name" (Rev 3:12). That is why we also see passages predicting God's presence being with His people: "Then have them make a sanctuary for Me, and I will dwell among them" (Exo 25:8). Ezekiel said, "The distance all around will be 18,000 cubits. And the name of the city from that time on will be: THE LORD IS THERE" (Ezek 48:35). Even Zecheriah joined in and prophesied, "'Shout and be glad, O Daughter of Zion. For I am coming, and I will live among you,' declares the LORD" (Zec 2:10). Just as Adam and Eve could walk and talk with God, we, too, in our glorified bodies will have the same blessed opportunity. What began in Genesis is reaching its fulfillment in Revelation. As Paul said, "What agreement is there between the temple of God and idols? For we are the temple of the living God. As God has said: 'I will live with them and walk among them, and I will be their God, and they will be My people'" (2 Cor 6:16).

In this new heaven and earth there will be no tears, as we have also seen predicted many times:
- "He will swallow up death forever. The Sovereign LORD will wipe away the tears from all faces; He will remove the disgrace of His people from all the earth. The LORD has spoken" (Isa 25:8).
- "and the ransomed of the LORD will return. They will enter Zion with singing; everlasting joy will crown their heads. Gladness and joy will overtake them, and sorrow and sighing will flee away" (Isa 35:10).
- "For the Lamb at the center of the throne will be their shepherd; He will lead them to springs of living water. And God will wipe away every tear from their eyes" (Rev 7:17).

The old order of things will have passed away and the new way of life will begin, and never end. However, as Christians we need to realize that this eternity has already begun. We are not waiting for an eternity to begin, we live it now, because death will have no power over us. We are in Christ Jesus and,

"Therefore, if anyone is in Christ, he is a new creation; *the old has gone, the new has come*" (2 Cor 5:17)!

Rev 21:6 He said to me: "It is done. I am the Alpha and the Omega, the Beginning and the End. To him who is thirsty I will give to drink without cost from the spring of the water of life. 21:7 He who overcomes will inherit all this, and I will be his God and he will be my son. 21:8 But the cowardly, the unbelieving, the vile, the murderers, the sexually immoral, those who practice magic arts, the idolaters and all liars-- their place will be in the fiery lake of burning sulfur. This is the second death."

Once the new heavens and earth are created, all things will be complete. Because of what we read in chapter 16, it is possible that all of this will take place right after the seventh bowl judgment, "The seventh angel poured out his bowl into the air, and out of the temple came a loud voice from the throne, saying, 'It is done'" (Rev 16:17)! After all, something ongoing should take place during the seventh bowl because something does for every other series of sevens.

Our heavenly reign will be the fulfillment of what Christ had been telling us all along: Come to Me if you are thirsty. Consider the following:

- "Come, all you who are thirsty, come to the waters; and you who have no money, come, buy and eat! Come, buy wine and milk without money and without cost" (Isa 55:1).
- "Jesus answered her, 'If you knew the gift of God and who it is that asks you for a drink, you would have asked Him and He would have given you living water. . . but whoever drinks the water I give him will never thirst. Indeed, the water I give him will become in him a spring of water welling up to eternal life'" (John 4:10,14).
- "On the last and greatest day of the Feast, Jesus stood and said in a loud voice, 'If anyone is thirsty, let him come to Me and drink. Whoever believes in Me, as the Scripture has said, streams of living water will flow from within him'" (John 7:37-38).

Once our thirst is quenched by eternal life, we are truly sons of God. Paul wrote to the Romans, "Those who are led by the Spirit of God are sons of God" (Rom 8:14). Right now, we can be sons of God when led by the Spirit.

Verse 8 goes on to explain that no evil will be allowed to stay in heaven. As in the parable of the wedding banquet, the man who was not wearing wedding clothes was cast into hell. Paul declared, "Do you not know that the wicked will not inherit the kingdom of God? Do not be deceived: Neither the sexually immoral nor idolaters nor adulterers nor male prostitutes nor homosexual offenders nor thieves nor the greedy nor drunkards nor slanderers nor swindlers will inherit the kingdom of God" (1 Cor 6:9-10). Also in Hebrews we read, "Make every effort to live in peace with all men and to be holy; without holiness no one will see the Lord" (Heb 12:14). This is precisely why we are given white linen to wear in heaven, because as we saw in chapter 19, white linen stands for the righteous acts of the saints. Through the blood of Christ we have been made holy. Without Christ, we have no way of entering heaven, because we have no way of attaining righteousness without Him. Praise God for His deliverance!

Rev 21:9 One of the seven angels who had the seven bowls full of the seven last plagues came and said to me, "Come, I will show you the bride, the wife of the Lamb." 21:10 And he carried me away in the Spirit to a mountain great and high, and showed me the Holy City, Jerusalem, coming down out of heaven from God. 21:11 It shone with the glory of God, and its brilliance was like that of a very precious jewel, like a jasper, clear as crystal. 21:12 It had a great, high wall with twelve gates, and with twelve angels at the gates. On the gates were written the names of the twelve tribes of Israel. 21:13 There were three gates on the east, three on the north, three on the south and three on the west. 21:14 The wall of the city had twelve foundations, and on them were the names of the twelve apostles of the Lamb.

One of the seven angels who HAD already poured out the bowl judgments told John to follow him, because he would show John the bride of Christ, or the Christian church.

Rather than following the angel, John was carried away by him in the Spirit. This was not the first time this happened to John as we saw it in 1:10, 4:2, and 17:3.

What John sees is astounding; a great high mountain and the Holy City of Jerusalem coming out of heaven. Ezekiel was shown the same vision as well, "In visions of God He took me to the land of Israel and set me on a very high mountain, on whose south side were some buildings that looked like a city. He took me there, and I saw a man whose appearance was like bronze; He was standing in the gateway with a linen cord and a measuring rod in His hand" (Ezek 40:2). This mountain is very interesting in that it seems to be Christ. In Daniel's vision of the end times this is what he saw happen to the golden statue, which represented the kingdoms of the earth: "While you were watching, a Rock was cut out, but not by human hands. It struck the statue on its feet of iron and clay and smashed them. Then the iron, the clay, the bronze, the silver and the gold were broken to pieces at the same time and became like chaff on a threshing floor in the summer. The wind swept them away without leaving a trace. But the Rock that struck the statue became a huge mountain and filled the whole earth" (Dan 2:34-35).

The above mountain, representing Christ, shows us why the city is so bright in verse 11, because Jesus is the light. In Isaiah we read, "Arise, shine, for your light has come, and the glory of the LORD rises upon you. See, darkness covers the earth and thick darkness is over the peoples, but the LORD rises upon you and His glory appears over you" (Isa 60:1-2). Ezekiel also wrote, "I saw the glory of the God of Israel coming *from the east*. His voice was like the roar of rushing waters, and the land was radiant with His glory. The vision I saw was like the vision I had seen when He came to destroy the city" (Ezek 43:2-3).

The city had 12 angels at 12 gates, and each gate bore a name of a tribe of Israel. Three of these gates were on the east, three on the west, three on the south and three on the north. From Ezekiel, we know that the city is divided up in this way because three tribes of Israel will live on each side. The names on each gate correspond to where they will live. We read, "These will be the exits of the city: Beginning on the north side, which is 4,500 cubits long, the gates of the city will be *named after the tribes of Israel*. The three gates on the north side will be the gate of Reuben, the gate of Judah and the gate of Levi. On the east side, which is 4,500 cubits long, will be three gates: the gate of Joseph, the gate of Benjamin and the gate of Dan. On the south side, which measures 4,500 cubits, will be three gates: the gate of Simeon, the gate of Issachar and the gate of Zebulun. On the west side, which is 4,500 cubits long, will be three gates: the gate of Gad, the gate of Asher and the gate of Naphtali. The distance all around will be 18,000 cubits. And the name of the city from that time on will be: THE LORD IS THERE" (Ezek 48:30-35). Once again we see that nothing in Scripture is an accident. Numbers 2 shows us that when in the wilderness, the Israelites also camped with three tribes on each side of the tabernacle to represent what would be seen in heaven. That is why we read in Hebrews, "They serve at a sanctuary that is a copy and shadow of what is in heaven. This is why Moses was warned when he was about to build the tabernacle: 'See to it that you make everything according to the pattern shown you on the mountain'" (Heb 8:5).

Besides the gates, the city also had twelve foundations, one for each of the apostles of Christ. Each foundation bore one of their names. We read in Ephesians, "Consequently, you are no longer foreigners and aliens, but fellow citizens with God's people and members of God's household, built on the foundation of the apostles and prophets, with Christ Jesus Himself as the chief cornerstone" (Eph 2:19-20). Speaking of Abraham, the author of Hebrews wrote, "For he was looking forward to the city with foundations, whose architect and builder is God" (Heb 11:10). The foundation of this city was talked about long before John saw it here in Revelation. Some wonder if Judas will have his name there. The answer is no! Judas did not have the proper foundation, which is why he was replaced, "Then they cast lots, and the lot fell to Matthias; so he was added to the eleven apostles" (Acts 1:26). Also, as discussed in the saint or sinner section, it is most probable that it will be Paul's name there, and not Matthias.

Rev 21:15 The angel who talked with me had a measuring rod of gold to measure the city, its gates and its walls. 21:16 The city was laid out like a square, as long as it was wide. He measured the city with the rod and found it to be 12,000 stadia in length, and as wide and high as it is long. 21:17 He measured its wall and it was 144 cubits thick, by man's measurement, which the angel was using. 21:18 The wall was made of jasper, and the city of pure gold, as pure as glass. 21:19 The foundations of the city walls were decorated with every kind of precious stone. The first

223

foundation was jasper, the second sapphire, the third chalcedony, the fourth emerald, 21:20 the fifth sardonyx, the sixth carnelian, the seventh chrysolite, the eighth beryl, the ninth topaz, the tenth chrysoprase, the eleventh jacinth, and the twelfth amethyst. 21:21 The twelve gates were twelve pearls, each gate made of a single pearl. The great street of the city was of pure gold, like transparent glass.

The same angel who brought John to see the city held a gold measuring rod to measure the city. Ezekiel saw the walls of Jerusalem being measured in Ezekiel 40:3ff. Zecheriah also saw an angel measuring Jerusalem, "I asked, 'Where are you going?' He answered me, 'To measure Jerusalem, to find out how wide and how long it is'" (Zec 2:2).

The city was found to be a perfect cube, just as Ezekiel had seen, each side being exactly 4500 cubits long (Ezek 48:16, 32-34). Again, it is no coincidence that the Most Holy Place in the temple of God was a perfect cube either. "For Christ did not enter a man-made sanctuary that was only a copy of the true one; *He entered heaven itself*, now to appear for us in God's presence. Nor did He enter heaven to offer Himself again and again, the way the high priest enters the Most Holy Place every year with blood that is not his own. . . Therefore, brothers, since *we have confidence to enter the Most Holy Place* by the blood of Jesus" (Heb 9:24-25,10:19).

To put the size of this city into perspective, its description suggests that it is 2,250,000 square miles at the base, 1500 miles high, wide, and long. That is about ten times larger than Germany and should hold about 100,000,000,000 people. Its walls were about 200 feet thick as well. This is no small city.

The city is pure gold, as pure as glass. We know that gold in its purest form is translucent. The astronauts had a layer of gold on their visors on their helmets, yet they could see through them. What a beautiful and amazing sight this must be. As Jesus said, "In My Father's house are many rooms; if it were not so, I would have told you. I am going there to prepare a place for you. And if I go and prepare a place for you, I will come back and take you to be with Me that you also may be where I am" (John 14:2-3). I can't wait!

The foundations of the city are decorated with twelve stones. Again, this is important even in Old Testament times. The breastplate of the priests had twelve stones on them: "Then mount four rows of precious stones on it. In the first row there shall be a ruby, a topaz and a beryl; in the second row a turquoise, a sapphire and an emerald; in the third row a jacinth, an agate and an amethyst; in the fourth row a chrysolite, an onyx and a jasper. Mount them in gold filigree settings. There are to be twelve stones, one for each of the names of the sons of Israel, each engraved like a seal with the name of one of the twelve tribes" (Exo 28:17-21). Even when the Israelites crossed the Jordan into the promised land they were to take 12 stones as a stone memorial for what God had done for them, "Choose twelve men from among the people, one from each tribe, and tell them to take up twelve stones from the middle of the Jordan from right where the priests stood and to carry them over with you and put them down at the place where you stay tonight. . . and said to them, 'Go over before the ark of the LORD your God into the middle of the Jordan. Each of you is to take up a stone on his shoulder, according to the number of the tribes of the Israelites'" (Josh 4:2-5). Isaiah described this place like this: "O afflicted city, lashed by storms and not comforted, I will build you with stones of turquoise, your foundations with sapphires. I will make your battlements of rubies, *your gates of sparkling jewels*, [see verse 21 and the pearly gates] and all your walls of precious stones. All your sons will be taught by the LORD, and great will be your children's peace" (Isa 54:11-13). It is also no accident that the garden of Eden had these same stones, "You were in Eden, the garden of God; every precious stone adorned you: ruby, topaz and emerald, chrysolite, onyx and jasper, sapphire, turquoise and beryl. Your settings and mountings were made of gold; on the day you were created they were prepared" (Ezek 28:13). As we mentioned at the beginning of this book, there are many parallels between the beginning and end of time. Genesis and Revelation are very close knit books.

Verse 21 talks about the pearly gates of heaven. It is from this verse that we hear this phrase used so often in the "heaven" jokes today. Each gate is made of only one pearl and, therefore, what a pearl it must be! Can you imagine the oyster that made that one? We also see once more that the streets are solid, transparent gold because of its pureness. Reader's Digest once told of a man who made a deal with God. The man had bargained with the Lord to allow him to bring just one suitcase of things with him to heaven. He kept the suitcase packed until the day he died. When he met St. Peter at the pearly gates, he was stopped and told he could not enter in with anything. The man assured Peter that he and God had made a deal, so Peter went to check it out. When Peter returned he told the man that it would be okay, but he needed to look inside first. Peter threw the suitcase upon a table and opened it up to see a suitcase filled with solid gold bars. Peter looked at the man puzzled and said, "Why did you want to bring in pavement?" The moral of the story is that the most precious thing on this earth will seem but nothing in heaven.

Rev 21:22 I did not see a temple in the city, because the Lord God Almighty and the Lamb are its temple. 21:23 The city does not need the sun or the moon to shine on it, for the glory of God gives it light, and the Lamb is its lamp. 21:24 The nations will walk by its light, and the kings of the earth will bring their splendor into it. 21:25 On no day will its gates ever be shut, for there will be no night there. 21:26 The glory and honor of the nations will be brought into it. 21:27 Nothing impure will ever enter it, nor will anyone who does what is shameful or deceitful, but only those whose names are written in the Lamb's book of life.

John tells us that there is no temple building in the NEW Jerusalem, because God is the temple. Thus, as we said earlier, when we are being made pillars into the temple of God, we are being made one in Christ. Jesus told the woman at the well, "Believe Me, woman, a time is coming when you will worship the Father neither on this mountain nor in Jerusalem" (John 4:21). Though the city talked about here is Jerusalem, it is the new Jerusalem, and Jesus's point is that we will not worship because of location or building, but we will worship in Spirit.

The city also has no need for the sun or moon to give light, because Jesus is the light of the world. Isaiah wrote of this day, "The moon will be abashed, the sun ashamed; for the LORD Almighty will reign on Mount Zion and in Jerusalem, and before its elders, gloriously" (Isa 24:23). Also, in chapter 60, "The sun will no more be your light by day, nor will the brightness of the moon shine on you, for the LORD will be your everlasting light, and your God will be your glory. Your sun will never set again, and your moon will wane no more; the LORD will be your everlasting light, and your days of sorrow will end. Then will all your people be righteous and they will possess the land *forever*. They are the shoot I have planted, the work of My hands, for the display of My splendor" (Isa 60:19-21). It is important to note that the people will possess this land FOREVER. We see the covenant God gave to Abraham many times in Genesis, and it is stated as eternal: "I will establish My covenant as an *everlasting covenant* between Me and you and your descendants after you for the generations to come, to be your God and the God of your descendants after you" (Gen 17:7). This has never been fulfilled because the Holy Land God is talking about in these verses has not yet completely belonged to God's people. It is at this point in Revelation that we see when this covenant will be fully answered.

Not only will God's glory give us light, but the kings of the earth will also bring their splendor into the city as well. We read in Daniel, "Those who are wise will shine like the brightness of the heavens, and those who lead many to righteousness, like the stars for ever and ever" (Dan 12:3). What a beautiful promise for us as saints.

No night means the gates of the city will never be shut, as Isaiah also attests, "Your gates will always stand open, they will never be shut, day or night, so that men may bring you the wealth of the nations-- their kings led in triumphal procession" (Isa 60:11). Indeed, the glory and honor of the nations will be brought into this great city (v. 26). Zecheriah explains, "It will be a unique day, without daytime or nighttime--a day known to the LORD. When evening comes, there will be light. On that day living water will flow out from Jerusalem, half to the eastern sea and half to the western sea, in summer and in winter. The LORD will be king over the whole earth. On that day there will be one LORD, and His name the only name. The whole land, from Geba to Rimmon, south of Jerusalem, will become like the Arabah. But Jerusalem will be raised up and remain in its place, from the Benjamin Gate to the site of the First Gate, to the Corner Gate, and from the Tower of Hananel to the royal winepresses. It will be inhabited; never again will it be destroyed. Jerusalem will be secure" (Zec 14:7-11). Not only do we see God's covenant with Abraham coming true with the land being restored forever, but we also see this time as being called "a day" and, "on that day." This fits well into our earlier discussion on how the Sabbath day of Creation foreshadowed our Sabbath day of rest to come in heaven. See explanation on 20:1-3.

Though the Garden of Eden foreshadowed our heavenly home, the real difference between the Garden and our eternal home, is that in our home, there will be no evil. Adam and Eve were created into an existence where they were able not to sin. Today, we are not able *not* to sin. But in heaven, we will not be able to sin. Whereas the Garden held the tree of knowledge and evil, Satan could roam freely, in heaven the tree is gone, Satan is thrown into hell, and there is no presence of evil of any kind. I have often felt that many parents have done their children a disservice because they introduce evil to their children, whether through their own entertainment, or because they do not want their children being ignorant of evil. As a teacher I have often heard the excuse, "I want my child to have choices, and besides, I want to prepare them for the things they will see in high school, so we are going to pull them from this Christian school and put them into a public school." Expose them to evil so they won't be naive when they get to high school? Being naive is good! The less you know of evil the closer you are to the Garden paradise where evil existed, but knowledge of it was not desired. In fact, they were commanded to stay away from it. At least in heaven there will be nothing to stay away from, it will all have been cast into hell. Everyone whose name is written in the Book of Life, belonging to Jesus, will have eternal life with the Lamb. Praise God for this deliverance from evil!

CHAPTER 22

Rev 22:1 Then the angel showed me the river of the water of life, as clear as crystal, flowing from the throne of God and of the Lamb. 22:2 down the middle of the great street of the city. On each side of the river stood the tree of life, bearing twelve crops of fruit, yielding its fruit every month. And the leaves of the tree are for the healing of the nations. 22:3 No longer will there be any curse. The throne of God and of the Lamb will be in the city, and his servants will serve him. 22:4 They will see his face, and his name will be on their foreheads. 22:5 There will be no more night. They will not need the light of a lamp or the light of the sun, for the Lord God will give them light. And they will reign for ever and ever.

Just as in the Garden of Eden, a river flowed from the center of the Garden, so, too, a river flows from the throne of God in the center of the city (remember the 12 tribes camped around the tabernacle, as in heaven they camp around the throne). This river is our delight as we see from Psalms, "They feast on the abundance of Your house; You give them drink from Your river of delights. For with You is the fountain of life; in Your light we see light" (Psa 36:8-9). Also, "There is a river whose streams make glad the city of God, the holy place where the Most High dwells" (Psa 46:4). Jesus said it best when He told the woman at the well, "whoever drinks the water I give him will never thirst. Indeed, the water I give him will become in him a spring of water welling up to eternal life" (John 4:14). Joel speaks of this fountain as well: "In that day the mountains will drip new wine, and the hills will flow with milk; all the ravines of Judah will run with water. A fountain will flow out of the Lord's house and will water the valley of acacias" (Joel 3:18). Zechariah recorded, "On that day living water will flow out from Jerusalem, half to the eastern sea and half to the western sea, in summer and in winter. The LORD will be king over the whole earth. On that day there will be one LORD, and His name the only name" (Zec 14:8-9). However, probably the best description comes from Ezekiel, some of which we cannot understand yet, but it will make complete sense when we see it:

> "The man brought me back to the entrance of the temple, and I saw water coming out from under the threshold of the temple toward the east (for the temple faced east). The water was coming down from under the south side of the temple, south of the altar. He then brought me out through the north gate and led me around the outside to the outer gate facing east, and the water was flowing from the south side. As the man went eastward with a measuring line in his hand, he measured off a thousand cubits and then led me through water that was ankle-deep. He measured off another thousand cubits and led me through water that was knee-deep. He measured off another thousand and led me through water that was up to the waist. He measured off another thousand, but now it was a river that I could not cross, because the water had risen and was deep enough to swim in--a river that no one

could cross. He asked me, 'Son of man, do you see this?' Then he led me back to the bank of the river. When I arrived there, I saw a great number of trees on each side of the river. He said to me, 'This water flows toward the eastern region and goes down into the Arabah, where it enters the Sea. When it empties into the Sea, the water there becomes fresh. Swarms of living creatures will live wherever the river flows. There will be large numbers of fish, because this water flows there and makes the salt water fresh; so where the river flows everything will live. Fishermen will stand along the shore; from En Gedi to En Eglaim there will be places for spreading nets. The fish will be of many kinds--like the fish of the Great Sea. But the swamps and marshes will not become fresh; they will be left for salt. Fruit trees of all kinds will grow on *both banks* of the river. Their leaves will not wither, nor will their fruit fail. Every month they will bear, because the water from the sanctuary flows to them. Their fruit will serve for food and their leaves for healing'" (Ezek 47:1-12).

Note that the tree of life will line both sides of the bank, just as verse two tells us. The tree bears a crop once a month for the "healing of the people." Because there is no sickness, death, or pain in heaven this "healing" can only be in reference to the "healing" that had been done by bringing the people into heaven. In other words, it is our access to the Tree of Life through Christ Jesus that has healed us. We may look at it from the point of view that Christ died on the cross for the healing of the nations. The tree will be an ongoing blessing, keeping us in perfect health without any chance of becoming sick. Nothing damaging can even exist in heaven.

Verse three tells us that there is no curse and, therefore, no sickness or problems. The throne of God is in the city as well. The picture described is almost exactly what the Garden of Eden was before its curse. We will see God's face and His name will be on our foreheads. The fact that we see God's face is an awesome encouragement for us today. Since the curse, no one has been able to see the face of God and live, because God is so holy. Nothing impure or unholy can be in His presence. The fact that we can see God face to face in heaven shows we are made holy. Job gives us a deeper understanding of this renewal when he said, "then his flesh is renewed like a child's; it is restored as in the days of his youth. He prays to God and finds favor with Him, he sees God's face and shouts for joy; he is restored by God to his righteous state" (Job 33:25). There are those that saw God "face to face," but not in God's full glory. Even Moses was kept from seeing God's face in full glory as we see God telling Moses, "'you cannot see My face, for no one may see Me and live.' Then the LORD said, 'There is a place near Me where you may stand on a rock. When My glory passes by, I will put you in a cleft in the rock and cover you with My hand until I have passed by. Then I will remove My hand and you will see My back; but My face must not be seen'" (Exo 33:20-23). When Miriam and Aaron were upset with Moses, God came to them and said, "Listen to My words: When a prophet of the LORD is among you, I reveal Myself to him in visions, I speak to him in dreams. But this is not true of My servant Moses; he is faithful in all My house. With him I speak face to face, clearly and not in riddles; he sees the *form of the LORD*. Why then were you not afraid to speak against My servant Moses" (Num 12:6-8)? If seeing God's form is that important, what glory will be revealed in us when we see God's form with His glory!

There are many Old Testament examples of the fear people had in seeing God's face. When Jacob wrestled with God (not in His full glory) Jacob named the place Peniel saying, "It is because I saw God face to face, and yet my life was spared" (Gen 32:30). We can have great hope and anticipation of this day when we will see God face to face in glory.

Verse five tells us there is no sun, for there is no need of it when there is the Son. Jesus, the light of the world, gives light for an eternity so there will be no more night, no more darkness, and no more evil. Just as at Creation, there was light on day one, but no sun until day four. Jesus was the light of the world then, and He will again be the literal light in heaven as well. God is glory! When Moses came down the mountain his face glowed from God's glory (Exo 34:10). Consider the following verses shedding light on God's glory:

- "When I smiled at them, they scarcely believed it; the light of My face was precious to them" (Job 29:24).
- "turn back his soul from the pit, that the light of life may shine on him" (Job 33:30).
- "Many are asking, 'Who can show us any good?' Let the light of Your face shine upon us, O LORD" (Psa 4:6).
- "It was not by their sword that they won the land, nor did their arm bring them victory; it was Your right hand, Your arm, and the light of Your face, for You loved them" (Psa 44:3).
- "For You have delivered me from death and my feet from stumbling, that I may walk before God in the *light of life*" (Psa 56:13).
- "You have set our iniquities before You, our secret sins in the light of Your presence" (Psa 90:8).
- "Come, O house of Jacob, let us walk in the light of the LORD" (Isa 2:5).
- "See to it, then, that the light within you is not darkness. Therefore, if your whole body is full of light, and no part of it dark, it will be completely lighted, as when the light of a lamp shines on you" (Luke 11:35-36).
- "In Him was life, and *that life was the light of men*" (John 1:4).
- "When Jesus spoke again to the people, He said, 'I am the light of the world. Whoever follows Me will never walk in darkness, but will have *the light of life*'" (John 8:12).

There can be no question that this light, of which we will live with, is none other than our life. The light is life! Jesus is the life as He said, "I am the way and the truth and the life. No one comes to the Father except through Me" (John 14:6).

Rev 22:6 The angel said to me, "These words are trustworthy and true. The Lord, the God of the spirits of the prophets, sent his angel to show his servants the things that must soon take place." 22:7 "Behold, I am coming soon! Blessed is he who keeps the words of the prophecy in this book." 22:8 I, John, am the one who heard and saw these things. And when I had heard and seen them, I fell down to worship at the feet of the angel who had been showing them to me. 22:9 But he said to me, "Do not do it! I am a fellow servant with you and with your brothers the prophets and of all who keep the words of this book. Worship God!"

To reassure us of these truths the angel tells John that these words are trustworthy and true. This message is not one that comes from John but, like the prophets, John is receiving it from the Spirit of God. We, too, get our strength from the Spirit of God: "Moreover, we have all had human fathers who disciplined us and we respected them for it. How much more should we submit to the *Father of our spirits* and live" (Heb 12:9)! Also like the prophets who often were to warn the Israelites of upcoming disaster, John was shown this message of Revelation, because it is to take place soon and we need to be prepared. Today, the gift of prophecy is something that we are told to seek and desire: "Follow the way of love and eagerly desire spiritual gifts, especially the gift of prophecy" (1 Cor 14:1). Paul gives other insight into how the Spirit works through these gifts: "For you can all prophesy in turn so that everyone may be instructed and encouraged. *The spirits of prophets are subject to the control of prophets.* For God is not a God of disorder but of peace" (1 Cor 14:31-33).

Verse seven shows one of the three times in chapter 22, that Jesus is coming soon. Blessed will be all who keep the words of this book. This "blessed" is the sixth of seven beatitudes in Revelation. Specifically, this promise is for the book of Revelation, but because of its tie into all of Scripture, this promise stands for any of the 66 books of Scripture.

Verse eight reaffirms that the apostle John was the one receiving this revelation and gift of prophecy. Once more, John does not try to hide his mistakes, but shows us his weakness openly when he bowed down to worship an angel. If he did this out of ignorance, or being overly excited, we do not know, however, it was the second time he did so. Look back at 19:10 for comments on this act there.

Rev 22:10 Then he told me, "Do not seal up the words of the prophecy of this book, because the time is near. 22:11 Let him who does wrong continue to do wrong; let him who is vile continue to be vile; let him who does right continue to do right; and let him who is holy continue to be holy."

John was told NOT to seal up the words of this book. He was to proclaim it far and wide because people needed to know what was going to happen soon. This is a contrast to Daniel, who was told, "The vision of the evenings and mornings that has been given you is true, but seal up the vision, for it concerns the distant future" (Dan 8:26). Since Daniel's vision was in the distant future, there was no need to share the message, yet John's message, however, is urgent! As Paul said to the Romans, "do this, understanding the present time. The hour has come for you to wake up from your slumber, because our salvation is nearer now than when we first believed. The night is nearly over; the day is almost here. So let us put aside the deeds of darkness and put on the armor of light. Let us behave decently, as in the daytime, not in orgies and drunkenness, not in sexual immorality and debauchery, not in dissension and jealousy. Rather, clothe yourselves with the Lord Jesus Christ, and do not think about how to gratify the desires of the sinful nature" (Rom 13:11-14).

Those who will ignore the words of this book will continue to do wrong, because they will not seek God, who gives them the strength to change. It is as Ezekiel said, "But when I speak to you, I will open your mouth and you shall say to them, 'This is what the Sovereign LORD says. Whoever will listen let him listen, and whoever will refuse let him refuse; for they are a rebellious house'" (Ezek 3:27). In Jeremiah we read, "This is what the LORD Almighty, the God of Israel, says: You and your wives have shown by your actions what you promised when you said, 'We will certainly carry out the vows we made to burn incense and pour out drink offerings to the Queen of Heaven.' Go ahead then, do what you promised! Keep your vows" (Jer 44:25). However, God continues in verse 27, "For I am watching over them for harm." Also Solomon wrote, "Be happy, young man, while you are young, and let your heart give you joy in the days of your youth. Follow the ways of your heart and whatever your eyes see, but know that for all these things God will bring you to judgment" (Eccl 11:9). This also includes those that are luke warm, as we saw in 3:16, for they will be spit out of God's mouth!

Those who do what is right are to continue in Christ and be holy through Him. They are to continue to "labor and strive" for godliness (1 Tim 4:8-10). Salvation is a gift, but godliness is a pursuit. Many believe that we will not understand this message. If that is true, why was John told not to seal up the message if the message was useless. Christ IS coming SOON, and we will understand, as I believe the Spirit of God is showing many active Bible reading and believing Christians just as He promised, "Many will be purified, made spotless and refined, but the wicked will continue to be wicked. None of the wicked will understand, *but those who are wise will understand*" (Dan 12:10).

Rev 22:12 "Behold, I am coming soon! My reward is with me, and I will give to everyone according to what he has done. 22:13 I am the Alpha and the Omega, the First and the Last, the Beginning and the End. 22:14 "Blessed are those who wash their robes, that they may have the right to the tree of life and may go through the gates into the city. 22:15 Outside are the dogs, those who practice magic arts, the sexually immoral, the murderers, the idolaters and everyone who loves and practices falsehood.

Verse 12 gives us the second urgent message that Christ is coming soon, and with Him will be His reward that everyone will receive according to what they have done. We have already given the scripture passages supporting that there are degrees of glory in heaven in 14:13, so you may go back to search that out. Those whose faith brought forth many good works will receive great rewards. Those whose faith brought forth few good works will receive a reward, but not as great. Christ is the Alpha and Omega, or the First and Last (Rev 1:8,17, 21:6). Since He is eternal, what He said is true, and He has the right to give His rewards out as He sees fit. Jesus said, "For the Son of Man is going to come in His Father's glory with His angels, and then He will reward each person according to what he has done" (Mat 16:27).

Isaiah also attests to this reward that Christ will bring, "See, the Sovereign LORD comes with power, and His arm rules for Him. See, His reward is with Him, and His recompense accompanies Him" (Isa 40:10). He said almost the same thing a few chapters later, "The LORD has made proclamation to the ends of the earth: 'Say to the Daughter of Zion, See, your Savior comes! See, His reward is with Him, and His recompense accompanies Him'" (Isa 62:11).

Verse 14 tells us that only those who have washed their robes may enter the city of eternal life. All those outside the city will be in hell. This fits well with the parable of the wedding banquet where the man who was not wearing wedding clothes was thrown "outside" where there was weeping and gnashing of teeth (Matt 22:11).

We know that the robes of these saints are washed in Christ's blood. That is what made them holy since the robes stand for the righteous acts of the saints (19:8). Earlier we read, "These are they who have come out of the great tribulation; they have washed their robes and made them white in the blood of the Lamb" (Rev 7:14). These people may enter through the gates into eternal life and have access to the Tree of Life, as seen earlier in this chapter.

On the other hand, all who are evil have no access to the gate, or the Tree of Life. As Paul said in Corinthians, "Do you not know that the wicked will not inherit the kingdom of God? Do not be deceived: Neither the sexually immoral nor idolaters nor adulterers nor male prostitutes nor homosexual offenders, nor thieves nor the greedy nor drunkards nor slanderers nor swindlers will inherit the kingdom of God" (1 Cor 6:9-10, see also Gal 5:19). These people would do well to take heed to the warning of Christ, "Put to death, therefore, whatever belongs to your earthly nature: sexual immorality, impurity, lust, evil desires and greed, which is idolatry. Because of these, the wrath of God is coming" (Col 3:5-6).

Rev 22:16 "I, Jesus, have sent my angel to give you this testimony for the churches. I am the Root and the Offspring of David, and the bright Morning Star." 22:17 The Spirit and the bride say, "Come!" And let him who hears say, "Come!" Whoever is thirsty, let him come; and whoever wishes, let him take the free gift of the water of life. 22:18 I warn everyone who hears the words of the prophecy of this book: If anyone adds anything to them, God will add to him the plagues described in this book. 22:19 And if anyone takes words away from this book of prophecy, God will take away from him his share in the tree of life and in the holy city, which are described in this book. 22:20 He who testifies to these things says, "Yes, I

am coming soon." Amen. Come, Lord Jesus. 22:21 The grace of the Lord Jesus be with God's people. Amen.

Verse 16 gives us the final message, that it that this message may have been brought by angels, but Christ Himself gave it to them to give to us. If you recall, the first few verses of Revelation explained the same thing, so Revelation is closing much like it began. To be sure we understand who Jesus is, we are told that He is the Root and Offspring of David, or the Bright Morning Star. I believe we are given this description of "Root" because of its great significance, both as identifying Christ as the Messiah who came, and also as the Savior who will come: "A shoot will come up from the stump of Jesse; from his roots a Branch will bear fruit. The Spirit of the LORD will rest on Him--. . . In that day the Root of Jesse will stand as a banner for the peoples; the nations will rally to Him, and His place of rest will be glorious. In that day the Lord will reach out His hand *a second time* to reclaim the remnant that is left" (Isa 11:1,10).

As for the offspring of David, we are told of Christ, "who as to His human nature was a descendant of David" (Rom 1:3). The very first verse of the New Testament says, "A record of the genealogy of Jesus Christ the son of David" (Mat 1:1). This one fact alone proves Christ to be the Messiah. Since 70 AD no one could come and prove he were the messiah because all the genealogical records were destroyed by Rome. It was prophesied over and over that the Christ would come from David, and indeed He did. This is just one more clear example where we see Christ is who He said He was.

The Bright Morning Star is a beautiful picture of God's glorious brightness, of which we will share. Regarding Christ, we read: "I see Him, but not now; I behold Him, but not near. A Star will come out of Jacob; a Scepter will rise out of Israel" (Num 24:17). In Phillipians we read, "we have the word of the prophets made more certain, and you will do well to pay attention to it, as to a light shining in a dark place, until the day dawns and the Morning Star rises in your hearts" (2 Pet 1:19). As for our future we see that, "you may become blameless and pure, children of God without fault in a crooked and depraved generation, in which you shine like stars in the universe as you hold out the word of life—" (Phil 2:15-16). Daniel said, "Those who are wise will shine like the brightness of the heavens, and those who lead many to righteousness, like the stars for ever and ever" (Dan 12:3). Perhaps this is the true meaning of the Light of the world shining upon us!

Verse 17 is a wonderful invitation for all to COME! If one thirsts, there is a free gift of eternal life. In John we read Jesus' words, "If you knew the gift of God and who it is that asks you for a drink, you would have asked Him and He would have given you living water" (John 4:10). From verse sixteen we know for sure who it is who is asking us to come, and if we ask Him, He will give us that free gift in our hearts. The gift is for everyone, and there is no limited supply, however, there is limited time.

A final warning is given after the invitation. If anyone hears the words of prophecy and adds to them, the plagues described in 15:6 – 16:21 will be put upon them. If they take away from these words, God will take away from them the free gift of salvation and their access to the tree of life. This is very similar to what God has told His people before, "Do not add to what I command you and do not subtract from it, but keep the commands of the LORD your God that I give you" (Deu 4:2, see also Deut 12:32 and Prov 30:6). I believe that many do these very things with Revelation, and need to be careful. Many books that I have read on this subject add to this book by saying things are "between the lines." If Scripture doesn't say it, be careful. Sometimes it is dissected to the point that one would think we could predict that Russia will do this and China that. The words Russia or China do not appear and, therefore, one must be careful in making predictions, rather be on your guard so that "this day should not surprise you" (1 Thess 4). Those that take away from it also need to be careful. They say this book is not understandable, or it is all symbolic, taking away the meaning, warnings, promises and truths that are written within it. They treat prophecy with contempt. In Thessalonians we are also warned, "Do not put out the Spirit's fire; do not treat prophecies with contempt. Test everything. Hold on to the good" (1 Th 5:19-21). If we believe something because our pastor, church, or family believes it, rather than searching the Scriptures ourselves, we "put out the Spirit's fire." The Catholic church used to (and to some extent many still do) rely upon the Pope to interpret the Scriptures for them. They did not need to read the Bible if the Pope would tell them what it said. Many churches have their doctrines that do the same thing. Their churches teach that you are to read your Bible, but this is how you must interpret it, according to our doctrine. If you stray from that doctrine, you may be looked down upon. In so doing,, we limit the power of the Spirit, because people go into the Scriptures with a bias and come out with a biased interpretation. Verse 18 tells us, "let Scripture interpret Scripture," not some doctrinal book that has added to, or taken away from His Word. He has given us all we need in the Bible, and contrary to many beliefs, it is very understandable when one studies the Bible itself, rather than studying someone's thoughts on it.

Verse 20 gives us our third and final promise, "YES, I am coming soon." I find great comfort, hope and joy in this promise. A few years ago I had a tremendous dream that really affected my life and view on things. In a shortened version, I was at my hometown of Plentywood, Montana when coming down out of the sky, cutting through the clouds, was Jesus. As He descended with arms open, He left a trail above Him tracing His path down through the clouds. He was descending in the east, about three miles away, yet He seemed very close. As soon as His body went behind the rolling hills, a smoke-like cloud came rushing towards me with great speed. As soon as it began coming towards me, I fell to my knees and began worshipping God. I did not know what I was saying, all I know is that my entire body, soul and spirit were praising. As soon as Christ reached me, my body turned while I was still on my knees, yet floating above the ground a bit. All of sudden there were four people around me. I was looking face to face at Barnabas. I was not introduced, but knew who he was. The others around me, although I was not looking at them but could see with my peripheral vision, were Bartholomew, Paul and Jesus. Again, I knew who they all were without having to ask. Barnabas looked as if he had not shaved for a few days and was missing some teeth, but in my dream this did not bother me. He had a great smile on his face, and as soon as I saw him, we hugged each other in great joy for seeing one another. It was as if I knew him. While hugging me, he spoke in my ear, "Brian, be patient, it's coming soon. It's coming soon!" Then I awoke. I prayed to go back to sleep and God answered my prayer, but I forgot to ask Him to put me back in that situation. You may believe what you like, but in my heart, this was more than an ordinary dream. God did not speak to me and this isn't God's Word, so I would never take this as doctrine, however, it did mean a lot to me. When I went over this dream I realized that there was no new information given, but everything was very Biblical, it meant even more to me. The disciples knew Moses and Elijah without being introduced, and I knew Barnabas, Bartholomew, etc.. At the time, believe it or not, I didn't know who Barnabas was. I thought his name might be in the Bible, and upon looking it up, I found him to be very close to Paul. His name means, "Son of encouragement." Let me tell you, I received great encouragement from this dream. Barnabas's missing teeth made me realize as well that Scripture doesn't say we get knew bodies until the resurrection. Jesus came in the east, in the clouds, and His *shekinah* glory came rushing towards me. (God's *shekinah* glory was the cloud that filled the temple and covered the mountain when the Ten Commandments were given). In my peripheral vision I saw that Paul was short and stocky. Two years later I found out that this is how he is traditionally described. I was just as happy to see them as they were me. I fell down and worshipped without thinking about it, it was just what I did. I have never experienced such peace and joy as I had while worshipping Christ at that moment. And finally, what was the message? The same message that we see here in the last chapter of Revelation three times: It is coming soon! I believe with all my heart that it is coming soon, and we do need to feel this urgent message, so that we may respond in telling people about God's Word boldly. I have many loved ones that I can no longer beat around the bush with. We need to stand firm in an uncompromising way, preaching the Gospel of Jesus Christ, crucified, and resurrected. If you knew the end was next week, what would you do today? Would your words to your loved ones change? Would your cares of this world be different? The answer to that question is what I got out of my dream, and that is the question Revelation causes one to think about! God wants us to to realize, "He is coming soon, hurry, go shout it from the mountain tops and prepare for His coming!" Praise be to God, Hallelujah!

    As we close this study I feel it important to remind us that we need to be careful in getting to caught up in the unwritten ideas of Revelation. I heard a great illustration once: What would you do if you hired someone to do a job and all he did was sit around waiting for the quitting bell to ring? Would you consider him a faithful worker? Would you say, well done, thou good and faithful servant? If all we do is sit around and wait for the quitting trumpet to blow, will Christ see us as faithful servants?

    Paul wrote to the Corinthians, "If anyone does not love the Lord--a curse be on him. Come, O Lord ! The grace of the Lord Jesus be with you" (1 Cor 16:22-23). We, too, can pray with confidence that the curse is not on us, but rather the curse has been taken away, at least for those who believe. We can say with confidence and joy, COME LORD JESUS, COME! With that, may the grace and peace of our Lord Jesus be with all of you as you go out to tell others this urgent message. AMEN! IT SHALL BE SO!

REVELATION

CHURCHES (CH 1-3) Each church 1)-Intro 2)-Attribute of Christ
3) Society attribute 4) urge to hear.

I- Ephesus (33-100 AD) Apostolic Age	"One who holds stars" 1:16
II- Smyrna (100-300 AD) Persecution	"First & Last who died yet lives" 1:17-18
III- Pergamum (300-500 AD) Mix church/state	"Two edged sword sees heart" 1:16; Heb 4:12
Begin to tolerate IV- Thyatira (500-1500 AD) Dark Ages-	"Eyes of fire, feet of bronze" 1:14-15
Tolerating V- Sardis (1500-1700 AD) Reformation	"Holds 7 spirits & stars" 1:16
Condemnation VI- Philadelphia (1700-1900 AD) Missionary	"Holy & True; holds key of David" 1:18
Post Reformation --------INTERLUDE?-------- VII- Laodicea (1900- Now) Luke-warm	"God as Creator, faithful & true witness" 1:17-18

        SEALS (CH 6 INTERLUDE CH 7)
        1- White Horse (Antichrist) Mat 24
        2- Red Horse (War)
        3- Black Horse (Famine)
        4- Pale Horse (Sword, plague, famine, beast)
              1/4 world affected. Ezek 14:21
        5- Scene in Heaven- "How long"
        6- Sun/Moon/Stars changed
              Joel 2:30; Is 13:9; 34:4; Hag 2:6
---------INTERLUDE 144,000 SEALED AND MULTITUDE
PRAISE GOD CH 7-----
        7- Trumpets- Prep for war (Num 10, 23; I Chron 16)

                TRUMPETS (CH 8-9 INTERLUDE CH 10-11)
                A- 1/3 burned
                B- 1/3 sea turns to blood and dies
                C- 1/3 water bitter
                D- 1/3 heavens destroyed
                E- Scorpions & locusts torture 5 months (no death)
                F- 2 million horsemen kill 1/3 men (Zec 13:9)

----------INTERLUDE: ANGEL & SCROLL; 2 WITNESSES (ZEC 4) --------
G- Reign begins (I Cor 15:51; I Thes 4:15) Temple opened for bowl judgments 11:9 & 15:5 (CH 12-14 may connect with same time period as interlude)

BOWLS (CH 15-18 INTERLUDE 16:18) Angels come out of temple
a- poured on land - painful sores
b- sea turns to blood and all in it die
c- rivers & springs turn to blood
d- sun/moon struck and there's intense heat
e- poured on throne of beast and he's cast into darkness (men curse God)
f- Euphrates dries up and spirits gather armies
-------INTERLUDE 16:15 LORD SPEAKS------
g- "It is done" cities destroyed

Suggested outline: Ch 1-6; 8-9; 15-18;19 on.
Ch 7, 10-14 interlude type but all seem to talk of same period.
(Main chronological order)   Ch 7, 14 deal with 144,000
                              Ch 11, 12, 13 all 3 1/2 years

1

144,000, 60, 61, 64, 65, 69, 74, 125, 129, 131, 132, 141, 231, 232

4

40, 13, 21, 27, 47, 51, 64, 86, 91, 100, 101, 102, 125, 131, 145, 149, 152, 186, 205, 214, 216, 226
42 months, 91, 119

6

666, 124, 125, 126

A

Abraham, 61, 99, 100, 102, 116, 136, 144, 180, 193, 215, 218
Abyss, 31, 75, 76, 78, 80, 95, 120, 161, 162, 189, 190, 202, 211
Achor, 115
Acts, 16, 21, 27, 83, 95, 97, 111, 138, 215
Antichrist, 4, 16, 50, 51, 55, 57, 59, 65, 92, 95, 96, 110, 111, 112, 117, 118, 119, 120, 123, 124, 125, 159, 162, 165, 166, 179, 194, 195, 203, 231
Antioches Epiphenes, 92
Armageddon, 71, 81, 140, 152, 153, 203

B

Babylon, 23, 24, 81, 117, 118, 132, 134, 138, 139, 153, 154, 157, 159, 160, 161, 162, 166, 167, 168, 169, 170, 171, 172, 174, 175, 187
Balaam, 24, 25, 26
Beast, 25, 28, 31, 39, 92, 95, 110, 117, 118, 119, 120, 121, 122, 123, 124, 125, 126, 127, 129, 135, 138, 142, 143, 144, 147, 149, 150, 151, 154, 158, 159, 160, 161, 162, 163, 164, 165, 166, 172, 184, 185, 189, 190, 194, 195, 203, 205, 211, 231, 232
Beatitudes, 5, 152, 224
Bird, 78, 151, 158, 167, 183, 205

Book of life, 29, 30, 31, 120, 121, 161, 162, 206, 207, 208, 217
Bowls, 10, 46, 69, 71, 104, 135, 139, 142, 143, 145, 146, 147, 150, 157, 214
Bride, 64, 109, 131, 143, 172, 173, 174, 176, 178, 211, 214, 227

C

Carnelian, 38, 216
Catholic, 31, 160
Cherubim, 40, 41, 43, 65, 89, 110
Colossians, 13, 32, 34, 60, 88, 111, 227
Constantine, 26
Corinthians, 27, 28, 32, 35, 36, 38, 39, 60, 64, 73, 98, 100, 101, 102, 113, 131, 137, 165, 168, 176, 194, 195, 207, 208, 209, 212, 213, 214, 224, 226, 230, 232
Creator, 17, 34, 36, 43, 48, 74, 85, 117, 122, 134, 135, 141, 231
Crown, 15, 22, 23, 32, 33, 39, 49, 50, 67, 79, 109, 137, 138, 179, 212
Cyrus, 29

D

Daniel, 10, 14, 15, 16, 23, 28, 31, 37, 47, 49, 54, 55, 59, 63, 65, 66, 87, 91, 92, 95, 103, 110, 111, 112, 115, 117, 118, 119, 120, 124, 137, 138, 144, 152, 153, 158, 159, 160, 161, 162, 165, 172, 184, 187, 194, 206, 209, 214, 215, 218, 225, 228
David, 31, 32, 45, 46, 62, 63, 102, 192, 196, 227, 231
Demons, 75, 76, 79, 80, 81, 82, 94, 98, 123, 124, 136, 149, 150, 151, 162, 165, 167, 168, 184, 189
Deuteronomy, 124, 147, 183, 207, 228
Diana, 21
Domitian, 14, 163
Doxology, 13, 43, 48, 65
Dragon, 50, 109, 110, 111, 112, 114, 116, 117, 118, 119, 120, 122, 123, 141, 150, 158, 161, 185, 189, 190, 203, 211

E

Eagle, 41, 42, 72, 92, 114, 115, 187
Earthquake, 34, 52, 69, 70, 97, 104, 145, 153, 182, 204
Eden, 5, 19, 22, 40, 80, 217, 219, 221, 222
Egypt, 24, 62, 63, 70, 71, 72, 76, 81, 94, 95, 98, 100, 102, 115, 122, 147, 148, 150, 151
Elijah, 93, 94, 95, 123, 125, 141, 187, 229
Enoch, 94, 165, 182
Ephesians, 16, 30, 33, 35, 60, 88, 113, 121, 122, 132, 178, 191, 215
Ephesus, 14, 15, 17, 21, 22, 23, 25, 26, 28, 30, 82, 231
Esclepis, 24, 25
Esther, 96
Euphrates, 80, 81, 98, 150, 151, 161, 172, 184, 232
Eusebius, 14
Exodus, 13, 16, 25, 39, 40, 52, 70, 71, 72, 76, 87, 94, 115, 119, 125, 126, 138, 144, 145, 146, 147, 148, 150, 154, 180, 206, 212, 216, 222, 223
Eyes, 5, 12, 15, 16, 26, 27, 28, 34, 35, 37, 39, 41, 42, 45, 46, 65, 67, 76, 91, 101, 121, 148, 166, 173, 180, 181, 194, 204, 211, 212, 225
Ezekiel, 10, 14, 15, 16, 38, 40, 41, 42, 51, 59, 62, 63, 70, 72, 85, 89, 90, 91, 96, 97, 102, 110, 121, 143, 154, 166, 167, 171, 172, 173, 178, 183, 187, 196, 203, 204, 205, 212, 214, 215, 216, 217, 221, 222, 225, 231

F

False Prophet, 117, 118, 122, 123, 124, 125, 142, 151, 164
Famine, 51, 55, 57, 231
Fifth seal, 51, 52, 56
foreshadowing, 19, 66, 69, 96, 98, 124, 139, 193, 219
Foreshadowing, 40, 99, 115, 171, 178
Fourth kingdom, 117, 118, 159

G

Galatians, 28, 99, 100, 146, 193, 226
Gentiles, 45, 61, 88, 89, 91, 101, 115, 119, 191, 193
Gog, 70, 202, 203, 204
Golden altar, 69, 80
Greek, 11, 12, 22, 33, 39, 69, 76, 78, 118, 126, 158

H

Hades, 16, 23, 32, 51, 75, 206
Hagar, 100
Haggai, 53, 231
Heb, 16, 28, 35, 36, 40, 47, 90, 93, 95, 99, 101, 111, 122, 126, 130, 136, 140, 146, 165, 180, 181, 192, 196, 211, 212, 214, 215, 216, 224, 231
Hebrews, 66
Horns, 5, 46, 69, 80, 109, 110, 117, 118, 119, 122, 158, 159, 160, 161, 162, 164, 165, 187
Hosea, 51, 54, 63, 86, 112, 114, 131, 193, 196

I

I am coming soon, 30, 32, 33, 35, 224, 225, 227, 228
Incense, 22, 40, 46, 63, 69, 70, 80, 170, 225
Isaac, 61, 99, 100, 102, 136
Isaiah, 12, 15, 16, 26, 29, 32, 35, 36, 38, 40, 42, 45, 47, 49, 53, 54, 62, 66, 67, 73, 75, 81, 96, 98, 101, 110, 114, 130, 131, 134, 135, 139, 145, 149, 150, 151, 154, 157, 167, 168, 169, 172, 173, 175, 178, 180, 181, 182, 184, 190, 202, 207, 208, 211, 212, 213, 215, 217, 218, 223, 226, 227, 231

J

Jacob, 61, 62, 100, 103, 109, 114, 130, 135, 149, 168, 193, 205, 223, 227
Jasper, 38, 214, 216, 217
Jeremiah, 49, 51, 59, 62, 63, 71, 77, 89, 94, 96, 105, 115, 121, 122, 131, 132, 135, 139, 144, 145, 148, 160, 161, 166, 167, 168, 169, 172, 173, 174, 183, 184, 196, 209, 225
Jericho, 98, 102

Jerusalem, 19, 32, 33, 38, 51, 52, 54, 59, 64, 67, 86, 91, 95, 96, 97, 100, 105, 129, 130, 131, 135, 139, 140, 142, 151, 152, 153, 154, 173, 178, 182, 202, 205, 211, 212, 214, 216, 217, 218, 221
Job, 79, 113, 114, 222, 223
Joel, 52, 76, 79, 80, 86, 93, 139, 140, 151, 153, 221, 231
Jonah, 97, 166, 186
Jordan, 102, 216
Joshua, 25, 102, 113, 126, 178, 192
Judah, 32, 45, 53, 60, 62, 63, 109, 130, 139, 173, 182, 193, 202, 215, 221
Jude, 47, 76, 94, 112, 113, 165, 182
Judges, 63

K

Kings, 27, 63, 80, 93, 94, 123, 187

L

Lake of fire, 23, 31, 75, 184, 185, 196, 206, 207
Lamb, 19, 31, 33, 36, 46, 47, 49, 50, 53, 63, 64, 65, 66, 99, 113, 121, 123, 125, 129, 131, 135, 137, 143, 144, 146, 147, 148, 151, 153, 164, 176, 178, 179, 180, 183, 195, 212, 214, 217, 219, 221, 226
Lampstand, 12, 21, 30, 93
Laodicea, 14, 15, 17, 23, 30, 33, 34, 35, 36, 37, 48, 74, 140, 231
Leopard, 117, 118, 182
Leviticus, 15, 52, 64, 143, 167
Life, 34, 77, 121, 206, 207, 208, 210, 219, 222, 226
Linen, 39, 64, 87, 91, 145, 146, 170, 171, 176, 177, 178, 181, 195, 214
Lion, 45, 46, 180
Locusts, 75, 76, 77, 78, 79, 80, 82, 189
Luke, 23, 36, 39, 46, 75, 85, 91, 94, 95, 99, 103, 113, 114, 123, 137, 139, 152, 160, 162, 168, 170, 179, 189, 195, 206, 208, 209, 223, 225, 231

M

Malachi, 85, 93, 145, 206

Mark, 22, 28, 39, 59, 71, 92, 111, 123, 124, 125, 127, 129, 135, 139, 147, 167, 180, 184, 194, 195
Matthew, 13, 14, 16, 22, 24, 31, 36, 39, 46, 49, 53, 54, 55, 59, 65, 85, 86, 87, 89, 90, 92, 93, 97, 98, 99, 110, 111, 112, 113, 121, 122, 124, 125, 131, 136, 137, 138, 151, 153, 160, 167, 174, 177, 183, 184, 186, 190, 194, 206, 207, 209, 226, 227, 231
Megiddo, 140, 153
Micah, 103
Michael, 31, 65, 87, 88, 94, 112, 113, 153, 206
Millenium, 185, 186, 190, 193, 194, 195, 196
Moon, 52, 53, 55, 56, 57, 72, 79, 80, 109, 139, 154, 193, 217, 218, 232
Morning Star, 16, 28, 227
Moses, 40, 70, 72, 93, 94, 95, 100, 102, 112, 113, 124, 141, 143, 144, 145, 150, 167, 180, 187, 215, 222, 223, 229
Most Holy Place, 40, 41, 46, 66, 69, 105, 146, 216
Mount Moriah, 99
Mt. Sinai, 13, 100
Mystery, 17, 32, 39, 61, 77, 87, 88, 89, 98, 102, 103, 161, 162, 178, 193

N

Nahum, 174
Nebuchadnezzar, 124, 125
Nero, 23, 163
New Jerusalem, 19, 33, 91, 100, 178, 218
Nicolaitans, 21, 22, 24, 25
Noah, 38, 76, 144, 189, 192, 211
Noah's Flood, 38, 76
North, 22, 24, 152, 172
Numbers, 25, 87, 101, 115, 223, 227, 231

O

Olives, 52, 55, 130, 152, 182

P

Papacy, 28

Pergamum, 14, 24, 25, 26, 27, 28, 30, 32, 231
Persecution, 4, 21, 22, 23, 24, 25, 66, 77, 78, 90, 112, 119, 195
Persian, 117, 118, 158
Peter, 13, 16, 23, 25, 33, 35, 39, 42, 76, 77, 88, 103, 113, 116, 121, 132, 189, 192, 196, 206, 211, 217, 227
Pharaoh, 94, 147
Philadelphia, 14, 30, 31, 32, 33, 34, 231
Philippians, 31, 33, 132, 145, 196, 206, 228
Pillar, 32, 33, 82, 197, 212
Polycarp, 22, 23
Prophecies, 51, 162, 169, 179, 228
Prostitute, 149, 157, 159, 165, 166, 175
Proverbs, 15, 72, 86, 133, 163, 228
Psa, 16, 31, 39, 47, 48, 70, 86, 89, 96, 102, 103, 111, 114, 129, 130, 131, 133, 134, 135, 136, 144, 145, 147, 161, 165, 167, 169, 176, 180, 182, 183, 205, 206, 208, 221, 223
Psalms, 13, 16, 40, 87, 131, 145, 148, 163

R

Rainbow, 38, 85, 143
Reformation, 33, 231
Reward, 29, 39, 89, 137, 148, 207, 209, 225, 226
Romans, 11, 13, 16, 29, 30, 31, 35, 36, 45, 48, 52, 54, 60, 61, 88, 89, 90, 100, 101, 102, 109, 111, 115, 116, 134, 145, 157, 189, 194, 207, 208, 213, 225, 227
Rome, 34, 54, 59, 117, 118, 140, 158, 159, 160, 161, 163, 171, 227

S

Sabbath day, 126, 192, 219
Sapphire, 40, 41, 143, 144, 216, 217
Sardis, 14, 29, 30, 31, 32, 132, 231
Scorpions, 75, 76, 78, 80, 98
Scroll, 14, 45, 46, 48, 52, 53, 74, 85, 86, 87, 89, 90, 141, 154, 172, 206
Seventh, 18, 45, 59, 64, 65, 69, 72, 74, 85, 86, 87, 88, 89, 90, 98, 102, 104, 126, 136, 138, 141, 142, 143, 145, 153, 164, 165, 176, 182, 191, 192, 193, 195, 213, 216
Seventy, 18, 23, 75
Sixth angel, 80, 150, 151, 203
Sixth seal, 50, 51, 52, 53, 66, 71
Smoke, 42, 52, 66, 69, 70, 75, 76, 80, 81, 82, 104, 123, 127, 130, 135, 145, 170, 171, 175, 189, 229
Smyrna, 14, 22, 23, 25, 26, 28, 30, 35, 231
Sodom, 60, 76, 82, 95, 136
Stars, 5, 15, 16, 17, 21, 29, 37, 52, 53, 56, 60, 71, 72, 75, 79, 80, 109, 110, 111, 113, 121, 132, 134, 137, 139, 193, 209, 218, 227, 228, 231
Sulfur, 70, 81, 82, 123, 135, 136, 147, 154, 184, 204, 205, 213
Sun, 15, 38, 52, 53, 56, 65, 66, 72, 75, 79, 80, 85, 109, 138, 139, 149, 150, 154, 183, 193, 217, 218, 221, 223, 232
Sword, 15, 16, 24, 37, 49, 51, 55, 57, 79, 91, 111, 115, 121, 122, 130, 135, 140, 180, 181, 182, 183, 184, 204, 223, 231
Symbol, 24, 64, 134, 160, 172
Symbolic, 5, 10, 12, 40, 48, 60, 74, 90, 105, 110, 140, 164, 166, 178, 183, 187, 228
Symbolism, 10, 12, 46, 115, 187

T

Temple, 13, 15, 32, 33, 40, 41, 42, 46, 65, 66, 86, 91, 92, 104, 119, 124, 130, 137, 138, 139, 143, 144, 145, 146, 147, 153, 168, 174, 178, 197, 212, 213, 216, 217, 218, 221, 229, 232
Ten, 15, 22, 23, 37, 40, 47, 62, 96, 101, 109, 110, 117, 118, 119, 121, 134, 137, 141, 145, 158, 159, 160, 161, 162, 164, 165, 168, 176, 179, 208, 209, 216, 229
Thessalonians, 14, 16, 30, 49, 88, 97, 98, 119, 123, 124, 132, 153, 170, 182, 196, 228
Thief, 29, 30, 35, 49, 152, 160, 170
Thirst, 65, 66, 148, 184, 213, 221
three and one-half years, 66, 87, 91, 92, 93, 94, 112, 114, 119, 120, 232

Thunder, 39, 42, 49, 69, 70, 86, 104, 129, 131, 139, 145, 153, 176
Thyatira, 14, 26, 27, 28, 30, 231
Tiberias, 163
Timothy, 13, 29, 39, 145, 151, 165, 167, 183, 188, 225
Tribulation, 33, 64, 65, 66, 92, 114, 120, 122, 141, 195, 226
Trinity, 12, 29, 34, 46
Trumpet, 14, 18, 37, 49, 56, 59, 64, 65, 69, 70, 71, 72, 73, 75, 76, 79, 80, 82, 85, 86, 87, 88, 89, 91, 98, 102, 103, 104, 130, 136, 138, 141, 142, 143, 145, 148, 153, 176, 189, 195, 196
Trumpets, 5, 10, 18, 37, 45, 49, 55, 56, 57, 64, 69, 70, 72, 74, 83, 90, 98, 104, 141, 142, 147, 179

U

UN, 166

W

Wedding banquet, 36, 64, 137, 146, 153, 176, 177, 178, 184, 195, 213, 226
White horse, 49, 179, 181, 183
Wings, 41, 42, 78, 80, 92, 109, 114, 115, 143, 187
Woman, 26, 27, 30, 79, 92, 100, 109, 110, 111, 112, 114, 115, 116, 131, 148, 154, 157, 158, 159, 160, 161, 162, 163, 165, 166, 167, 169, 170, 171, 172, 218, 221
Wormwood, 71

Z

Zecheriah, 12, 14, 15, 50, 51, 52, 91, 93, 103, 113, 114, 130, 152, 178, 182, 212, 216, 218, 221, 231
Zephaniah, 132, 147, 152, 169
Zeus, 24, 25
Zion, 52, 61, 66, 67, 86, 103, 129, 130, 134, 138, 139, 140, 153, 154, 161, 193, 202, 205, 212, 218, 226

About the Author:

Brian Young is the founder and director of the Creation Instruction Association, and is currently a principal of a Christian School. Brian speaks around the country on issues dealing with the Creation/Evolution debate and publishes a quarterly newsletter called, *From the Beginning*. He has authored other books in similar areas, including, The Stars: God's Word in the Sky; Genesis: Yesterday's Answers to Today's Problems; and Doubts About Creation? Not After This! His topics cover a wide range of areas in which he has done research; while at the same time, stresses Biblical Creationism as the foundation for good education.

About the Cover:

This book cover is a detail of a painting entitled, *MARANATHA!*, done by Stephen Gjertson (American born, 1949). *MARANATHA!*, 1987-00 is an oil on paper mounted to board, 40 X 67, and is a collection of Mr. and Mrs. Galen Carlson. It was taken from Revelation 19:11-16 where it states, "And I saw the opened heaven. And consider this. A horse, a white one, and He who is seated upon it who is called Faithful and Dependable. And in righteousness He administers justice and makes war. And His eyes were a flame of fire. And upon His head there were royal crowns, many of them. He has a name which has been written which no one knows except He himself. And He is clothed with a garment which has been stained with blood. And His name has been called, and the name is on record, The Word of God. And the armies which are in heaven kept following Him [in a steady procession, rank after rank] upon white horses, clothed in fine linen, shining, bright, clean. And out of His mouth there proceeds a sword, a sharp one, in order that with it He would strike down the nations. And He himself treads the wine press of the wine of the wrath of the anger of God, the Omnipotent. And He has upon His garment and upon His thigh a name which has been written, King of kings and Lord of lords." (*An Expanded Translation*, by Kenneth S. Wuest).

On the back cover we have the full painting of MARANATHA, showing Christ's glorious return with His saints.